ST ANTONY'S SERIES
General Editor: Alex Pravda, Fellow of St Antony's College, Oxford

Recent titles include:

Mark D. Alleyne
INTERNATIONAL POWER AND INTERNATIONAL COMMUNICATION

Daniel A. Bell, David Brown, Kanishka Jayasuriya and David Martin Jones
TOWARDS ILLIBERAL DEMOCRACY IN PACIFIC ASIA

Judith M. Brown and Rosemary Foot (*editors*)
MIGRATION: The Asian Experience

Sir Alec Cairncross
MANAGING THE BRITISH ECONOMY IN THE 1960s: A Treasury
Perspective

Alex Danchev and Thomas Halverson (*editors*)
INTERNATIONAL PERSPECTIVES ON THE YUGOSLAV CONFLICT

Anne Deighton (*editor*)
BUILDING POSTWAR EUROPE: National Decision-Makers and European
Institutions, 1948–63

Simon Duke
THE NEW EUROPEAN SECURITY DISORDER

Y. Hakan Erdem
SLAVERY IN THE OTTOMAN EMPIRE AND ITS DEMISE, 1800–1909

Christoph Gassenschmidt
JEWISH LIBERAL POLITICS IN TSARIST RUSSIA, 1900–14: The
Modernization of Russian Jewry

Amitzur Ilan
THE ORIGIN OF THE ARAB–ISRAELI ARMS RACE: Arms, Embargo,
Military Power and Decision in the 1948 Palestine War

Hiroshi Ishida
SOCIAL MOBILITY IN CONTEMPORARY JAPAN

Austen Ivereigh
CATHOLICISM AND POLITICS IN ARGENTINA, 1910–60

Leroy Jin
MONETARY POLICY AND THE DESIGN OF FINANCIAL INSTITUTIONS
IN CHINA, 1978–90

Social Citizenship Rights

A Critique of F. A. Hayek and Raymond Plant

João Carlos Espada
Research Fellow, Institute of Social Sciences
University of Lisbon

Foreword by

Lord Dahrendorf

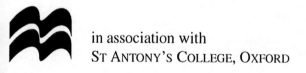

in association with
ST ANTONY'S COLLEGE, OXFORD

First published in Great Britain 1996 by
MACMILLAN PRESS LTD
Houndmills, Basingstoke, Hampshire RG21 6XS
and London
Companies and representatives
throughout the world

This title is published in the *St Antony's Series*
General Editor: Alex Pravda

A catalogue record for this book is available
from the British Library.

ISBN 0–333–65315–7

First published in the United States of America 1996 by
ST. MARTIN'S PRESS, INC.,
Scholarly and Reference Division,
175 Fifth Avenue,
New York, N.Y. 10010

ISBN 0–312–15976–5

Library of Congress Cataloging-in-Publication Data
Espada, João Carlos.
Social citizenship rights : a critique of F. A. Hayek and Raymond
Plant / João Carlos Espada.
p.   cm. — (St. Antony's series)
Includes bibliographical references (p.   ) and index.
ISBN 0–312–15976–5
1. Citizenship.   2. Basic needs.   3. Social justice.   4. Social
policy.   5. Hayek, Friedrich A. (Friedrich August), 1899–1992.
6. Plant, Raymond.   I. Title.   II. Series.
JF801.E87   1996
323.6—dc20   96–10389
                                                           CIP

10   9   8   7   6   5   4   3   2   1
05   04   03   02   01   00   99   98   97   96

Printed and bound in Great Britain by
Antony Rowe Ltd, Chippenham, Wiltshire

To my parents,
who first introduced me to the
Anglo-American civilization
of liberty and personal responsibility

To my wife, Graça, and our daughters,
Isabel and Diana, who have embarked
upon this British adventure with me

Contents

Foreword

This book is an important contribution to a difficult and topical debate. Its subject is the notion of social rights as part of an emphatic notion of citizenship. What exactly do we mean when we speak of social rights? What are we doing when we postulate their existence? What follows not just in political theory but in practical politics from our answers to these questions? As tends to be the case with good books, João Espada does not just ask such questions out of abstract interest, but has a real concern. He is looking for ways of breaking out of the alternative of socialism vs. liberalism, not so much a third way as a plausible intellectual case for a position which is as concerned about civil liberties as it is about the social policies which sustain them.

T. H. Marshall's seminal lectures on *Citizenship and Social Class* first introduced the notion of social rights alongside civil and political rights. Marshall's abiding interest in social policy and the welfare state made him place provisions for all – Beveridge's justly famous plan – alongside equality before the law and universal suffrage, or more generally, the rule of law and democracy. The complete civilized state – the state of citizens in the full sense – combines the rule of law with political democracy and the welfare state.

Many have taken this view of modern developments for granted. More recently, some have tried to set social rights against civil rights and argued that poverty is a violation of human rights just like detention without trial. Almost every recent author, and certainly all international organizations and most political leaders have accepted the notion of social rights. Espada takes the scholarly view and wonders whether they are right.

His analysis focuses in the first instance on F. A. Hayek. He has in mind Hayek the political theorist more than Hayek the economist. Clearly Hayek was unhappy with the notion of social rights, as with any idea of 'positive freedom'. For him it was all a part of the 'fatal conceit' which leads people, especially politicians, to think that they can do something to bring about freedom, when in fact doing nothing is the only

contribution that politicians can make for freedom to become
real. Espada's sympathetic and yet highly critical analysis of
Hayek is in itself a notable intellectual achievement and
certainly worth reading.

The author did not find it easy to identify one person to
make the opposing case, a Hayek of the Left (if that is not too
absurd an idea). Raymond Plant, whose work was eventually
singled out, is too sophisticated to fit into any simple categor-
ization. He combines a commitment to social improvement
with Christian roots of his thinking and with a thorough knowledge of the contemporary debate on these issues. However,
Plant has no doubt about the usefulness of the concept of
social rights, and is therefore an author whose work allows a
critical examination of this concept. At times one feels that
Espada shares some of Lord Plant's sentiments but will not
allow his critical mind to go along with the resulting conclusions.

So where do we go from here? João Espada has emerged
from the new liberty of his home country, Portugal, as a man
committed to the constitution of liberty, and impressed by
the fact that many of those who fought with him for a free
Portugal were socialists. He has since immersed himself in the
West and the great debates which are waging in Britain, in the
United States, in all Western democracies (of which Portugal
is now one). His commitment to civil and political liberties is
strong and never in dispute. He also wants to advance social
well-being. But he is no longer sure that the concept of social
rights achieves this end.

Many conversations with the author have helped me sharpen
my own view on this important question. Partly in response to
the unfortunate tendency to try and balance civil and social
rights as one worries about human rights, partly as a result of
further reflection on Isaiah Berlin's distinction between
'positive' and 'negative freedom', I have come to conclusions
which are similar to those at which Espada hints towards the
end of his study. All rights are individual rights, and they all
go back to the two essentials, inviolability of the person and
freedom of expression. It is a fact that many people – many
citizens – cannot make effective use of these rights for reasons
which are in the widest sense social. Social changes, and in
many cases social policies, are needed in order to enable human
beings to be citizens. But these social policies are in some ways

additional to, if essential for rights. They are not rights of the same order. When Sanjay Gandhi tried a programme of mass sterilization he violated rights which even the poor village people of India regarded as inviolable. Conversely, Amartya Sen has shown that where freedom of the press prevails, famines are unlikely. Even extreme social deprivation can be a result of the absence of primary civil rights. Thus social policy is important, even very important, but neither more important nor on the same level of entitlements as the basic civil and political rights of every citizen.

These are far-reaching and passionate statements. Indeed, they may be misleading, even wrong. Anyone who wants to engage in the debate of these issues however will find João Espada's book a stimulus and a guide.

Ralf Dahrendorf
Oxford, June 1995

Acknowledgements

This book is based on the DPhil. thesis that I submitted in Oxford, in July 1994. For its sake, I and my wife, accompanied by our two daughters, left our relatively comfortable positions in Lisbon to embark upon an adventure in a country whose history we loved, but with whose language we were not at ease and with whose day-to-day life we were not familiar. This is the kind of adventure one usually undertakes at an earlier stage in life. But later is better than never, and I do not regret having done it in my mid and late thirties: the adventure was rewarding and even thrilling. Having arrived at Oxford as committed friends of Britain and all that she stands for, we left four years later with a deeper love for this country, her traditions and institutions, her incredibly free and civilized people. Living in Britain, as well as studying in Oxford, was an irreplaceable intensive course on the fundamentals of liberty and the rule of law. This education has been fortunately extended with two further years abroad, in the United States, at Brown and Stanford Universities, where a Luso-American Development Foundation visiting professorship brought me and my family.

My first words of thanks go to my wife and daughters, who have embarked upon this adventure with me. My wife has discussed with me every step of my intellectual exploration, and her criticisms, as well as our general discussions about politics have contributed greatly to the progress of this book. To my parents, I owe more than can be expressed. They were the first to introduce me to the Anglo-American civilization of liberty and personal responsibility, and they have always encouraged me to pursue my intellectual explorations according to my own lights. Without their warm support, our adventure abroad, of which this book is a result, would not have been possible.

My intellectual education is also primarily indebted to the work of three men: Raymond Aron, Ralf Dahrendorf and Karl Popper, two of whom I was privileged to meet.

Sir Karl Popper may be said to have changed my life: not only did his *Open Society* change my intellectual outlook, but also, without him, I would not have decided to go to Britain. Since

1987, when I first met him, Sir Karl Popper supported me more than I could have dreamt of. Sir Karl acceded to my request that he be my referee in my application to Oxford, and he introduced me to Lord Dahrendorf (then Sir Ralf) who kindly agreed to be my supervisor. Ever since my arrival in Oxford, in September 1990, Sir Karl regularly received me in his lovely home in Kenley, and patiently discussed my countless doubts and questions. His assistant, Mrs Melitta Mew, also supported me warmly. In January 1992, I was privileged to represent Sir Karl in a Tribute to F. A. Hayek organized by the Annual Meeting of the American Economic Association in New Orleans, where I read Sir Karl's paper 'The Communist Road to Self-Enslavement'. Sir Karl's death, in September 1994, was a terrible loss.

To Lord Dahrendorf, I am also immensely indebted. In 1982, when I first wrote a paper on his active view of liberalism, I could not imagine I would come to meet him, not to mention work under his supervision. Over the four years in Oxford, he always supported and encouraged me, patiently criticizing every draft of each chapter, suggesting what I should read next, but always allowing my thoughts to flow their own way. As my research developed, I wrote him numerous letters, to which he always patiently replied. He and his wife, Lady Dahrendorf, were our perfect hosts. Like the work of Sir Karl, I claim the work of Lord Dahrendorf to be the underlying inspiration of the views presented in this book. Needless to say, however, this is a personal view and neither of them is responsible for the errors this work may contain.

A word of thanks is also due to Dr John Gray and Professor Steven Lukes, my examiners in Oxford, who have recommended my thesis for publication. I have tried to incorporate their comments and suggestions in this final version, but again they are not responsible for any flaws it may contain. During our stay in Oxford, we were helped and supported by many friends, all of whom it would be impossible to enumerate here. Mr Herminio Martins and his wife Margaret, as well as Dr Roger Hood, his wife Nancy, and his father Ronald, have been the best of representatives of British hospitality.

I must also thank St Antony's College for the marvellous environment of study and social intercourse it has provided me with. A special word of thanks goes to Mrs Stevens, the

Warden's secretary, Mrs Flitter, the College secretary, and Miss Campbell, the chief librarian, for their tireless help and warm support.

* * *

This book would not have been possible were it not for the support of several institutions and individuals. Dr Alex Pravda has included it in the Macmillan/St Antony's series, which he edits. I also benefited from the attention of Mr T. M. Farmiloe, Publishing Director, and Ms Gráinne Twomey, Commissioning Editor, at Macmillan, as well as from the careful editorial services of Ms Anne Rafique. The British Council in Lisbon awarded me an FCO grant to attend St Antony's College and the University of Oxford from 1990 to 1994. The Calouste Gulbenkian Foundation in Lisbon provided me with a grant for living expenses. The Luso-American Foundation for Development granted me a loan under favourable conditions and has supported me ever since. The European University Institute in Florence, by request of Professor Steven Lukes, invited me for a research visit which proved very helpful and pleasant. The Instituto de Ciencias Sociais da Universidade de Lisboa seconded my stay in Oxford.

* * *

Acknowledgements and thanks are due to Mrs Melitta Mew for permission to quote from *The Open Society and Its Enemies* and *Conjectures and Refutations* by Sir Karl Popper; and to Routledge & Kegan Paul for permission to quote from the works of F. A. Hayek: *The Constitution of Liberty*; *Studies in Philosophy, Politics and Economics*; *Law Legislation and Liberty Vol. I, Rules and Order*; *Law, Legislation and Liberty Vol. II The Mirage of Social Justice*; *Law, Legislation and Liberty Vol. III The Political Order of a Free People*; *New Studies in Philosophy, Politics, Economics and the History of Ideas*; *Law, Legislation and Liberty*, one-volume edition with corrections and revised Preface; *The Fatal Conceit: The Errors of Socialism*, first volume of The Collected Works of Friedrich August Hayek, edited by W. W. Bartley.

Providence, Rhode Island
July 1995

Introduction: Equal Citizenship and Social Inequality

Should we welcome the extension of the traditional idea of the rights of man to the political and social field? Or should we deplore that those rights have lost (or seem to have lost) their unconditional and even sacred character? We should probably accept both conclusions: our epoch has the merit of having extended the number of subjects and objects of rights which are claimed to be universal, but this extension has weakened these rights.

Raymond Aron, *Political Studies*, 1972

ARE THERE OR SHOULD THERE BE ANY SOCIAL RIGHTS?

The idea that individuals have rights which are prior to, and compelling over, governments has a long and well-established tradition in political theory, especially within families of thought with liberal affiliation. Although it has never ceased to be a controversial tradition, its acceptance seems to have enlarged during the second half of the twentieth century. And yet, this apparently growing acceptance has not brought controversies to an end. Somehow, it has produced only a metamorphosis in the framework within which the discussion evolves: now, not so much between those who do and those who do not accept the idea that individuals have rights, but mainly between different interpretations of this idea; and also between different views on what should or should not be the realm of rights.

This study discusses one of the several topics that have fostered recent controversies: the nature of what is usually called social and economic rights, also known as welfare rights, or social citizenship rights, sometimes also as second generation rights. Roughly speaking, these rights involve claims to certain social, economic and cultural goods – such as, for example, education, social security, housing, health care and, in general, a standard of living that might be perceived as decent. As claims to the provision of certain goods they are often called 'positive' rights, as contrasted with the 'negative' ones, which are the traditional civil and political rights – generally perceived, although

1

perhaps not always accurately, as demanding only negative forbearance from others, not positive action.

Unlike traditional rights, which are now widely accepted, social rights have been surrounded by deep scepticism. Should they be considered as a constitutive part of the rights of individuals? Can they be compatible with civil and political rights? Even if they are compatible, should they be bestowed with the same dignity as the traditional rights, or should they be perceived as somehow subordinate? And what do social rights consist of: a safety net, a common floor over which social inequalities can blossom, or rather an expression of a common principle of distribution that ascribes to each one the share of the general output to which he is perceived as being entitled?

These constitute the sort of questions which will be discussed here. The method chosen has been the critical analysis of the arguments conveyed by two rival views, which might be called Neo-liberalism and Socialism. In order to allow a systematic discussion of the consistency of each view, two authors who are considered as representatives of the views under analysis have been selected. Among neo-liberals, in fact among twentieth-century political authors in general, Friedrich A. Hayek is certainly one of the most powerful and original thinkers. As for socialist authors, Raymond Plant, now Lord Plant, was chosen because of his special concern with the subject of social rights and for his specific proposal of renovation of the socialist programme on the basis of the concept of citizenship, namely social citizenship. However, other socialist oriented authors will be called into the discussion, whenever this seems appropriate.[1]

Basically, it can be said that neo-liberals refuse to admit the concept of social rights, whereas socialists argue for their recognition. Neo-liberals – and particularly Friedrich A. Hayek, who has produced a strong case against social rights – think that there is an insuperable contradiction between the nature of traditional rights, civil and political ones, and the nature of social rights. The proper enforcement of social rights, Hayek maintained, would lead to the destruction of that liberal order whose maintenance traditional rights are aimed at. Socialists, on the contrary, maintain that social rights are the necessary extension of traditional rights, without which the effectiveness of traditional rights would be undermined.

After a careful scrutiny of the arguments underpinning each

of these views, it will be argued here that both Neo-liberalism and Socialism share a misleading assumption about social rights: they both perceive them as being an expression, or a component, of a general criterion of distribution or social justice. On the contrary, and according to the view presented here – which, if it deserves any label, could simply be called Liberal – social rights should not be associated with any overall theory of justice whatever.[2] They should be perceived as giving rise to a common floor below which nobody needs fear to fall, but above which social inequalities may flourish. This common status of citizenship may thus be seen as an expression of the political will to avoid injustice, and above all exclusion, but this by no means entails an overall theory of justice or a common pattern of distribution. If, and only if, this distinction is allowed, social rights can and should be perceived as a constitutive part of the rights of individuals, in tune with the traditional civil and political rights.

* * *

This study comprises three Parts: the first one is devoted to F. A. Hayek's critique of social rights, the second to Raymond Plant's and the socialist case for these rights, the third and final one to the conclusions of the discussion previously undertaken. Parts I and II are organized in a similar way. They both comprise three chapters, and both start with one (Chapters 1 and 4) devoted to the presentation – as fair and impartial as possible – of each author's argument. Each Part then moves on to a further chapter (2 and 5) in which the argument previously presented is discussed and criticized. A third and final chapter (3 and 6) then closes each Part, with an attempt to define the origins of the flaws detected by the critique developed in the intermediate chapter.

The net result of this method is that the last chapters of Parts I and II go considerably beyond the scope of a discussion on social rights alone. In fact, Chapters 3 and 6 focus on what is called 'the background assumptions' of each view on social rights. In this sense, it might be said that they include a general critique of neo-liberalism and socialism or, at least, of the general work of the two authors who have been chosen as representative of those currents of thought. Although this is partially true, it is worth noting that the main goal of the critique developed here is the elucidation of the problem under scrutiny: the problem of social citizenship rights.

Before we embark upon the discussion of this problem, however, it is still necessary to define the scope of the problem in greater detail. The next section will recall two pioneer contributions to its discussion. After that, some relevant concepts will be defined.

ALFRED MARSHALL AND T. H. MARSHALL

Debates on social rights refer almost inevitably to T. H. Marshall's famous lectures given at Cambridge in 1949 and published in the following year under the title 'Citizenship and Social Class'.[3] In these lectures, T. H. Marshall reflected on the progress of what he called the rights of citizenship, and addressed the main question of whether or not this progress was compatible with the maintenance of a market economy and corresponding social inequalities. Marshall was delivering the Alfred Marshall lectures, and he used the occasion to present his own topic of citizenship 'with the assistance of' Alfred Marshall's paper on 'The Future of the Working Classes'.[4] It is worth recalling the main issues at stake in these reflections of the two great scholars.

'The Future of the Working Classes' was a paper read by Alfred Marshall also in Cambridge, at the Reform Club in 1873, and it was republished by A. C. Pigou in the volume he edited under the title *Memorials of Alfred Marshall*.[5] Alfred Marshall was quite clear on the question he wanted to address, as well as on the answer he wanted to uphold:

> The question for us to-night . . . is not whether all men will ultimately be equal – that they certainly will not – but whether progress may not go on steadily if slowly, till the official distinction between working man and gentleman has passed away; till, by occupation at least, every man is a gentleman. I hold that it may, and that it will.[6]

In 1949, T. H. Marshall addressed the same problem but he introduced two alterations. Where Alfred Marshall had used the term 'gentleman', Thomas Humphrey Marshall proposed the term 'civilized', 'for it is clear that he (Alfred Marshall) was taking as the standard of civilized life the conditions regarded by his generation as appropriate to a gentleman'.[7] Then T. H. Marshall adds a further alteration: 'We can go on to say that the claim of all to enjoy these conditions (of a civilised or a gentleman's life) is a claim to be admitted to a share in the social heritage, which in turn means a claim to be accepted as full members of the society, that is, as citizens.'[8]

Having thus introduced the concept of citizenship, T. H. Marshall embarks upon an historical survey of the evolution of the concept and its application in the last 250 years. His three-fold scheme of citizenship rights and their corresponding institutions is now well known. The emergence of civil, political and social rights would have roughly corresponded to the eighteenth, nineteenth and twentieth centuries; their institutional counterparts would have been the courts of justice (civil rights), parliament and councils of local government (political rights), and finally the educational system and the social services (social rights).

Civil rights, according to T. H. Marshall, are composed of 'the rights necessary for individual freedom – liberty of the person, freedom of speech, thought and faith, the right to own property and to conclude valid contracts, and the right to justice'. Political rights, on the other hand, include 'the right to participate in the exercise of political power, as a member of a body invested with political authority or as an elector of the members of such a body'. Finally, social rights involve 'the whole range from the right to a modicum of economic welfare and security to the right to share to the full in the social heritage and to live the life of a civilized being according to the standards prevailing in the society'.[9]

Although Alfred Marshall had not mentioned the concept of citizenship as such, T. H. Marshall maintained that a basic sociological hypothesis was underlying his Cambridge paper of 1873:

> It postulates that there is a kind of basic human equality associated with the concept of full membership of a community – or, as I should say, of citizenship – which is not inconsistent with the inequalities which distinguish the various economic levels in the society. In other words, the inequality of the

social class system may be acceptable provided the equality of citizenship is recognised.[10]

This would have been the sociological hypothesis implied in Alfred Marshall's paper of 1873. Seventy-six years later, again in Cambridge, T. H. Marshall addressed the same problem and posed his predecessor's question afresh. 'The basic human equality of membership', he observed, 'has been enriched with new substance and invested with a formidable array of rights'. The questions stemming from this evolution go without saying:

> Is it still true that the basic equality, when enriched in substance and embodied in the formal rights of citizenship, is consistent with the inequalities of social class? . . . Is it still true that basic equality can be created and preserved without invading the freedom of the competitive market?[11]

T. H. Marshall's answer to these questions were both qualified. He thought that equality of citizenship was still compatible with class inequality, but only with certain inequalities: 'citizenship, he maintained, has itself become, in certain respects, the architect of legitimate inequalities.'[12] As for the market system, Marshall thought that the advancement of citizenship had transformed it into a 'socialist system', although, he added, 'it is equally obvious that the market still functions – within limits'.[13] Marshall saw this conflict as a creative one, giving rise to what he called a hyphenated society, the welfare-capitalist society. This is mainly characterized by a progressive divorce between real and money incomes. Social services provide individuals with the access to goods which are not directly proportionate to their purchasing power in the market. 'The advantages obtained by having a larger money income do not disappear, but they are confined to a limited area of consumption,'[14] Marshall concluded.

This conflict between social citizenship and the market – a conflict of principles which, Marshall asserted, 'springs from the very roots of our social order in the present development of democratic citizenship'[15] – will be with us throughout this study. Even though the approach adopted here is different from the one adopted by T. H. Marshall – his being sociological and historical, ours being analytical, to say nothing of the fact that his view was social-democratic whereas ours is liberal – much of the argument presented here will build on the foundations provided by Marshall. His distinction between civil, political and social rights will be accepted. His main question about the conflict between equal citizenship and social inequality will also be present, although most of the time the conflict under scrutiny will be the one allegedly existing between traditional and social rights.

Eventually, we shall come back to Marshall's own solution for this conflict and a slightly different view will be presented. Whereas Marshall saw that the inequality of the social class system can be acceptable provided the equality of citizenship is recognized, it will be argued here that the equality of citizenship is desirable provided social inequality is accepted.

But let us not rush into the conclusions. A long discussion lies ahead, before Alfred Marshall and Thomas Humphrey Marshall are called again onto the stage. For the time being, certain concepts which are instrumental for our discussion must be clarified.

HAVING A RIGHT

The growing use of the language of rights made the expression 'having a right' particularly casual and, thus, elusive. Legal scholars have become particularly aware of this elusiveness, and in the twentieth century an increasing discussion, aimed at giving preciseness to the language of legal rights, has taken place. This discussion has produced a vast literature whose analysis lies beyond the scope of this study.[16] But the clarification of certain basic concepts is indispensable to a serious discussion on social citizenship rights.

The first distinction which is worth retaining is the one between 'rights in a strict or narrow sense', also called 'claim-rights', and 'mere liberties' or 'privileges'.[17] When one says that 'A is at liberty to do X', this should be understood as 'A has no duty not to do X'. But when one says that 'A has a right to do X', this has necessarily a stronger connotation. Even in day-to-day language, it is assumed that the fact that 'A has a right to do X' somehow implies that others have a corresponding duty to respect A's right. Joel Feinberg says that 'a legal right is a claim to performance, either action or forbearance as the case may be, usually against other private persons. It is also a claim against the state to recognition and enforcement.'[18]

As Feinberg also points out, what the claim-right adds to the liberty is the duty of others.[19] Not surprisingly, then, the main distinctions within claim-rights are related to the duties entailed by them.[20] These distinctions are usually made between *in personam* and *in rem* rights, between *positive* and *negative* rights, and between *active* and *passive* negative rights.

In personam and *in rem* rights differ in relation to whom their corresponding duties apply to. The former entail specific duties of certain individuals, as in the case of the right of a creditor against his debtor. By contrast, *in rem* rights involve duties of all the others, or of 'the whole world', towards the right-holder. This is the case of the right to property, according to which everyone has a duty of forbearance or of non-interference in someone's property.

Positive and *negative* rights differ to the extent that they entail either positive or negative duties, that is to say, (negative) duties to refrain from doing something, or (positive) duties to do something. The usual example of a positive right is the right of the creditor against his debtor, which entails the latter's positive duty to pay his debt. The right of someone to his own property is mainly a negative right which entails the negative duty of others not to interfere with his property. In these two examples, as well as in most of the cases, negative rights tend to be *in rem*, and positive ones tend to be *in personam*. Joel Feinberg recalls, however, that there are some, although perhaps not many, examples of both negative *in personam* rights and positive *in rem* rights.[21]

A final distinction, which applies only within negative rights, is between active and passive ones. Unlike the first two classes of claim-rights, this distinction refers mainly to the action of the right-holder, not to the nature of the corresponding duty – which, in both cases, is a negative duty. As Feinberg puts it, 'active rights are rights to act or not to act as one chooses; passive rights are rights not to be done to by others in certain ways.'[22] Active rights are usually part of 'the right to liberty', including the right to leave one's country, to free speech, etc. Passive rights are part of 'the right to security', namely the right to be left alone, or to enjoy one's property.

* * *

According to the elementary classification recalled here, it is already possible to say that our discussion about social citizenship rights will focus on a particular kind of rights: they will certainly be *in rem*, positive claim-rights. Social rights are claims, and not only liberties, since they should entail the duty of others to provide some sort of goods which the right-holder is perceived as being entitled to. Because the duty they entail is not a negative one, but a positive duty to act, namely to provide goods and services (or access to goods and services), social rights must be positive rights. And finally, because they do not entail duties of specific individuals, but, in principle, they demand action, or contribution to action, from all the others towards the right-holder, social rights are expected to be *in rem*. It will be observed, in due course, that none of these features is undisputed; in fact, the debate is whether or not there can be social rights that can be simultaneously *in rem*, positive, claim-rights, and whether or not their enforcement can be compatible with the traditional civil and political rights.

A final distinction which is worth explaining refers to the term citizenship. Why do we use the expression social citizenship rights, and not only social rights? The reason is not merely semantic. Social rights have been introduced as part of human rights, which became widely known after a Universal Declaration of Human Rights was adopted by the United Nations Organization in 1948.[23] The chief feature of human rights is that they are moral rights (that is, 'rights that are held to exist prior to, or independently of, any legal or institutional rules'[24]) of a special species: they apply to all human beings as human beings, unconditionally and unalterably. By choosing the expression 'social citizenship rights', and by choosing T. H. Marshall's reflections on citizenship as a starting point, the scope of the discussion undertaken here is intentionally limited. Issues of justification, content and enforcement of social rights are not addressed in terms of universal human rights, but in a much humbler way: they should always be understood as applying to individuals who are citizens of states (as a rule, nation-states) that in turn have already accepted and enforced civil and political rights – states which are sometimes called liberal-democratic. As Raymond Aron once recalled, 'the Jews of my generation cannot forget how fragile these human rights become when they no longer correspond with citizenship rights.'[25]

That the argument developed here might one day apply to a world civil society, the dream of Immanuel Kant in his 'Idea for a Universal History with a Cosmopolitan Purpose', is something that I can only hope for. But the problem of a world civil society is not addressed here: social rights of citizenship, such as we know it nowadays, will remain our subject-matter throughout the pages that follow.

Part I
Friedrich A. Hayek and Neo-Liberalism

1 Presentation: The Mirage of Social Justice

To reject his half of the truth because he overlooked the other half, would be to fall into his error without having his excuse. For our own part, we have a large tolerance for one-eyed men, provided their one eye is a penetrating one: if they saw more, they probably would not see so keenly, nor so eagerly pursue one course of inquiry. Almost all rich veins of original and striking speculation have been opened by systematic half-thinkers.

John Stuart Mill, 'Bentham', 1838

F. A. Hayek's views on social and economic rights, as well as on many others issues, are quite clear and straightforward. He unequivocally maintains that:

The old civil rights and the new social and economic rights cannot be achieved at the same time but are in fact incompatible; the new rights could not be enforced by law without at the same time destroying that liberal order at which the old civil rights aim.[1]

The reasoning that underpins this alleged incompatibility is based on two main statements: (1) there is an accusation of 'vagueness and abstraction' directly addressed towards the UN Declaration,[2] which would only decree rights without caring to know how and by whom they would be enforced; (2) there is the assumption that, if these new rights were to give rise to effective *duties* ascribed to effective *agents*, the results would be the destruction of the liberal order that allowed traditional rights to flourish *and* the destruction of the material wealth which is associated with that order.

SOCIAL RIGHTS ARE VAGUE AND ABSTRACT

The first statement of Hayek's argument refers to the 'vagueness and abstraction' of the UN Declaration and it is derived from Hayek's view of traditional rights. He does not explicitly discuss the concept of traditional rights. He accepts them as something which results from 'rules of just individual conduct'.[3]

13

There is a sense of the noun 'right' in which every rule of just individual conduct creates a corresponding right of individuals. So far as rules of conduct delimit individual domains, the individual will have a right to his domain, and in defence of it will have the sympathy and the support of his fellows. And where men have formed organizations such as government for enforcing rules of conduct, the individual will have a claim in justice on government that his right be protected and infringements made good.[4]

Hayek elucidates next the fact that three conditions are needed in order to consider those claims as 'claims in justice or rights': (1) that those claims are addressed to some person or organization (such as government); (2) that such person or organization is capable of action; (3) and that one or the other is bound in its actions by rules of just conduct.[5] If we exclude temporarily the third condition, which is not fundamental at this stage, we see that Hayek demands basically of a 'right' that it gives rise to a *duty* on the part of someone with *power* or *capacity* to fulfil that duty. This is undoubtedly the sense of Hayek's statement that 'it is meaningless to speak of a right to a condition which nobody has the duty, or perhaps the power, to bring about.'[6] Then Hayek recalls that we have no right that our houses do not burn down, nor a right that our products or services find a buyer, nor that any particular goods or services be provided for us.

These two crucial requirements of rights – that they generate corresponding duties on the part of concrete agents and that these agents are capable of enforcing them – are precisely those that, according to Hayek, the UN Declaration does not fulfil. On the one hand this declaration states social and economic rights[7] 'without at the same time placing on anyone the duty or burden of providing them'.[8] On the other hand, 'the document completely fails to define these rights in such a manner that a court could possibly determine what their contents are in a particular instance.'[9] Hayek then concludes:

The conception of a 'universal right' which assures to the peasant, to the Eskimo and presumably to the Abominable Snowman 'periodic holidays with pay' shows the absurdity of the whole thing.[10]

Still according to Hayek, this vague and abstract manner of conceiving social and economic rights would be an expression of a fundamental delusion: 'The naive prejudice that we can create any state of affairs which we think to be desirable by simply decreeing that it ought to exist.'[11] And the practical consequence of this delusion would be 'to play an irresponsible game with the concept of 'right' which could result only in destroying the respect for it'.[12]

THE CONSEQUENCES OF MAKING THEM LESS VAGUE AND ABSTRACT

The second statement of Hayek's argument against the concept of social and economic rights is based on the author's evaluation of the foreseeable consequences which would follow from the attempt to give effectiveness to those rights; in other words, the consequences which would follow the attempt to correct the defect of 'vagueness and abstraction', which Hayek himself has pointed out in the way those rights were defined by the UN Declaration. Here Hayek's central point is no longer the impossibility of enforcing these rights but the moral non-desirability of the consequences of the attempt to enforce them. Those consequences would be of two different sorts: (1) liberal societies would become totalitarian and (2) they would no longer be able to provide the wealth that they can provide only because, and as long as, they are liberal.

This double forecast of Hayek's on the consequences of the attempt to enforce social and economic rights is founded on a basic distinction between these new rights and the traditional ones. Social and economic rights constitute 'claims to particular benefits' or 'to a particular state of affairs', whereas civil and political rights 'constitute essentially a demand that, so far as the power of government extends, it ought to be used justly'.[13] From these traditional rights, Hayek adds, no positive powers can be derived which the government ought to have in order to determine a particular state of affairs. By contrast, social and economic rights, because they are claims to particular benefits or to a particular state of affairs, 'demand as their counterpart a decision that somebody (a person or organization) should have the duty of providing what the others are to have'.[14] And Hayek concludes:

> If such claims are to be met, the spontaneous order which we call society must be replaced by a deliberately directed organization; the cosmos of the market would have to be replaced by a taxis whose members would have to do what they are instructed to do. They could not be allowed to use their knowledge for their own purposes but would have to carry out the plan which their rulers have designed to meet the needs to be satisfied.[15]

In other words, having pointed out the *different nature* of the traditional rights and the new ones, Hayek maintains that the measures needed in order to extend traditional rights to the new ones would involve the annihilation of those features which, according to him, define a liberal order. This is where the incompatibility between the two sets of rights lies, since the purpose of traditional rights is precisely to sustain that liberal order.

There is, however, still another consequence, apparently of second order. That is that the material affluence which characterizes the liberal order is, in great part, a product of the fact that the liberal order allows individuals to use their own knowledge for their own purposes. Since the application of social and economic rights would necessarily annul this main feature of a liberal order, this would mean the simultaneously annulment of the source of economic wealth which, still according to Hayek, has constituted the main device for the improvement of citizens' economic situations in liberal societies. These are the words of Hayek:

> The fundamental fact that these illusions disregard is that the availability of all those benefits which we wish as many people as possible to have depends on these same people using for their production their own best knowledge.[16]

HAYEK'S GLOBAL CRITIQUE

Having presented the main steps of Hayek's argument against the concept of social rights, we should now be able to capture the core of Hayek's critique. Keeping the terminology which has been used so far, one could say that what has been presented as the two main statements of Hayek's argument may, in fact, be subsumed in the first one – the one which consists of the alleged 'vagueness and abstraction of social rights'.

One may recall that that critique was based on the assumption that three conditions are needed in order to consider any claims as claims in justice or rights: (1) that those claims are addressed to some person or organization; (2) that such a person or organization is capable of action; (3) and that one or the other is bound in its actions by rules of just conduct.[17] Hayek started by pointing out that social rights, as presented by the UN Declaration, did not fulfil the first two requirements. Later, in what has been called here his second main statement, Hayek analysed the foreseeable results of the endeavour to make social rights fulfil those two requirements. It has been seen that, still according to Hayek, this endeavour was bound to lead to the assignment to someone of the power of 'providing what the others are to have'. This 'duty' would then entail the substitution of an organization for the spontaneous order which characterizes liberal societies. In other words, we would lose a system whose members only obey general rules equal for all, and we would obtain, probably unwillingly, a system whose members are to obey particular commands about what they have to do.[18]

Returning to what has been called the first main statement of Hayek, we shall now realize that its third requirement – that a person or organization with the duty to enforce a right is bound in its actions by rules of just conduct – would be drastically infringed by the attempt to give effectiveness to the social rights. The enforcement of these rights involves a person or an organization becoming responsible for bringing about a particular state of affairs. This in turn involves that person or organization not being bound in their actions by rules of just conduct. Conversely, if they were, they would not have the power to enforce social rights. The latter would remain vague and abstract declarations of intention. Finally, if those insubstantial declarations may be considered to be much less harmful than the totalitarian menace engendered by the attempt to enforce social rights, the insubstantial declarations have themselves their consequences: by playing an irresponsible game with the concept of 'right', they would destroy the respect for such a concept.

In other words, Hayek's argument about the incompatibility between traditional and social rights may be summarized as follows:

(1) The enforcement of social rights demands as their counterpart the power of somebody to provide what others are to have;

(2) This new power may not be bound in its actions by rules of just conduct;

(3) As a consequence, the main feature of a liberal or spontaneous order will give way to the main feature of an organization; thus, the main aim of civil and political rights – which is to protect a liberal order – will be destroyed.

In order to clarify the reasoning that underpins these three contentions, and thus pave the way to the critical discussion of Hayek's argument, two diversions will now be introduced: the presentation of Hayek's distinction between a spontaneous order and an organization, and the presentation of his argument on the meaninglessness of the concept of 'social justice' in a spontaneous order.

ONE PRINCIPLE AND THREE KINDS OF RULES

The power and freshness of Hayek's argument against a common pattern of distribution in a liberal society has been widely appreciated as one of the crucial ideas of his political philosophy. According to this argument, there is no common pattern, no unique hierarchy of values capable of measuring the value, the merit, the deserts or even the needs of each member of a free society.

However powerful this idea may be – and it certainly is – there are nevertheless some problems in its very definition. The idea seems to designate three different types of rules which, although stating the same principle, have nonetheless different natures. There is in the first place a *moral rule* which expresses a normative demand of liberal societies: in a society of free men *there ought not to be* any common pattern of distribution, because otherwise the requirement of equality before the law would necessarily be infringed. There seems to be, secondly, a *natural rule* or a *natural law,* in the sense of a regularity of behaviour that might be observed in market societies: in such societies *it is a fact* that there are no common patterns of distribution, in the sense that such patterns cannot be discovered, but only artificially created. Finally, and thirdly, there seems to be a *rule of economic expediency or efficiency*: if a pattern of distribution is tentatively imposed upon a market system, the result will necessarily be a fatal interference in the spontaneous process of regulation which, in its turn, happens to be the decisive mechanism of economic growth.

It is not easy to establish what the logical relationship is between these three types of rules. Hayek hardly acknowledges the distinction between them. What happens is that, in one work or another, in one chapter or another, Hayek approaches the same principle from different angles. It may be said that the normative angle is mainly present in *The Constitution of Liberty*[19] and in the essay on liberalism published in *New Studies in Philosophy, Politics, Economics and the History of Ideas*.[20] In the three volumes of *Law, Legislation and Liberty*,[21] as well as in the essay entitled 'The Atavism of Social Justice'[22] the three different types of rules are simultaneously adopted in a peaceful and harmonious coexistence that does not obviously constitute a problem for the author. Finally, in *The Fatal Conceit: The Errors of Socialism*,[23] Hayek fully adopts a naturalist and evolutionist approach which, having not been absent in his previous works, was by no means entailed by them. We shall return later to this overlapping problem and to the role that it plays in Hayek's political philosophy.

For the time being, our main concern is to explain the Hayekian principle according to which there is no common pattern of distribution in a free society. We already know that this 'there is no common pattern' means simultaneously three different things: *there ought not to be, there is no,* and *it would necessarily be* too costly to impose a particular pattern of distribution in a free society. As far as this overlapping problem allows, we shall try to explain the principle.

EQUALITY BEFORE THE LAW

In chapter 5 of *The Constitution of Liberty*[24] Hayek mainly explains why there ought not to be, in the sense of not being morally desirable that there be, such a pattern of distribution. The elegance of the argument is quite striking.

The author explains that the fact of his condemning the imposition of patterns of distribution, namely egalitarian patterns, does not mean that he does not consider a more even or just distribution to be desirable. He even adds that 'one may well feel attracted to a community in which there are no extreme contrasts between rich and poor and may welcome the fact that the general increase in wealth seems gradually to reduce those differences'.[25] In fact, Hayek explains, he opposes the introduction of patterns of distribution on their own: either they are egalitarian or inequalitarian.

So what is Hayek's argument against the introduction of such patterns? The answer has its starting point in the following assumption: 'if we wish to preserve a free society, it is essential that we recognize that the desirability of a particular object is not sufficient justification for the use of coercion.'[26]

Hayek does not of course believe that there is no coercion or ought not to be any in a free society. He knows that the abolition of coercion is logically paradoxical as well as is the concept of unlimited freedom.[27] But, having first presented the normative case for freedom understood as 'independence of the arbitrary will of another', Hayek presents the liberal ideal as that of 'a state of liberty or freedom', that is to say, 'that condition of men in which coercion of some by others is reduced as much as is possible in society'.[28] His problem is not therefore to abolish coercion altogether, but to reduce it as far as possible.

In its turn, this reduction is only possible 'by conferring the monopoly of coercion on the state and by attempting to limit this power of the state to instances where it is required to prevent coercion by private persons'.[29] How can we limit the power of the state? The answer of Hayek runs as follows:

> This is possible only by the state's protecting known private spheres of the individuals against interference by others and delimiting these private spheres, not by specific assignation, but by creating conditions under which the individual can determine his own sphere by relying on rules which tell him what the government will do in different types of situation.[30]

These rules, which allow the individual to know what the government will do in different situations, are the laws. The liberal ideal of reducing coercion as much as possible is then the ideal of government limited by laws. These laws must, in their turn, be equal for all. 'The great aim of the struggle for liberty has been equality before the law', says Hayek, adding that this is also 'the only equality which we can secure without destroying liberty'.[31]

Laws are then the ultimate guarantee that government will not become an instrument of coercion at the caprice of those in office. But why should laws be equal for all? Hayek has two main normative reasons for this. The first consists of saying that, although the history of liberty has been the history of the achievement of particular liberties, liberty is actually one. It is only secured when each individual is subject to the same laws as his fellow citizens and, therefore, immune from the arbitrary coercion of others.

But the fact that individuals should be equal before the law does not mean that they actually are equals among themselves. Hayek stresses that he fully recognizes the fact that individuals are very different. In this respect, he explains, his legal egalitarianism is much more radical than the Utopian egalitarianism of those who intend to underpin the egalitarian ideal on the assumption of an alleged equality that would actually exist among men. Saying this, these egalitarians tacitly imply that an actual inequality among men might entail inequality before the law. On the contrary, Hayek's normative egalitarianism is based on the argument that differences between individuals do not constitute justification for the government to treat them differently.

* * *

It is now possible to reconstruct Hayek's normative argument against the introduction of common patterns of distribution in a society of free men. Even if those patterns were desirable on their own (for instance, the reduction of inequalities), it would be necessary to weigh up whether that desirability was enough to justify the use of coercion. Aiming at the reduction of coercion to a bare minimum, but knowing that coercion cannot be altogether avoided, a society of free men ascribes its monopoly to the government. But, in order to avoid the abuse of that power, it is now indispensable that the government be limited by laws. For these laws actually to protect the liberty of all, they have to be equal for all: individuals have to be treated equally before the law, even if they are actually rather different among themselves.

The decisive step comes now: the desirability of a common pattern of distribution is not sufficient to justify the use of coercion, because, in order to introduce that pattern, the government would have to treat individuals differently.

> from the fact that people are very different it follows that, if we treat them equally, the result must be inequality in their actual position, and that the only way to place them in an equal position would be to treat them differently. Equality before the law and material equality are therefore not only different but are in conflict with each other; and we can achieve either the one or the other, but not both at the same time.[32]

The same argument against an egalitarian pattern of distribution is presented by Hayek sixteen years later, in the second volume of *Law, Legislation and Liberty*:

> To assure the same material position to people who differ greatly [...], the government would clearly have to treat them very differently to compensate for those disadvantages and deficiencies it could not directly alter [...][33]

VALUE AND MERIT

One might however reply that, although Hayek has shown that the goal of material equality is not compatible with the principle of equality before the law, this does not mean that *all common patterns of distribution* necessarily conflict with equality before the law. Hayek himself acknowledges this difficulty and discusses other possible patterns. One of these is, of course, merit: each one should receive from society a reward according to his merit, or according to the merit ascribed to his own contribution to society.

Hayek then recalls that merit has to mean here 'assessable merit', since it would not be possible to establish rewards which could not be ascertained by all. 'Assessable merit' then presupposes that we are able to say of someone that not only has he acted correctly – that is to say, according to rules of just conduct – but also that he has made a serious effort, has worked hard, and has had more than pure luck. And we have to be able to compare and evaluate different merits from different individuals.

The problem is that each one's effort cannot be measured by each one's results. 'Merit', Hayek recalls, 'is not a matter of the objective outcome but of subjective effort.'[34] Not only equally good results may arise from quite different merits, but also a worse result may well be achieved by a person who has made much more effort than another, who has simply had more luck. The classical example chosen by Hayek consists of saying that 'among those who try to climb Mount Everest or to reach the Moon, we also honour not those who made the greatest efforts, but those who got there first.'[35] And he concludes:

> We do not necessarily admire all activities whose product we value; and in most instances where we value what we get, we are in no position to assess the merit of those who have provided it for us.[36]

Hayek stresses that the idea according to which market economies reward merit is widespread among popular opinion and has even been presented by some authors as a decisive argument for the defence of markets. But that belief is based on two major mistakes. One, which has been referred to, consists of identifying success in the achievement of a result with the effort or the merit invested in it. We have already seen that we are only able to assess results, not compare merits among different individuals. The other mistake consists of an abusive generalization: from the potentially true statement according to which the improvement of an individual's well-being depends primarily on his own efforts and decisions, many people erroneously infer that the material success achieved is the reward either of each one's merit or his effort. This view has become 'largely the basis of the self-esteem of the businessman', Hayek observes, and it 'often gives him an air of self-righteousness which does not make him more popular'. Because, Hayek adds, 'to those who regard themselves (and perhaps are) equally able but have failed, this generalization must appear as a bitter irony and severe provocation'.[37]

According to Hayek, therefore, market economies do not

necessarily reward merit – about which we cannot be sure – but only reward results, the value of those results. But it is important to be accurate about this notion of 'value'. Hayek recalls 'the futile medieval search for the just price and just wage' and warns against the resumption of that search in the form of the concept of 'value to society'. The value to which Hayek is referring, as opposed to merit, is not the so-called 'value to society' as a whole: this simply does not exist, Hayek maintains. The only value we can assess is the value of something for those who consume that something which in turn has been produced by others.

> Services can have value only to particular people (or an organization) and any particular service will have very different values for different members of the same society. [. . .] The remunerations which the individuals and groups receive in the market are thus determined by what these services are worth to those who receive them (or, strictly speaking, to the last pressing demand for them which can still be satisfied by the available supply) and not by some fictitious 'value to society'.[38]

*　*　*

It might perhaps be noticed that a transition has been occurring throughout this section as regards the absence of a common pattern of distribution in a society of free men. Having started with the normative case for equality before the law, we have observed that an egalitarian distribution, or one only based on merit, would have produced insuperable obstacles to the application of the legal egalitarian principle. We have then moved to Hayek's distinction between value to society and value for those who avail themselves of a certain service. In this case, Hayek is not only discussing *what ought to be*. He refers to what is, to what the market system actually does; and, although one might understand that Hayek is implying that *what the market does* is actually *what the market ought to do*, this linkage has not been explicit. In order to understand it, and to complete the presentation of Hayek's argument, we need a second diversion: why the concept of social justice has no meaning in a market order.

COSMOS AND TAXIS

One of the crucial distinctions in Hayek's political thought – which has often been referred to, but not yet presented – concerns the difference between a spontaneous order and an organization. Although this distinction mainly refers to human societies, it may be properly understood with reference to a broader distinction between two general types of orders, including natural orders: the distinction between a *grown order*, which Hayek also calls spontaneous order or Cosmos, and a *made order*, which Hayek also calls organization or Taxis.[39]

Hayek introduces this distinction in the second chapter of volume I of *Law, Legislation and Liberty*. He starts by saying that the distinction between *grown order* and *made order* is primarily based on the origins or sources of each: whereas a grown order presents 'an equilibrium set up from within' (or endogenously), a made order 'can only be created by forces outside the system' (or exogenously). Besides that, while a made order results from the action of some external agent, who puts the elements of a set in their places or directs their movements, the place of each element in a grown order is not only unpredictable but also undetermined. The general character of that order is its sole predictable feature, not the particular position of its elements.

To illustrate what he understands by a grown order or Cosmos, Hayek recalls that

> we can never produce a crystal or a complex organic compound by placing the individual atoms in such a position that they will form the lattice of a crystal or the system based on benzol rings which make up an organic compound. But we can create the conditions in which they will arrange themselves in such a manner.[40]

This is intended to illustrate the idea that only the general character of a grown order – such as that of the crystal or the compound – may be predicted, not the particular positions of its elements. The same happens with the well-known school experiment in which iron filings on a sheet of paper are made to arrange themselves along some of the lines of force of a magnet placed below:

We can predict the general shape of the chains that will be formed, but we cannot predict along which ones of the family of an infinite number of such curves that define the magnetic field these chains will place themselves.[41]

These examples highlight one of the main aspects of the distinction between a *grown order* and a *made* one: although there are regularities in the behaviour of the elements which belong to each, and although those regularities influence the final position of those elements in both orders, this final position of the elements is predictable solely in the *made order*. In a *grown order* the final position of the elements is unpredictable.

The reason for this is interesting. The final position of the elements in both orders depends upon two common factors: the general rules which govern the behaviour of each element, and, of course, the initial position of each element. But in the grown order there is a further factor. The final position of its elements will also depend upon 'all the particular circumstances of the immediate environment to which each of the elements will react in the course of the formation of that order.'[42] Hayek explains the importance of this point in a clear-cut manner:

The important point is that the regularity of the conduct of the elements will determine the general character of the resulting order but not all the details of its particular manifestation [...] The order, in other words, will always be an adaptation to a large number of particular facts which will not be known in their totality to anyone.[43]

One may notice that this involves a superior capability of the grown order to deal with information. Since its elements only obey general rules, and their particular positions are not fixed in advance, the information is dealt with in a decentralized way by each of the elements of the grown order. The amount of information that a grown order is able to deal with is therefore much bigger than the one of a made order. Conversely, however, the power of an external agent to change the positions of each element is much wider in a made order: whereas in this kind of order particular places are externally set, in a grown order one may only alter general rules – whereby one may hope to achieve a change of particular places of the elements. But even this is only a hope, however likely it is to occur.

RULES: NOMOS AND THESIS

Another important distinction may be inferred from what has just been said. If both a made and a grown order are governed by rules, but if those rules govern them in two opposing ways, it is reasonable to think that those rules must be different. Hayek wants to define these differences as far as possible.

He uses the Greek term 'nomos' to designate the rules of a spontaneous order, and 'thesis' to refer to those of an organization. Hayek mentions John Burnet's 'Law and nature in Greek Ethics' and quotes him as saying that 'in contrast to "nomos", which originally meant "use", "thesis" may mean either the giving of law or the adoption of laws so given'.[44]

The main characteristic of 'thesis', or rules of organization, is that 'they must be rules for the performance of assigned tasks':

> They presuppose that the place of each individual in a fixed structure is determined by command and that the rules each individual must obey depend on the place which he has been assigned and on the particular ends which have been indicated for him by the commanding authority. The rules will thus regulate merely the detail of the action of appointed functionaries or agencies of government.[45]

Three main consequences arise from this nature of rules of an organization. First, 'they are necessarily subsidiary to commands, filling the gaps left by commands'. Secondly, 'they will be different for the different members of the organization, according to the different roles which have been assigned to them'. And, thirdly, 'they will have to be interpreted in the light of the purposes determined by the commands'.[46]

By contrast, Hayek defines rules of a spontaneous order in the following way:

> They must be independent of purpose and be the same, if not necessarily for all members, at least for whole classes of members not individually designated by name. They must [...] be rules applicable to an unknown and indeterminable number of persons and instances. They will have to be applied by the individuals in the light of their respective knowledge and purposes; and their application will be

independent of any common purpose, which the individual need not even know.[47]

Hayek will later identify 'nomos', or the rules of a spontaneous order, with the private law, and 'thesis', or the rules of an organization, with public law. He concedes that the distinction is hard to draw, but maintains that it should not be overlooked. Private law is mainly concerned with rules of just conduct, thus allowing the individuals 'to pursue their respective individual ends and merely aiming at so confining individual actions that they will in the result serve the general interest'.[48] Public law, by contrast, is mainly concerned with what particular officers or agencies of government are required to do – the reason why Hayek would prefer to call it 'regulations or by-laws of government'. According to Anglo-Saxon but contrary to continental-European practice, Hayek places criminal law under private rather than public law.

ACTION AND DESIGN

We have discussed the differences between the rules of a grown order and a made one. But we had seen before that one of the main distinctions between the two orders concerned their origin. What about the origin of the rules? Is their origin also different? Should the rules of a spontaneous or grown order also be a spontaneous product in themselves? Or might they be intentionally designed, namely with the specific purpose either of creating or of protecting and improving a spontaneous order? In other words, does the spontaneous nature of a grown order entail that the origin of its rules be itself spontaneous?

We shall see later that Hayek is by no means consistent in dealing with this problem. But at this stage one should note that, when introducing the concept of grown order in volume II of *Law, Legislation and Liberty*, Hayek maintains absolutely that 'the spontaneous character of the resulting order must be distinguished from the spontaneous origin of the rules on which it rests'. It is worth quoting this passage:

> While the rules on which a spontaneous order rests may also be of spontaneous origin, this need not be always the case. Although undoubtedly an order originally formed itself spontaneously because the individuals followed rules which

had not been deliberately made but had arisen spontaneously, people gradually learned to improve those rules; and it is at least conceivable that the formation of a spontaneous order relies entirely on rules that were deliberately made.[49]

According to this observation, it seems necessary to consider as being at least awkward one of the other designations Hayek has chosen for a grown or spontaneous order: an order that 'results from the interplay of *human actions* and not of *human design*'.[50] This has led several authors, and sometimes Hayek himself, to consider that the rules of a spontaneous order must themselves be a result of 'human actions' and not of 'human design'. In other words, rules of a spontaneous order would differ from rules of a made order not only by their features but also by their origin: 'spontaneous rules', like spontaneous orders, would have emerged undesigned, whereas 'made rules', like 'made orders', would have been the product of an agent's design.

The truth is, however, that, when discussing the distinction between rules of a spontaneous order and a made one, Hayek has not discussed their origin but simply their different characteristics. And, as we have just seen, he himself has stressed the distinction between the 'spontaneous character of the resulting order' and the 'spontaneous origin of the rules on which it rests'. This allows one to think that a spontaneous order might be entirely a product of human design: for example, of a liberal human design which would aim at the creation and improvement of rules which guarantee to each individual the most extensive liberty of movements compatible with an equal liberty of movements to all the others. This hypothesis of a spontaneous order created by liberal design is theoretically admitted by Hayek. He says that 'it is possible that an order which would still have to be described as spontaneous rests on rules which are entirely the result of deliberate design'.[51]

We shall see later that this nuance is in no way irrelevant.

THE ROLE OF RULES IN A SPONTANEOUS ORDER

We are now able to understand the nature of the process of 'distribution' which, according to Hayek, is at work in a market order or in a liberal society. One should even note that Hayek dislikes this term 'distribution process', for it somehow suggests that there is a 'distribution agent'. There is no such thing. Hayek maintains that the essential feature of 'distribution' in a liberal society – in a spontaneous order or a market system – is precisely that such distribution in rigour does not exist: there is no intentional nor predictable distribution of the share which each individual will have. A liberal order is only concerned with the general rules that individuals have to observe – it says nothing about the results emerging from their observance. These results are the product of an infinite number of exchanges between individuals and organizations who try to use their own knowledge to pursue their particular purposes.[52]

We have already seen that the general rules of a spontaneous order are distinguished from those of an organization at a crucial point: whereas the latter aim at particular purposes, the former are end-independent. They are simply procedural rules of conduct. This is at the origin of one important advantage of an economic system which may be based on a spontaneous order: only restrained by general rules of good conduct, which are independent of particular ends or purposes, individuals in this system are able to use freely all their best knowledge, or information, in order to pursue their own particular purposes.

This advantage should be understood in two different respects. First, there is a large open field for social and economic experiments, as individuals are free to act without previous authorization or the agreement of authorities, or simply of their fellow-citizens. So long as they comply with general rules of behaviour, they are free to pursue their own purposes. Secondly, as a consequence, the amount of information which will be used at each moment by this decentralized system is always much larger than the one that might ever be used by one single mind, or one single centre of coordination.

Hayek maintains that, for this decentralized process to work efficiently, it is indispensable that it is not troubled by arbitrary interferences. These would necessarily distort the system of signals that individuals use to take economic decisions – signals consisting, of course, of prices and wages. In this respect it is particularly important that the principle of 'negative feed-back' be allowed to work, that is to say, the principle which entails that 'some must suffer unmerited disappointment'.

The importance of particular prices and wages, and therefore of the incomes of the different groups and individuals, is not due chiefly to the effects of the prices on all of those who receive them, but to the effects of the prices on those for whom they act as signals to change the direction of their efforts. Their function is not so much to reward people for what they have done as to tell them what in their own as well as in general interest they ought to do.[53]

The importance of this principle of negative feed-back effect may be seen from two different points of view. From a normative point of view, Hayek suggests that this is likely to be the only way in which free people may be prevented from doing certain things – things that are anyway harmful for them, but that they would still do if others told them not to.[54] From the point of view of economic efficiency, the action of the negative feed-back effect in the impersonal process of the market allows the maximization of the general outcome as well as that of each individual's share:

> We use an impersonal process to determine the allocation of benefits precisely because through its operation we can bring about a structure of relative prices and remunerations that will determine a size and composition of the total output which assures that the real equivalent of each individual's share that accident or skill assigns to him will be as large as we know how to make it.[55]

SOCIAL JUSTICE IS MEANINGLESS

What might a spontaneous order be like if it were ordered in accordance with principles of social justice? Hayek's response is unambiguous: it might not be. Spontaneous order and social justice are incompatible concepts, for the simple reason that, in a spontaneous order, the concept of social justice is literally meaningless – in the same sense that the concept of a 'moral stone' is meaningless.[56]

This contention of Hayek's is based on relatively simple reasoning. We do not say that situations whose responsibility cannot be ascribed to anyone – such as natural catastrophes or mere absence of luck – are unjust. Although we are impressed by the harshness with which life sometimes deals with certain people, we do not use the term 'injustice' in these cases. This is because there is nobody who can be made responsible for those situations. And Hayek then adds:

> There is no difference with regard to the general feeling of injustice about the distribution of material goods in a society of free men. Though we are in this case less ready to admit it, our complaints about the outcome of the market as unjust do not really assert that somebody has been unjust.[57]

Hayek says that the market outcome could be unjust if it were the result of a deliberate allocation to particular people. But that is not the case, he underlines, because 'those shares are the outcome of a process the effect of which on particular people was neither intended nor foreseen by anyone'.[58] According to Hayek, the attribute of justice may be predicated about the intended results of human action, but not about circumstances which have not deliberately been brought about by men. For that reason, the concept of social justice cannot apply to the results of the market.

> Justice requires that in the 'treatment' of another person or persons, i.e. in the intentional actions affecting the well-being of other persons, certain uniform rules of conduct be observed. It clearly has no application to the manner in which the impersonal process of the market allocates command over goods and services to particular people: this can be neither just nor unjust, because *the results are not intended or foreseen,* and *depend on a multitude of circumstances not known in their totality to anybody.*[59]

A reply to this argument of Hayek's could obviously be as follows: if a system recurrently generates situations which we intuitively perceive to be unjust, but which cannot be avoided or minimized because there is nobody responsible for them, then the system must be to blame. The market system is responsible for those kinds of situations and therefore it must be changed. As a matter of fact, Hayek himself thinks that this is the real issue at stake in the proposals for social justice. In the last instance, social justice is nothing but the alibi for socialism, whose true motive is the destruction of liberal societies based on market economies.

The only blame implicit in those complaints is that we tolerate a system in which each is allowed to choose his occupation and therefore nobody can have the power and the duty to see that the result corresponds to our wishes.[60]

Nevertheless, Hayek adds, this critique of the market economy is itself inconsistent. It rests on the assumption that some other system could provide a better standard of living for individuals. But the market system is the one that brings about 'a greater satisfaction of human desires than any deliberate human organization can achieve'.[61] This system was not created by design, but men learnt gradually how to improve it after having discovered 'how it increased the efficiency of men in the groups who evolved it'.[62] What men did not yet understand is that the maintenance of this system, capable of generating wealth, has its price also:

> The fact is simply that we consent to retain, and agree to enforce, uniform rules for a procedure which has greatly improved the chances of all to have their wants satisfied, but at the price of all individuals and groups incurring the risk of unmerited failure.[63]

RULES AND PATTERNS

According to Hayek, the concept of social justice has no meaning in a market order because the outcome of such order is neither intended nor foreseen. This is the price we have to pay for having an impersonal process which is capable of maximizing the chances of everyone, as well as of preserving their individual liberty. But there is still a third motive for which the concept of social justice has no meaning in a market order:

> There are no principles of individual conduct which would produce a pattern of distribution which as such could be called just, and therefore also no possibility for the individual to know what he would have to do to secure a just remuneration of his fellows.[64]

The non-existence of principles of this kind is maintained by Hayek with recourse to two main arguments. The first consists of saying that there are no impersonal patterns capable of gathering the agreement of everyone, to assess what is due to each one. We have seen that patterns such as merit and value for society could never be ascertained on common grounds. The second argument, which we already know as well, is that any attempt to establish rules of conduct with the aim of producing particular results, or particular states of affairs, is bound to fail. The only rule which could produce certainty about final particular results is the rule which attributes the power and the duty of bringing these about to a central authority. This rule is however incompatible with the liberal principle according to which each individual must be free to use the best of his knowledge for his own purposes. This principle, in its turn, allows the efficient use, for the benefit of all, of information widely dispersed among millions of men.

Moreover, it should be noted that none of these difficulties would be removed if, instead of aiming at 'social justice', individuals had only adopted the minimalist aim of avoiding 'social injustice'.

> There can be no test by which we can discover what is 'socially unjust' because there is no subject by which such an injustice can be committed, and there are no rules of individual conduct the observance of which in the market order would secure to the individuals and groups the position which as such (as distinguished from the procedure by which it is determined) would appear just to us.[65]

HAYEK'S ARGUMENT: AN OVERVIEW

Starting with a critique of the alleged vagueness and abstraction of social and economic rights, F. A. Hayek has maintained that it would be impossible to correct these defects in a liberal society. According to him, the attempt to make social rights less vague and less abstract would involve a person or an organization becoming responsible for bringing about a particular state of affairs. This, in turn, involves this person or organization not being bound in their actions by rules of just conduct. We are now able to understand why, according to Hayek, things should be like that.

In a liberal society or a spontaneous order, as opposed to an organization, individuals obey general and end-independent rules of just conduct, which allow them the liberty to use the best of their knowledge in pursuit of their own purposes. Because of this, the results brought about by free exchanges between them are not intended nor foreseen. Nobody may therefore be said to be responsible for the shares that – out of skill, luck or by accident – each of the individuals will obtain. In such a system there are no common patterns of distribution and there is no real distribution, since there is no agent responsible for it.

The concept of social rights would involve the adoption of common patterns of distribution. But there is no way of introducing such artificial patterns without, at the same time, destroying a spontaneous order. Those patterns, like merit or equality or value to society, would in the first place infringe the fundamental liberal requirement of equality before the law. Secondly, they would interfere with the system of signals which allow the market order to maximize economic efficiency. For that reason, and because they would interfere with the negative feed-back effect, artificial patterns of distribution would destroy the principle of an individual's responsibility for his actions. Finally, such patterns of distribution or of social justice could never be mere rules of just conduct: nobody would know which general criteria should rule his actions in order to produce the particular results that would fit the patterns of distribution. Without general rules of just conduct, society would remain at the mercy of the mighty or of the rulers. The liberal goals, which civil and political rights have aimed at, would therefore be destroyed by the introduction or the pursuit of social and economic rights.

2 Discussion: The Dualism of Facts and Standards

The dualism of facts and standards is, I contend, one of the bases of the liberal tradition. For an essential part of this tradition is the recognition of the injustice that does exist in this world, and the resolve to try to help those who are its victims. This means that there is, or that there may be, a conflict, or at least a gap, between facts and standards ... Liberalism is based upon the dualism of facts and standards in the sense that it believes in searching for ever better standards, especially in the field of politics and of legislation.

Karl R. Popper, Addenda to
The Open Society and its Enemies, 1961

IS SOCIAL JUSTICE MEANINGLESS?

One of F. A. Hayek's contentions about the concept of social rights is that it entails the concept of social or distributive justice. According to Hayek, the concept of social justice is simply meaningless in a market order: 'social justice does not belong to the category of error but to that of nonsense, like the term of a "moral stone".'[1] It is important to stress this point. Hayek has also criticized some particular views of social justice, the ones entailing common patterns of distribution, but he has been always keen on highlighting the fact that he is not basing that critique upon a particular defence of any specific pattern of distribution as opposed to other specific ones. What he wants to assert is that the discussion about the justice or injustice of results in a market order is meaningless. In other words, Hayek maintains that he is not embracing his own particular conception of social justice as opposed to other particular ones. According to him, the very idea of social justice is meaningless, that is to say, social justice has no meaning as subject-matter, regardless of the particular view on social justice one wants to uphold:[2]

The concept of 'social justice' *is* necessarily empty and meaningless[3]

and:

The differences in rewards simply *cannot* meaningfully be described as just or unjust[4]

and:

Justice clearly *has no* application to the manner in which the impersonal process of the market allocates command over goods and services to particular people.[5]

It is worth noting, however, that this concept of 'meaninglessness' may be understood in at least two different ways. One is that the subject-matter of 'social justice' *is* meaningless, in the sense that it actually has no meaning in a *market order*. The other is that the subject-matter of 'social justice' *ought not* to have meaning in a *liberal society*.

In the first case we have a statement of fact, a description of how things actually occur in a market order. There is no moral prescription involved. It may be true or false, depending on the accordance between the descriptive information given by the statement and the facts which that description refers to. One may then discuss whether or not the market allocates resources in a neutral way in terms of 'social justice'. Whatever the resulting conclusion may be, it is of course pointless to discuss whether or not one agrees with that market feature: the normative evaluation of the feature is not at stake. Hayek has argued that the market allocates rewards on a neutral basis, and it is now widely admitted that he has produced invaluable insights in this regard.

But in the second case, that 'social justice' *ought not* to have meaning in a *liberal society*, there is a normative evaluation: facing the fact that social justice has no meaning in the market place, Hayek believes that there are good reasons not to interfere with that reality and so he concludes that social justice *ought not* to be applied to a *liberal society*. Let us assume that Hayek's argument is cogent and that he actually manages reasonably to show that the concept *is* meaningless in a *market order*. Is that sufficient to rule out a discussion about the subject-matter of social justice in a *liberal society*? In other words, can we derive an *ought to* from an *is*? Would it not be the case that Hayek is being trapped in the 'is/ought dichotomy' detected by David Hume?[6] There are reasons to think so. Hayek seems to be erroneously confusing both levels – what is, and what ought to be – and thus he is paying a disservice to his own free-market cause.

It was mentioned before that there is a simple counter-argument which immediately comes to mind about this insistence of Hayek's on the meaninglessness of social justice. One might say that, if a given system, like the market one, produces situations which we intuitively perceive to be unjust, and if that system does not allow us to correct them, or even discuss them, because there is nobody responsible for them, then one might say that the factor pre-eminently responsible for the allegedly unjust situations is the market itself. This system is then perceived as having to be altogether removed in order to allow the correction of unjust situations. In other words, if the *market order is* ethically neutral, a *liberal society*, if we want it to be ethically just, should get rid of the market system.

It must be noted that the reply to this argument may no longer rest with the repetition of the contention that 'social justice is meaningless in a market order'. One cannot deduce from this assertion that the subject-matter of social justice has no moral meaning at all, or that it is morally desirable that it has no such meaning. Wishing to avoid a discussion on social justice, Hayek could probably reply that it is worthless morally to condemn the market order, since this is the most efficient and, therefore, that it is bound to prevail. In this sense, the moral condemnation of the market order would necessarily be a defeated cause, and, for that reason, it should be abandoned.[7]

However, in this reasoning there is a third term which has been omitted. When one says that 'it is worthless morally to evaluate the market order for this is anyway the winning system', the justification makes sense only if one had previously decided that one would support only winning causes. But this decision, in its turn, is very difficult to justify in moral terms. The idea that we ought to support only winning causes really excludes room for moral judgements: for me to choose my moral cause, I just have to know which cause will be winning tomorrow. But what is the moral virtue, or the moral value, of that cause that justifies that I *ought* to support it?[8]

WHAT IS AND WHAT OUGHT TO BE

Arguing against the concept of social justice, Hayek at a certain point quotes P. H. Wicksteed in a passage which is particularly clarifying:

It is idle to assume that ethically desirable results will necessarily be produced by an ethically indifferent instrument.[9]

Hayek quotes this excerpt in order to illustrate his assertion
that: 'it is a sign of the immaturity of our minds that we have
not yet outgrown these primitive concepts and still demand
from an impersonal process [. . .] that it conforms to the moral
precepts men have evolved for the guidance of their individual
actions.'[10] The truth however is that the quotation referred to
is by no means clear about the *normative consequences* of the fact
that the market is 'an ethically indifferent instrument'. Shall
we conclude from this that *we ought not* to judge market results
according to any standards of social justice, and that these
results *ought simply to be accepted*? Or shall we conclude that,
precisely because the market is an ethically neutral instrument,
there is no reason to accept its results as ethically valid? The
truth is that both conclusions are possible, precisely because
one cannot derive one and only one normative judgement
from a statement of fact. Several moral judgements – we have
seen two – are simultaneously mutually contradictory and yet
compatible with the same statement of fact. Only the introduction of moral standards, by reference to which we *decide* the
attitude to adopt towards the facts, allows us to derive moral
conclusions. Information about facts or states of affairs are just
that: information. They say nothing about how we ought to act
given these facts.

Hayek has tried to escape this inescapable dualism of facts
and standards. But of course he has not succeeded. In order
to conclude that the 'ethically neutral instrument' of the market
ought to be respected, he himself has to justify this normative
choice by resort to the normative virtues he attributes to the
market system, including its results:

> an impersonal process which brings about *a greater satisfac-
> tion of human desires* than any deliberate human organization
> could achieve.[11]

or a set of institutions:

> which we then permitted to continue because it was found
> that *they improve for all or most the prospects of having their needs
> satisfied.*[12]

or still:

> a procedure which has *greatly improved the chances of all* to have their wants satisfied . . .[13]

and again:

> the only procedure yet discovered in which information widely dispersed among millions of men can be *effectively utilised for the benefit of all* – and used by *assuring to all an individual liberty* desirable for itself on ethical grounds.[14]

and quite conclusively:

> we use an impersonal process to determine the allocation of benefits *precisely because* through its operation we can *bring about* a structure of relative prices and remunerations that will determine *a size and composition of the total output* which assures that the real equivalent of each individual's share that accident or skill assigns to him will be *as large as we know how to make it*'[15]

It is interesting to observe that, while using these arguments to justify the moral desirability of the market order, Hayek is indeed discussing the results of that order in terms of the subject-matter of social justice – although, of course, his view on this subject-matter is that no overall pattern of distribution or social justice should be imposed on the market results. In other words, he is trying to show that *the benefits* produced by a 'game of skill and chance' are highly superior to those that would be produced by any other kind of system in which there was a common pattern of distribution. But this, in turn, is not due to the fact that, the market being 'an ethically neutral instrument', the discussion about the subject-matter of results and rewards becomes meaningless. On the contrary, this is due to the fact that, when we start discussing the normative value of such a system, including its results and rewards, we observe that it maximizes the chances of better results and rewards for all – even if the assignment of each reward to each person does not correspond to any ethical pattern of merit, desert, need, etc. The moral neutrality of the market system of distribution is then accepted, and even praised, for normative reasons: reasons which mainly consist of Hayek considering a system that maximizes the chances of better rewards for all as normatively preferable.[16]

HAYEK'S REFUTATION OF HIS OWN ARGUMENT

What should now be noticed is that, when justifying the market order for its ability to maximize rewards, Hayek is refuting some of the arguments he had presented to maintain that social justice is meaningless as a subject-matter. It will be recalled that there were two main arguments:

(1) The attribute of justice may thus be predicated about the intended results of human action, but not about circumstances which have not deliberately been brought about by men.[17]

(2) It [social justice] clearly has no application to the manner in which the impersonal process of the market allocates command over goods and services to particular people: this can be neither just nor unjust, because *the results are not intended or foreseen*, and depend on a multitude of circumstances not known in their totality to anybody.[18]

Now it is possible to note, as Kenneth Hoover and Raymond Plant have highlighted, that Hayek has refuted at least one of these arguments: that market results are not foreseen. Having justified the market system of rewards on the basis that it maximizes the chances of better rewards for all, Hayek is foreseeing the general or global structure of those results, although of course he is right when maintaining that it is not possible to foresee the particular reward that each individual will obtain.[19]

This seems sufficient, I believe, to say that Hayek's argument is in this respect ill-conceived. It is not because the results of the market are unforeseen that the concept or subject-matter of social justice does not apply to market rewards. It is because, among other reasons, one can foresee that the market will maximize the chances of better rewards for all that we consider as just, or normatively acceptable, an impersonal system of allocation of resources in which the rewards that each individual obtains do not obey a common pattern of distribution – and, for that reason, may be said to be unintended. But, if it may also be said that each of these rewards is unforeseen, the truth is that the general structure of rewards is foreseeable. And it was this foreseeability that allowed Hayek to justify the moral desirability of the market system of rewards on the basis that, through this system, 'we can bring about a structure of relative prices and remunerations that will determine a size and composition of the total output which assures that the real equivalent of each individual's share that accident or skill assigns to him will be as large as we know how to make it.'[20]

One can go even further. Hayek's first assumption, according to which justice does not apply to circumstances that have not been deliberately brought about by men, is also partially refuted by himself. Hayek now and again argues for a government protection guarantee for everybody against situations of severe deprivation in a form of an assured minimum income, or a floor below which nobody needs to descend:

> To enter into such an insurance against extreme misfortune may well be in the interest of all; or it may be felt to be a clear moral duty of all to assist, within the organized community, those who cannot help themselves.[21]

It is worth noting that this 'extreme misfortune' was not the product of deliberate actions of other individuals. Nevertheless, Hayek accepts that helping people in these circumstances 'may be felt to be a clear moral duty'. This seems to refute his thesis according to which 'the attribute of justice may not be predicated about circumstances which have not deliberately been brought about by men'.

As a matter of fact, Hayek's thesis seems to be once more ill-formulated. Once again, it seems that Raymond Plant has produced a reasonable critique here. He accepts that the attribute of justice may be predicated about the intended results of human actions, but maintains that the conclusion Hayek derives from this is mistaken. The only possible conclusion would be that, the 'extreme misfortune' not having been deliberately brought about, one cannot say that the cause of this misfortune is unjust: this cause may have been simply lack of luck, or a complicated series of circumstances for which nobody is responsible. Hence, one cannot say that 'extreme misfortune' is unjust. But this, in its turn, does not mean that *my absence of action* in the face of that extreme misfortune, or my refusal to act in order to avoid or minimize human suffering, is justifiable. In short, although a situation of 'extreme misfortune' may not be unjust, my intentional absence of action towards those individuals who happen to be in such situations may well become unjust. Only this can explain that Hayek himself considers that 'it may be felt to be a clear moral duty of all to assist, within the organized community, those who cannot help themselves'. A similar point is presented by Judith N. Shklar in her book *The Faces of Injustice*:

> It is evident that when we can alleviate suffering, whatever its cause, it is passively unjust to stand by and do nothing. It is not the origin of injury, but the possibility of preventing and reducing its costs, that allows us to judge whether it was or was not unjustifiable passivity in the face of disaster.[22]

METHODOLOGICAL REMARK: AN OVERVIEW

Hayek has observed the market system closely and discovered that the system of rewards it embodies does not obey any common pattern of distribution, or any common pattern of social justice. Markets allow people to exchange utilities, and each producer obtains a reward corresponding to the value his product has for those who consume it – not corresponding to the so-called merit of those who produce it, nor to their needs, not even to the value of the product to society.

Hayek deduced from this the erroneous conclusion that there is no meaning in a discussion about social justice in a liberal society, in other words, that the subject-matter of social justice is meaningless in a market order as well as in a liberal society. He used two main arguments: (1) that market results are unintended and unforeseen; (2) that the concept of social justice only applies to intentional human actions and not to circumstances which were not deliberately brought about by men.

Three main methodological mistakes in Hayek's reasoning have then been pointed out. The first was an illustration of *Hume's fork*. Hayek misleadingly identified the information about the ethically neutral nature of markets as systems of rewards with the alleged compulsory moral acceptance of that neutrality. He then thought it would be possible to rule out all discussion on the subject-matter of social justice. In fact, however, Hayek has accepted the fact of market neutrality because this neutrality appears to be desirable in terms of his own standards of social justice, that is, standards applying to the general structure of market results.

This was so because Hayek simultaneously acknowledged that, its being impossible to foresee a particular reward that the market procedure will allocate to each particular individual, it is nonetheless possible to foresee the global tendency, or the general structure, of rewards. These rewards tend to maximize the chances of everyone having their needs satisfied, and this is achieved by assuring to all an individual liberty desirable on ethical grounds. For these reasons – the first of which being a reason related to results and thus to the subject-matter of social justice – Hayek has accepted as morally valid the fact of moral neutrality of market procedures.

Having shown that Hayek's reasoning was actually thus, his second methodological mistake became apparent: he has misleadingly identified particular rewards – which are not foreseeable – with the global character of rewards, which are foreseen by himself. A third methodological mistake consisted of identifying *situations* with *human action (or absence of action) towards individuals in certain situations.* The fact that certain situations of extreme deprivation have not been deliberately brought about by men does not prevent Hayek from accepting that 'it may be felt to be a clear moral duty of all to assist, within the organized community, those who cannot help themselves'. Hence, to avoid or to minimize avoidable or minimizable human suffering – even if that suffering has not been deliberately brought about by other men – may well provide justification for a moral duty.[23]

Since it is possible, as we have indicated in the second methodological mistake, to foresee the general structure of rewards in a market order, a consequence derives from this: if, as Hayek himself has admitted, it is possible to foresee that situations of extreme deprivation may occur in a market order – and even though these situations have not been deliberately brought about by men – then we have the moral duty to create and improve procedures that can minimize the human suffering inherent in those situations of extreme deprivation.

A TEST FOR THE LEGITIMATE USE OF COERCION

Could this moral duty of helping those who cannot help themselves give rise to a moral right of the kind we first defined as 'social rights'? This is our next problem in the discussion of Hayek's argument against social rights.

There are two different issues at stake here. The first consists of investigating in what circumstances a duty might give rise to a right. For reasons of methodological convenience, we shall discuss it later, in Part II, where Raymond Plant's and socialist views are under scrutiny. For the time being, we shall keep suspended the response to this question, although we can admit the possibility that this duty actually gives rise to a right, since Hayek has not produced any argument against this possibility. In due course, the question will be addressed in full.

The second issue consists of investigating whether or not this moral duty, or the hypothetical right, passes the test put forward by Hayek in order to restrain the use of coercion in a free society. This test, we shall recall, was needed because 'if we wish to preserve a free society, it is essential that we recognize that the desirability of a particular object is not sufficient justification for the use of coercion'.[24] Applied to the moral duty referred to above, this test should then consist of three main stages:

(1) Does the moral duty, which is, in a way, a demand of minimal distributive justice, entail the power of somebody to assign particular shares of the product of society to different individuals or groups?

(2) Is this moral duty incompatible with the rule of laws of just conduct?

(3) Finally, does this moral duty entail the transformation of a spontaneous order into an organization?

These three stages will be discussed next.

TWO MEANINGS OF A MORAL DUTY

The first stage consists of finding out whether our moral duty 'demands as its counterpart a decision that somebody (a person or organization) should have the duty of providing what the others are to have'.[25] It will be recalled that, according to Hayek, this duty of providing what the others are to have would necessarily entail the transformation of a spontaneous order into an organization:

If such claims are to be met, the spontaneous order which we call society must be replaced by a deliberately directed organization; the cosmos of the market would have to be replaced by a taxis whose members would have to do what they are instructed to do. They could not be allowed to use their own knowledge for their own purposes but would have to carry out the plan which their rulers have designed to meet the needs to be satisfied.[26]

The problem at stake here consists of finding out whether the moral duty of helping those who cannot help themselves would have these same consequences and, as a first point, whether it would 'demand as its counterpart a decision that somebody (a person or organization) should have the duty of providing what the others are to have'. This problem has been called the first stage, or the first requirement, of the Hayekian test for the legitimate use of coercion in a free society.

We should start by noting that the formulation of this first step is ambiguous. 'The duty of providing what the others are to have' may be understood in at least two different ways, depending upon the meaning one attributes to the expression 'what the others are to have'. This ambiguity is far from being simply semantic.

If one understands 'what the others are to have' as 'everything or most of the things that everyone is to have', we will arrive at a situation which is dramatically different from the one we would get from the other possible meaning: 'some of the basic things that everyone is to have'. In the first case we have the typical consequence (which was brilliantly denounced by Hayek) of a decision to impose a common pattern of distribution, or of social justice. If one believes that every single share the market attributes to each person must not be accepted as morally valid – perhaps because the market is an 'ethically neutral instrument' – then a consequence becomes inevitable: one has to substitute a central authority (either a central one, or the authority of all joined together), in charge of attributing to each individual or group particular shares of the global outcome, for the 'game of skill and chance' of the market.

As Hayek correctly highlights, the particular criterion of distribution is irrelevant here. It can be 'merit', or 'desert', 'needs', or 'value to society', or equality, but there will always be a common pattern of distribution. This demands that some-body, or all joined together, decides what everyone is to have in the sense of 'everything or most of the things that everyone is to have'. Spontaneous exchanges among individuals, as well as individual responsibility for one's actions would inevitably lose the central place that Hayek rightly attributes to them in a society of free men. As he has pointed out, individuals 'could not be allowed to use their knowledge for their own purposes but would have to carry out the plan which their rulers have designed to meet the needs to be satisfied'.

But the second meaning of the expression 'what the others are to have' – when it is interpreted as 'some of the basic things that everyone is to have, or that everyone must not be deprived of' – produces rather different consequences. There is no *positive* common pattern of distribution, no attempt to establish what kind of reward or share is to be allotted to each individual. On the contrary, there is only what we could call a *negative, residual* or *basic* pattern of distribution, which only refers to *that minimum that people must not be deprived of.* It will be recalled that Hayek used precisely a negative formulation to refer to the moral duty of helping those who cannot help themselves: 'a floor below which nobody need descend'.

One should note that there is no room here for any person or organization to decide what each individual is to have. There is only a decision about the minimum that everybody cannot be deprived of. All the rest above this minimum is not subject to any kind of collective or central decision. Hence there is no central overall allocation of resources and, for that reason, there is no motive for the transformation of a spontaneous order into an organization. Hayek himself acknowledges this distinction, although he does not derive from it all due consequences:

> So long as such a uniform minimum income is provided out-side the market to all those who, for any reason, are unable to earn in the market an adequate maintenance, this need not lead to a restriction of freedom, or conflict with the Rule of Law. The problems with which we are here concerned arise *only* when the remuneration for services rendered is determined by authority, and the impersonal mechanism of the market which guides the direction of individual efforts is thus suspended.[27]

SOCIAL INJUSTICE VERSUS SOCIAL JUSTICE

It is worth investigating which are the consequences that Hayek is not able to derive from this distinction which he himself acknowledges. Basically, these consequences are that a similar distinction may be made between a positive and a negative or basic conception of social rights, a positive and a negative conception of social justice.

In other words, Hayek is right when maintaining that a common pattern of distribution or social justice entails the creation of a central authority that arbitrarily decides what each one should obtain. But he does not notice that this is a *positive* pattern of distribution. Such consequences do not arise from a *negative, residual* or *basic* pattern of social justice, a pattern that only *forbids* morally undesirable situations of extreme deprivation, instead of *prescribing* morally desirable situations based on general criterions such as well-being, merit, needs, etc.

Using the same terminology of Hayek, there is, therefore, a crucial distinction between 'gradually approaching social justice' and 'persistently eliminating social injustice'. Unfortunately, Hayek explicitly denies this distinction:

> It might be objected that [. . .] we might not know what is 'socially just' yet know quite well what is 'socially unjust'; and by persistently eliminating 'social injustice' whenever we encounter it, gradually approach 'social justice'. This, however, does not provide a way out of the basic difficulty.[28]

We now have the conceptual instruments to show that the reason put forward by Hayek to deny the relevance of 'social injustice' as a negative concept is not valid:

> There can be no test by which we can discover what is 'socially unjust' because (1) there is no subject by which such an injustice can be committed, and (2) there are no rules of individual conduct the observance of which in the market order would secure to the individuals and groups the position which as such (as distinguished from the procedure by which it is determined) would appear as *just* to us.[29]

The first argument ('there is no subject by which such an injustice can be committed') was refuted in a previous section with the assistance of Raymond Plant and Judith N. Shklar.

We have then seen that it was based on a confusion between a *situation of deprivation* and *human actions* towards those who happen to be in such a situation. Whereas the situation may well not be unjust in itself, our inaction in the face of people in that situation is unjust and morally condemnable.

The second argument maintains that 'there are no rules of just conduct the observance of which in the market order would secure the position which as such [...] would appear as *just* to us'. It must be immediately noted that this formulation is not accurate. From the standpoint of 'persistently eliminating injustice' – which is the issue discussed here by Hayek as contrasted with 'promoting social justice' – we need not know 'which positions would appear as *just* to us'. It suffices to know which positions would appear as *unjust*. And, although it is necessary to discuss the notion of 'unjust' – namely to prevent the abuse of this notion by politicians and interest groups eager to interfere in the market order – there is no doubt that we can to a great extent agree on a common notion of 'unjust'. Hayek himself provided a reasonable approximation to this notion:

> There is no reason why in a free society government should not assure to all *protection against severe deprivation* in the form of an assured minimum income, or floor below which nobody need descend. To enter into such an insurance *against* extreme misfortune may well be in the interest of all; or it may be felt to be a clear moral duty of all to assist, within the organized community, *those who cannot help themselves.*[30]

This shows that, still according to Hayek, it is possible to define unjust situations without resorting to a common or positive pattern of distribution, or social justice. Furthermore, it is even possible to show that Hayek himself has sometimes acknowledged this crucial distinction, even though he has been unable to draw all the necessary conclusions. It is worth quoting his own words:

> It is true, of course, that even the provision of a uniform minimum for all those who cannot provide for themselves involves some redistribution of income. But there is a great deal of difference between the provision of such a minimum for all those who cannot maintain themselves on their earnings in

a normally functioning market and a redistribution aiming
at a 'just' remuneration in all the more important occupa-
tions – between a redistribution wherein the great majority
earning their living agree to give to those unable to do so,
and a redistribution wherein a great majority takes from a
minority because the latter has more. The former preserves
the impersonal method of adjustment under which people
can choose their occupation; the latter brings us nearer and
nearer to a system under which people will have to be told
by authority what to do.[31]

After this, one can reasonably say that the first stage of the
Hayekian test for the legitimate use of coercion in a free society
has been overtaken: because the moral duty to assist those who
cannot help themselves does not entail any general criterion
of distribution, it does not demand either that somebody (a
person or an organization) should have the power to decide
what each individual is to have.

We are then left with the problem of knowing whether this
moral duty of helping those who cannot help themselves is
compatible with the rule of laws of just conduct, the second
stage of what has been called the Hayekian test.[32]

RULES: FORMAL CHARACTER AND CONTENT

The second requirement or stage of what has been called the
Hayekian test for the legitimate use of coercion in a society of
free men consists of finding out whether or not the pursuit
of a given purpose, including the political measures needed to
achieve it, is compatible with the rule of law. This requirement
is closely linked with the previous one, but it is still independent. The first requirement concerns the *amount* of power, as it
were, which a central authority would have to have in order to
guarantee a certain minimum to each individual. The second
requirement concerns the *manner* in which this power is to be
exercised: is it to be exercised by way of general rules, equal for
and predictable by all, or is it to be exercised through specific
commands which are going to vary according to the goals of
the rulers and, for that reason, are going to be unpredictable
for the ordinary citizen?

Hayek seems to believe, or at least he did so at the time of writing *The Constitution of Liberty*, published in 1960, that a power which is exercised through laws and not through specific commands is necessarily non-arbitrary and liberal. For that reason he might have considered as unnecessary the distinction presented here between the first and the second requirements of the 'Hayekian test' for the legitimate use of coercion in a free society. In order to evaluate whether or not a government is arbitrary, the second requirement (the rule of law) would probably suffice. Nevertheless this is disputable.

It has been suggested that most of the formal characteristics that Hayek attributes to the rule of law could be respected by an illiberal government which could still be said not to be arbitrary, in the sense that it could still obey general rules. In an essay on Hayek's *The Constitution of Liberty*, entitled 'La definition liberale de la liberté', Raymond Aron has observed that 'a law which in fact is arbitrary may be formulated in such terms that it presents all the characteristics of generality and abstraction. If a law forbids every citizen to travel abroad, it is not discriminatory; yet it is illiberal.'[33] This led Aron to conclude that one has to add the analysis of the concrete character of each prohibition imposed by a law to the analysis of the formal properties of generality and abstractness. A similar point was made by Samuel Brittan.[34]

According to these reflections of Raymond Aron and Samuel Brittan, it appears to be necessary to discuss separately the first two requirements of the Hayekian test for the legitimate use of coercion in a free society. In the previous section we have discussed the requirement concerning the 'amount of power' involved in the moral duty of helping those who cannot help themselves. It was then temporarily assumed, for reasons of methodological convenience, that this duty could give rise to a special type of social right, which was then called a *basic social right*. Moreover it was argued that, interpreted in a basic or negative sense, this social right would not demand as its counterpart any such power that would deny individuals the freedom to use their best knowledge in the pursuit of their own purposes. It was then concluded that, for this reason, the concept of basic social rights could perfectly satisfy the first requirement of the Hayekian test for the legitimate use of coercion in a free society.

The second requirement of this test should now be discussed: not the 'amount of power', but the 'manner' in which it is exercised. Will the concept of basic social rights still be compatible with a power limited by general and abstract laws? This is our present problem.

BASIC SOCIAL RIGHTS AND THE RULE OF LAW

In *The Constitution of Liberty*, Hayek wrote that 'Law in its ideal form might be described as a 'once-and-for-all' command that is directed to unknown people and that is abstracted from all particular circumstances of time and place and refers only to such conditions as may occur anywhere and at any time.'[35] Hayek was trying to contrast the concept of law with that of command and, as we have seen in Chapter 1, he associated laws with the rules of a spontaneous order and commands with the rules of an organization.

In the same book, Hayek attempted to define several characteristics of the law as opposed to those of a command. He said that laws must be, in general terms, 'general, abstract and equal for all'. But he added at least five characteristics which would illustrate this general character of generality, abstractness and equality: laws must be negative, independent of particular purposes, equal to or at least accepted by all, and must apply to those who lay them down and those who apply them.

The negative character of laws means that:

> General and abstract rules specify that in certain circumstances action must satisfy certain conditions; but all the many kinds of action that satisfy these conditions are permissible; [...] though they eliminate certain choices open to [the individual], they do not, as a rule, limit the choice to some specific action that somebody else wants him to take.[36]

Hayek maintains, secondly, that laws must not aim at particular situations or particular cases. 'Because the rule is laid down in ignorance of the particular case', he says, 'and no man's will decides the coercion used to enforce it, the law is not arbitrary.'[37] But this aspect is true only if, he adds, rules apply equally to all: 'As a true law should not name any particulars, so it should especially not single out any specific person or groups of persons.'[38] This is the third characteristic of laws.

There is, however, some qualification to be made in this principle of equality. Hayek observes that 'it does not mean that sometimes special rules may not apply to different classes of people if they refer to properties that only some possess'[39] – this is the case, for example, of women, or people above certain age, or the disabled, etc. In most of these circumstances laws need not name these classes of people, since only they are in the specific situations, or have the specific properties the law is referring to. (For instance, only women can have babies.) Anyway, the problem consists here of finding out in what conditions laws that apply to different classes of people may be considered as legitimate:

> Such distinctions will not be arbitrary, will not subject one group to the will of others, if they are equally recognized as justified by those inside and those outside the group. This does not mean that there must be unanimity as to the desirability of the distinction, but merely that individual views will not depend on whether the individual is in the group or not.[40]

We have then a fourth principle which has to be added or qualify the principle of equality: that the laws, when they apply to different groups of people, must be susceptible to the approval of all, irrespective of whether they are inside or outside the group. Finally Hayek adds a last safeguard against the possibility that laws restrict freedom unnecessarily: 'That the rules must apply to those who lay them down and those who apply them – and that nobody has the power to grant exceptions.'[41]

These are, briefly, the five characteristics which distinguish general and abstract laws, also the property of a spontaneous order, as opposed to specific commands which are the property of an organization. The problem now consists of finding out whether what has been called 'basic social rights' – rights we have temporarily admitted as arising from the duty of helping those who cannot help themselves – may be enforced through general and abstract laws, or, on the contrary, whether they demand specific commands.

The reasonable answer seems to be that it all depends. Basic social rights may be enforced either by general laws or by specific commands. This will depend upon the political will and the political traditions of the society in which these rights are to be enforced. One must admit that an illiberal political culture will allow a strong temptation to introduce basic social rights with recourse to specific commands. But one must also admit that there is nothing in the nature of basic social rights that prevents them from being enforced by general and abstract laws.

This versatility of basic social rights is at the origin of enduring debates about the procedures of their enforcement. Liberals have, as a rule, favoured measures that respect what Hayek calls the negative characteristic of laws. They usually want welfare benefits to be paid in cash, and not in kind, in order to allow the recipient the freedom to choose how best to use the help he receives. Also because liberals want to restrict the apparatus of bureaucracy, and because they want to give individuals power to choose, they usually favour voucher schemes rather than state provision of services – this is the case with education and health. Ideally, welfare provisions would be produced by the market and subject to market competition, and people in need would be directly subsidized by vouchers.

In order that laws might be independent of particular situations or particular cases, liberals tend to support the universality of welfare provision. The idea of a minimum income guarantee – which is to be distinguished from a minimum wage, which directly interferes with market signals – seems to have been designed precisely to fit the requirement of general application irrespective of particular circumstances.

Such is also the case of equality before the law. Liberals usually refuse to accept that welfare provisions are dependent upon correlative duties of the recipients – such as working for the state, or voting, etc. – which are not the universal duties of all citizens. This is probably one of the reasons liberals also oppose the so-called 'right to work'. This would lead to the obligation of accepting the work provided by the state, and would thus infringe the principle of an equal right to choose whatever job one wants. In this respect, a right not to work is much more important, from a liberal standpoint, than the so-called right to work.

One might probably reply that basic social rights do not treat individuals as equals, since they consist of transfers of resources from the better-off to the worse-off by means of taxation and subsidies. But here we are confronted by the fourth characteristic of Hayek's definition of general laws: that laws, when applying to different groups or people, must be susceptible to the approval of all, irrespective of whether they are inside or outside the group. This approval, which Hayek rightly distinguishes from unanimity, is compatible with the idea of a universal insurance against extreme misfortune. Its acceptance does not depend upon whether or not the individual is inside the group of those who happen to have experienced extreme misfortune: everyone may be in such a situation in the unknown future and, therefore, all have reasonable motives to accept the principle of supporting those who happen to be in a situation of extreme misfortune, or deprivation.

Needless to say, this only applies to social rights interpreted in the negative or basic sense presented here, as will be extensively argued in Part II. A view of social rights which is inspired by a positive pattern of distribution or social justice, does not satisfy, and never will, the requirements of a 'thought experiment' in which individuals are counted as equals. Under a Rawlsian 'veil of ignorance', individuals would never reach unanimity to implement a policy of what Samuel Brittan rightly called 'reassignment' as opposed to redistribution. As has been previously argued, reassignment is a typical example of a policy inspired by a positive pattern of distribution or social justice. Redistribution, in its turn, may only be inspired by a negative concept of justice, in the sense that it may merely arise from the moral imperative of helping those who cannot help themselves, and not necessarily from any preconception about a positive pattern of social justice.

A CRITIQUE OF HAYEK'S ARGUMENT: AN OVERVIEW

This chapter started with a methodological remark: that Hayek was trapped in the 'is/ought' dichotomy detected by David Hume. Observing that the *market* is an ethically neutral instrument, in which the concept or subject-matter of social justice *is* meaningless, he concluded that this concept *ought* to be meaningless in a *liberal society*. It was then pointed out that Hayek himself had accepted the fact of market neutrality because this neutrality appeared to be normatively desirable in terms of the results it brings about. It was also recalled that Hayek himself admitted that 'it may be felt to be a clear moral duty of all to assist, within the organized community, those who cannot help themselves'. And it was then concluded that, if it is possible to foresee that situations of extreme misfortune may recurrently occur in a market order, then, taking Hayek seriously, we should have the moral duty to create and improve procedures that can minimize the human suffering inherent in those situations.

Whether or not this moral duty could give rise to a correspondent social right (to be helped, so to speak) then became our next problem. Two major issues were at stake here: (1) to discuss in what circumstances a duty might give rise to a right, and (2) to investigate whether or not such duty would be compatible with the 'Hayekian test' for the legitimate use of coercion in a free society. It was then proposed, for reasons of methodological convenience, to postpone the discussion of the first issue, although one could temporarily admit that a social right might be produced by this moral duty, since Hayek did not object to that possibility. The discussion then focused on the second issue: could this moral duty, or this hypothetical social right pass the 'Hayekian test'?

According to the presentation of Hayek's argument included in Chapter 1, the 'Hayekian test' was then defined by three main requirements. The first requirement consisted of knowing whether or not a certain right 'demands as its counterpart a decision that somebody should have the duty of providing what the others are to have'. It was argued that 'what the others are to have' could be interpreted in two different ways. The positive one would certainly entail the substitution of a central authority for the market order. But the negative one would not. A distinction between a positive and a negative or basic conception of social rights was then suggested, and it was proposed that a similar distinction could be made between 'promoting social justice' and 'eliminating social injustice'. Hayek's argument against the relevance of this distinction was then refuted – once again, by resort to his own arguments. It was then presented how other authors, such as Samuel Brittan, Ralf Dahrendorf and Karl Popper, have somehow acknowledged this distinction between a negative criterion of social justice (or a criterion of social injustice) and a positive one. The conclusion of this point was, of course, that our temporarily admitted social right had passed the first stage of the 'Hayekian test'.

The second stage consisted of finding out whether or not the enforcement of this hypothetical basic social right would be compatible with the rule of law. Hayek's five main characteristics of the law, as opposed to the characteristics of specific commands, were then recalled. And it was argued that basic social rights, as opposed to positive ones, are not necessarily incompatible with the rule of law, even though they are also compatible with government by specific commands. Liberals need not, therefore, rule out the enforcement of basic social rights by way of law. On the contrary, it is reasonable to assume that they should argue for this.

Now, the conclusion of our discussion of the 'Hayekian test' for the legitimate use of coercion in a free society seems to be clear: basic social rights, and only these, have passed the test. But, even before investigating whether Hayek's moral duty actually gives rise to a social right – which will be done in Part II – we now face another problem: if basic social rights pass the 'Hayekian test', why did he exclude them? This question will be discussed in the next chapter, which is dedicated to an evaluation of Hayek's argument.

3 An Evaluation: Civilization Based on Personal Decisions

The latter-day liberals fell into the same error as Marx. Only they became apologists for instead of opponents of the status quo.
Walter Lippmann, *The Good Society*, 1938

Sometimes we find among liberals – as among Marxists – a tendency to believe that the world order permits the conciliation of reality with our aspirations. This confidence is not without a certain grandeur. Allow me to admire it, without imitating it.
Raymond Aron, *Political Studies*, 1972

We may become the makers of our fate when we have ceased to pose as its prophets.
Karl Popper, *The Open Society and its Enemies*, 1945

WHY DID HAYEK RULE OUT BASIC SOCIAL RIGHTS?

If a negative view of social rights or, as we have also called it, a conception of basic social rights, has passed the 'Hayekian test' for the use of legitimate coercion in a free society, why did Hayek exclude it? Because he did not take seriously his own normative arguments in favour of the rule of law, and because he has gradually detached himself from those arguments, exchanging them for an evolutionist theory which rules out all moral and normative considerations, including the 'Hayekian test' itself. However peculiar and perhaps even daring this contention may sound, this final chapter on Hayek's argument will present the case for it.

The argument presented here will be that Hayek's normative defence of classical liberalism is powerful and outstanding, but it has been undermined by his dogmatic evolutionism. On the particular subject of social rights, Hayek has acutely shown the contradiction between a positive view of these rights – the one which identifies them with a positive pattern of distribution or social justice – and the classical liberal conception of civil and political rights. But his insights would have been perfectly compatible with what has been called here a negative view of social rights, as was shown in the previous chapter. If Hayek failed to grasp that compatibility, this is not due to his normative view of liberalism – namely his view of liberty as absence of coercion, or his defence of the spontaneous order of the market – but to the fact that he has yielded to the allure of the other component of his doctrine: the naturalistic and somehow historicist theory of evolution. This yielding may be illustrated by his instrumental view of the rule of law, and, moreover, by his untenable ambition to discard the need of personal decision on moral issues or, to put it shortly, by his historicist theory of cultural evolution.

SPONTANEOUS ORDER AND THE RULE OF LAW

The internal tension in Hayek's political theory becomes apparent in his distinction between rules of a spontaneous or 'grown' order and rules of an organization or 'made' order. As was mentioned in Chapter 1, one of the main distinctions between the two orders concerns their origin. The spontaneous order results gradually from a process that is neither intended nor planned by anyone, whereas the organization is made by design. The same problem about origins might then apply to the rules which govern the functioning of these orders. Are their origins also different? Should the rules of a spontaneous order also be a spontaneous product in themselves? Or might they be intentionally designed, namely with the specific purpose of creating or of protecting and improving a spontaneous order? In other words, does the spontaneous nature of a 'grown' order demand that the origin of its rules be itself spontaneous?

Hayek has actually answered these questions in a contradictory way. Conceptually, he has maintained absolutely that 'while the rules on which a spontaneous order rests may also be of spontaneous origin, this need not always be the case. [. . .] And it is at least conceivable that the formulation of a spontaneous order relies entirely on rules that were deliberately made'.[1] But, later, Hayek ends by contradicting this assertion when he identifies the rules of a spontaneous order – 'nomos', or the law of liberty – with that body of law that emerges from the separate decisions of judges in a process of spontaneous adjustment. He calls the law of liberty 'the lawyer's law' and he explicitly identifies it with the English tradition of the 'common law'.[2] Hayek is thus applying the criterion of origins – which he used to distinguish a spontaneous order from an organization – to the very rules that regulate each one of these orders. The law of liberty is itself a product of a spontaneous evolution, whereas legislation, the rules of organization – is produced by design.

The first comment that might be made on this conception is that it is too closely related to the English experience. American Founding Fathers' liberalism would hardly recognize itself in this evolutionist and anti-design view of Hayek's liberalism. It is apparent throughout *The Federalist Papers* that the makers of the American Constitution were committed to the making of fundamental laws by design. They wished to create those laws which would best suit the protection of a liberal order, or, as Hayek would say, 'a state of liberty or freedom', 'that condition of men in which coercion of some by others is reduced as much as is possible in society'.[3] This was acutely pointed out by James Buchanan:

> The European classical liberal, who is well represented by Hayek, can and perhaps should stress the evolutionary sources of many of the institutions that stand as bulwarks of individual freedom. The American cannot, and should not, neglect the fact that his own heritage of freedom, although owing much to its European antecedents, was deliberately constructed in large part by James Madison and his compatriots. Theirs were no invisible hands. They set out to construct a constitutional framework for 'the good society', which they defined implicitly as 'free relations among free men.[4]

The second comment that might be made on Hayek's view consists of recalling that he himself underlines the fact that a spontaneous order – and namely the spontaneous order of the market – cannot survive without the protection of an appropriate framework of laws. Moreover, the whole of Hayek's defence of a liberal conception of liberty is underpinned by the principle that liberty must not be misleadingly identified with licence, nor with the pure absence of norms. Rules of law are the condition of the existence of liberty, and of a free market, rather than its product. However, if the law is a condition of the existence of a spontaneous order, how could the same spontaneous order alone produce the laws on which it depends? This would imply that all orders based on unconstrained exchange between individuals would necessarily produce rules appropriate to the protection of free exchange between individuals. But this is hardly plausible, as Karl Popper has pointed out:

> It is clear that the idea of a free market is paradoxical. If the state does not interfere, then other semi-political organizations such as monopolies, trusts, unions, etc, may interfere, reducing the freedom of the market to a fiction.[5]

Popper does not infer from this that the ideal of a free market is nothing but an illusion. He wants to show that, in order to safeguard the desirable (in liberal terms) freedom of the market, it is indispensable to intervene to protect it. If intervention to protect liberty is not guaranteed by the rule of law, other interventions will take place, reducing the freedom of the market to a fiction.

> It is most important to realize that without a *carefully protected free market*, the whole economic system must cease to serve its only rational purpose, that is, to satisfy the demands of the consumer.[6]

The same problem, approached from a different angle, has been presented by James Buchanan. Having recalled the concept of 'external diseconomies', Buchanan points out that there may be both 'spontaneous orders' and 'spontaneous disorders':

> The results produced by the operation of the invisible hand, by the independent and separate utility maximizing behaviour of persons, are not necessarily efficient in the economic sense. [. . .] The principle of spontaneous order, as such, is fully neutral in this respect. It need not be exclusively or even primarily limited to explanations of unplanned and unintended outcomes that are socially efficient.[7]

For the same reason, Buchanan denies that the simple fact that some institutions have evolved spontaneously, through the independent responses of persons to the choices that they faced, might constitute a guarantee that these institutions embody efficiency attributes. The same principle leads him to say that he sees 'no reason to expect that the evolution of law made by independent judges ensures efficiency or optimality'.[8]

EVOLUTION AND RULES OF JUST CONDUCT

At the end of the third volume of *Law, Legislation and Liberty*, Hayek includes an Epilogue entitled 'The Three Sources of Human Values'.[9] And in the Preface to the one-volume edition of the work, dated 1982, Hayek underlines the scope of the considerations he had included in that Epilogue:

> The Epilogue I added to that volume before publication indicates that even during the period of restricted activity my ideas have continued to develop imperceptibly more than I was aware of before I attempted to sketch my present general view of the whole position in a public lecture. As I said in the concluding words of the present text, it became clear to me that the Epilogue has become the outline of a new book of which I have now completed a first draft.[10]

The book Hayek is referring to would see the daylight in 1988 with the title *The Fatal Conceit: The Errors of Socialism*, as the first of 22 volumes of Hayek's collected works to be edited by W. W. Bartley III. In this book, Hayek presents his general theory of cultural evolution, which he had just sketched in the Epilogue of *Law, Legislation and Liberty*. His central question consists of finding out the origin of the rules of just conduct whose observance allowed the flourishing of market economies and liberal societies. Hayek's answer, usually designated as a non-justificationist theory of morals, is briefly presented at the very start of his Introduction to *The Fatal Conceit*:

> This book argues that our civilisation depends, not only for its origin but also for its preservation, on what can be precisely described only as the extended order of human cooperation, an order more commonly, if somewhat misleadingly, known as capitalism. To understand our civilisation, one must appreciate that the extended order resulted not from human design or intention but spontaneously: it arose from unintentionally conforming to certain traditional and largely *moral* practices, many of which men tend to dislike, whose significance they usually fail to understand, whose validity they cannot prove, and which have nonetheless fairly rapidly spread by means of an evolutionary selection – the comparative increase of population and wealth – of

those groups that happened to follow them. The unwitting, reluctant, even painful adoption of these practices kept these groups together, increased their access to valuable information of all sorts, and enabled them to be 'fruitful and multiply, and replenish the earth, and subdue it' (*Genesis* 1:28). This process is perhaps the least appreciated facet of human evolution.[11]

The starting-point of this conception of Hayek's seems to be once again his critique of what he calls the illusions of constructivist rationalism. This rationalism, he maintains, wants to reject all the traditions that cannot rationally be justified. He adds that this ambition is logically inconsistent and empirically irrelevant.

In order to show that this justificationist ambition is logically inconsistent, Hayek cites the philosophical work of Karl Popper. He recalls Popper's falsificationist theory first presented in *The Logic of Scientific Discovery*,[12] according to which scientific theories are not susceptible of positive demonstration but only of negative falsification, or refutation. Theories which are able to resist crucial experiments – conceived as tests to refute the empirical consequences which stem from the theories – do not become proved theories. They are only corroborated, and may still be refuted by a future crucial experiment:

> It is indeed true not only that our current scientific laws are not justified or justifiable in the way that constructivist methodologists demand, but that we have reason to suppose that we shall eventually learn that many of our present scientific conjectures are untrue. Any conception that guides us more successfully than what we hitherto believed may, moreover, although a great advance, be in substance as mistaken as its predecessor. As we have learnt from Karl Popper (1934/1959), our aim must be to make our successive mistakes as quickly as possible.[13]

Hayek also quotes a lecture of Karl Popper's on the nature of traditions[14] and recalls that Popper criticizes the ambition to eliminate all traditions that cannot be rationally justified. And Hayek concludes:

> If we were meanwhile to abandon all present conjectures that we cannot prove to be true, we would soon be back at

the level of the savage who trusts only his instincts. Yet this is what all versions of scientism have advised – from Cartesian rationalism to modern positivism.'[15]

Having said that, Hayek maintains that the origin of moral rules really lies in an evolutionary process whereby the practices of those groups which prevail are copied and adopted by the others. 'Such new rules', Hayek explains, 'would spread not because men understood that they were more effective, or could calculate that they would lead to expansion, but simply because they enabled those groups practising them to procreate more successfully and to include outsiders.'[16]

The problem remains to know how and why these 'successful rules' were initially adopted by those pioneer groups who did not have the experience of other groups to copy. Hayek insists that even in these pioneer cases – as would have been those of ancient Athens and Rome, the Renaissance Italian towns, or seventeenth-century England and Holland – there was no awareness of the reasons whereby those rules were followed:

> Disliking these constraints so much, we can hardly be said to have selected them; rather, these constraints selected us: they enabled us to survive. [. . .] All this is possible because we stand in a great framework of institutions and traditions – economic, legal, and moral – into which we fit ourselves by obeying certain rules of conduct that we never made, and which we have never understood in the sense in which we understand how the things we manufacture function.[17]

The question that stems from this is formulated by Hayek himself about one hundred pages later:

> How could traditions which people do not like or understand, whose effects they usually do not appreciate and can neither see nor foresee, and which they are still ardently combating, continue to have been passed on from generation to generation? More important, how were they preserved against the strong opposition of instinct and, more recently, from the assaults of reason?[18]

Hayek's answer to this problem is not conciliatory:

> We owe it partially to mystical and religious beliefs, and, I believe, particularly to the main monotheistic ones, that

beneficial traditions have been preserved and transmitted at least long enough to enable those groups following them to grow, and to have the opportunity to spread by natural or cultural selection. This means that, like it or not, we owe the persistence of certain practices, and the civilisation that resulted from them, in part to support from beliefs which are not true – or verifiable or testable – in the same sense as are scientific statements, and which are certainly not the result of rational argumentation. I sometimes think that it might be appropriate to call at least some of them, in at least a gesture of appreciation, 'symbolic truths', since they did help their adherents to 'be fruitful and multiply and replenish the earth and subdue it' (*Genesis* 1:28).[19]

TRADITION AND REASON

Friedrich Hayek has based his critique of the constructivist ambition about moral traditions on the philosophical work of Karl Popper, by which he acknowledges other main issues of his doctrine to have been inspired. It is not clear, however, that he has properly applied the 'critical rationalism' of Karl Popper, namely in what concerns the attitude towards traditions.

Popper presents himself as a 'rationalist of sorts'. In *The Open Society and its Enemies*, he maintained:

> The issue between rationalism and irrationalism is of long standing. [. . .] In this issue, I am entirely on the side of rationalism. This is so much the case that even where I feel that rationalism has gone too far I still sympathize with it, holding as I do that an excess in this direction (as long as we exclude the intellectual immodesty of Plato's pseudo-rationalism) is harmless, the only way in which excessive rationalism is likely to prove harmful is that it tends to undermine its own position and thus to further an irrationalist reaction.[20]

In fact Popper has strongly criticized some rationalist excess, and he established a distinction between an 'uncritical or comprehensive rationalism', which he criticizes, and a 'critical rationalism', which he sustains. This difference lies mainly in the role and limits of reason. Uncritical rationalism holds the principle that 'any assumption which cannot be supported either by argument or by experience is to be discarded'[21] Popper then shows this principle to be inconsistent, 'for since it cannot, in its turn, be supported by argument or by experience, it implies that it should itself be discarded'. He then concludes that 'uncritical rationalism' is logically untenable and adds:

> This criticism may be generalized. Since all argument must proceed from assumptions, it is plainly impossible to demand that all assumptions should be based on argument. The demand raised by many philosophers that we should start with no assumptions whatever and never assume anything without 'sufficient reason', and even the weaker demand that we should start with a very small set of assumptions ('categories'), are both in this form inconsistent. For they themselves rest upon the truly colossal assumption that it is possible to start without, or with only a few assumptions, and still obtain results that are worth while. (Indeed this principle of avoiding all presuppositions is not, as some may think, a counsel of perfection, but a form of the paradox of the liar).[22]

In his Oxford lecture 'Towards a Rational Theory of Tradition', Popper develops the views on critical rationalism which he had already presented in *The Open Society*. The paper may be seen as a brilliantly powerful case for rationalism, against two main other conceptions, which Popper calls traditionalist irrationalism, and uncritical or comprehensive rationalism. He presents himself again as 'rationalist of sorts' who counters anti-rationalist traditionalism in a special way, which he is not sure that his listeners will accept. Curiously enough, Popper defines anti-rationalism in a way that could apply to some of Hayek's views, especially some of those presented in *The Fatal Conceit*. Here are his own words:

> The anti-rationalists in the field of politics, social theory, and so on, usually suggest that this problem [of tradition] cannot be tackled by any kind of rational theory. Their attitude is to accept tradition as something just given. You have to take it; you cannot rationalize it; it plays an important role in society, and you can only understand its significance and accept it. The most important name associated with this anti-rationalist view is that of Edmund Burke.[23]

Popper recalls next that the 'traditional' (it is his expression) view of rationalists consists of maintaining total or global hostility to tradition. A 'traditional rationalist' would say:

I am not interested in tradition. I want to judge everything on its own merits; I want to find out its merits and demerits, and I want to do this quite independently of any tradition. I want to judge with my own brain, and not with the brains of other people who lived long ago.[24]

This idea, of submitting to critical doubt *all* traditions before accepting them, is then going to be criticized by Karl Popper in two main issues. The first consists of observing that we do hundreds of things daily under the influence of traditions that we are not even aware of. (If I wear my watch on my left wrist, I need not be conscious that I am accepting a tradition, Poppers recalls.) And the second point is even more decisive. It consists of recognizing that the existence of traditions and their acceptance as *starting points* is absolutely indispensable to scientific activity itself – and, as we shall see, to the very critique of traditions.

As referred to above, Karl Popper had presented this idea in *The Open Society*, asserting that the ambition to base all assumptions on argument was logically inconsistent. In his Oxford lecture, he approaches the problem in a slightly different way. He recalls his own theory of knowledge and science in order to show that all that science does is to start from problems and then to question reality from their standpoint. Mere multiplication of observations does not constitute science since we would not even know what to conclude from observations which were not themselves oriented and selected by previous problems. In fact, we would not even know what to observe.

The next problem goes without saying: from where do problems arise? They arise, Popper asserts, from real problems, problems existing objectively, from questions that we ask about those real problems and which we answer tentatively, afterwards trying to test these answers with experience. But the truth is also that each problem we are able to put forward is formulated according to, or on the basis of, the *scientific tradition* hitherto accumulated, the whole of the answers hitherto accepted and the new problems those answers have produced. It is indeed true that the conjectural solution for a new problem may put into question the whole system of scientific traditions hitherto accepted – and thus oblige a complete change in those traditions. But it is no less true that this is only possible because the new problems were formulated on the basis of existing traditions and not on the basis of no traditions at all, or of a radical critique of all traditions. Such an operation is simply not possible for, as it was noted, we would not be able to formulate that radical critique. Thus, the acceptance of *tradition* as a working basis, as it were, for the critical discussion of problems and of particular *traditions*, is indispensable to the progress of science.

> It is a very simple and a decisive point, but nevertheless one that is often not sufficiently realized by rationalists – that we cannot start afresh; that we must make use of what people before us have done in science. If we start afresh, then, when we die, we shall be about as far as neanderthal man. [. . .] We do not know where or how to start our analysis of this world. There is no wisdom to tell us. Even the scientific tradition does not tell us. It only tells us where and how other people started and where they got to. [. . .] It serves us as a kind of network, as a system of co-ordinates to which we can refer the various complexities of this world.[25]

For this very same reason, Popper demolished the authoritarian intellectualist dream of Plato 'to clean the canvas' and start afresh a brand new rational world ruled by the philosopher-king. For the same reason, Popper demolished the Utopian dreams of the radical left.

*   *   *

It might be said that this argument of Popper's strongly corroborates Hayek's own view. If we cannot justify or demonstrate traditions, and if we act under the influence of traditions which we are not even aware of, are not these the best arguments for Hayek's non-justificationist theory of tradition and morals? Not really. Popper indeed asserts that we cannot justify traditions, but the same applies to almost everything, scientific theories included. They cannot be positively demonstrated, but only negatively falsified. And the fact is that, if we cannot positively demonstrate or justify traditions as well as scientific theories, we can still discuss both. Popper maintains that we can discuss traditions, not of course all traditions at the same time, but in turn and on the basis of problems. Moreover, he maintains that it is this attitude of *discussing*, of *criticizing*, that really launched the scientific attitude, or the *scientific tradition*.

Popper is not satisfied with the current explanation that attributes the invention of a rational philosophy – the creation of a scientific tradition somewhere in Greece in the sixth and fifth centuries before Christ – to the fact that Greek philosophers were the first to try to *understand* what happens in nature. He observes that the more primitive myth-makers before them also tried to understand what happens in nature. Their myths were attempts to explain thunderstorms or rough seas.

> I think that the innovation which the early Greek philosophers introduced was roughly this: they began to discuss these matters. Instead of accepting the religious tradition uncritically, and as unalterable, instead of merely handing on tradition, they challenged it, and sometimes even invented a new myth in place of the old one [. . .]. The Greek philosophers invented a *new tradition* – the tradition of adopting a critical attitude towards the myths, the tradition of discussing them; the tradition of not only telling a myth, but also of being challenged by the man to whom it is told. [. . .]
>
> My thesis is that what we call 'science' is differentiated from the older myths not by being something distinct from a myth, but by being accompanied by a second-order tradition – that of critically discussing the myth. [. . .] This second-order tradition was the critical or argumentative attitude. It was, I believe, a new thing, and it is still the fundamentally important thing about scientific tradition.[26]

This then leads Karl Popper to define the attitude of his critical rationalism towards tradition. Instead of wishing to abolish all traditions which cannot be rationally demonstrated and start afresh, instead of looking for justifications without previous assumptions, critical rationalism proposes the critical discussion of traditions.

> I do not think that we could ever free ourselves entirely from the bond of tradition. The so-called freeing is really only a change from one tradition to another. But we can free

ourselves from the *taboos* of a tradition; and we can do that not only by rejecting it but also by *critically* accepting it. We free ourselves from the taboo if we *think* about it, and if we ask ourselves whether we should accept it or reject it.[27]

This is the crucial point where the sharp distinction between Popper's and Hayek's theories of tradition is revealed. They both agree that traditions cannot be justified without initial assumptions, and that we cannot free ourselves from the bond of tradition. But Popper maintains that we can still *discuss* traditions, thus refusing to accept them as *taboos*. And it was this refusal of *taboos* that was at the origin of the scientific tradition. On the contrary, Hayek thinks that:

> Custom and tradition, both non-rational adaptations to the environment, are more likely to guide group selection when supported by *totem and taboo*, or *magical* and religious beliefs – beliefs that themselves grew from the tendency to interpret any order men encountered in an animistic manner.[28]

And Hayek adds a little later:

> If we bear these things in mind, we can better understand and appreciate those clerics who are said to have become somewhat sceptical of the validity of some of their teachings and who yet continued to teach them because they feared that a loss of faith would lead to a decline of morals. No doubt they were right; and even an agnostic ought to concede that we owe our morals, and the tradition that has provided not only our civilisation but our very lives, to the acceptance of such scientifically unacceptable factual claims.[29]

If one wants to grasp the abyss that in this regard separates Popper from Hayek, one ought to recall that the same Open Society or Extended Order, which Hayek wants to preserve by recourse to taboo, is defined by Karl Popper on the basis of the very rupture with taboo:

> The magical attitude towards social custom has been discussed before. Its main element is the lack of distinction between the customary or conventional regularities of social life and the regularities found in 'nature'; and this often goes together with the belief that both are enforced by a supernatural will. [. . .] There are few problems in this form of life, and nothing

really equivalent to moral problems. [. . .] The right way is always determined, though difficulties must be overcome in following it. It is determined by taboos, by magical tribal institutions which can never become objects of critical consideration. [. . .] Based upon the collective tribal tradition, the institutions leave no room for personal responsibility.

   [. . .] In what follows, the magical or tribal or collectivist society will also be called *the closed society* and the society in which individuals are confronted with personal decisions, *the open society*.[30]

A MORALIST OF SORTS

Having observed how Hayek's views on traditions sharply contrast with those of Popper's, in spite of the important issues they both agree with, we are now able to embark upon the discussion of the whole of Hayek's theory of cultural evolution. According to this theory, the extended order of what is called capitalism resulted not from human design but spontaneously, that is to say, men unintentionally conformed to certain traditional and largely moral practices. These practices mainly consist of what David Hume called the 'three fundamental laws of nature': 'the stability of possessions, of its transference by consent and of the performance of promises'.

   It must be noted that people tend to dislike these rules, since they restrain them from instinctive behaviour. And they usually fail to understand their significance, let alone their beneficial effects in the long run. Nevertheless, these rules have spread fairly rapidly because they enabled those groups that first adopted them to prevail. Observing their comparative increase of population and wealth, other groups tend to imitate them. We do not, and cannot, know why and how the pioneer groups started to follow these three fundamental laws of nature. We only know that they were not able to anticipate the beneficial results which would arise from those rules. And we know also that these rules were linked to magical and religious beliefs that oblige people to conform to them. Thus, if these beneficial traditions have been preserved and transmitted for long enough to enable the groups following them to grow, and to have the opportunity to spread by cultural selection, this is due to mystical and religious beliefs, particularly to the main monotheistic ones. For this reason, Hayek concludes that

> We have never been able to choose our morals. Though there is a tendency to interpret goodness in a utilitarian way, to claim that 'good' is what brings about desired results, this claim is neither true nor useful. Even if we restrict ourselves to common usage, we find that the word 'good' generally refers to what tradition tells us we ought to do without knowing why – which is not to deny that justifications are always being invented for particular traditions.[31]

Hayek adds, none the less, that we can ask in retrospect 'which among the many and conflicting rules that tradition treats as good tend, under particular conditions, to preserve and multiply those groups that follow them'.[32] Rather obviously, these efficient rules – which may be called 'good' because they are efficient – are the rules of the market economy: chiefly rules of property and contract, securing the personal domain of the individual. These rules, that were selected by natural and spontaneous evolution, are themselves rules of a spontaneous order. And a spontaneous order is itself superior to a centralized one for it allows the treatment of an amount of information infinitely larger than the amount that a centralized one can afford.

Thus we come to the justification whereby we must not only defend a *spontaneous order* but also a *spontaneous evolution* based on traditions: the worst menace against a spontaneous order is the constructivist invention of new rules to bring about every particular result which is considered to be desirable. The best shelter against constructivism is then *not to intervene* in the spontaneous order, that is to say, to allow the spontaneous evolution to take its course.

*   *   *

The main difficulty in Hayek's theory of evolution is that, in spite of himself, he is not able to justify the requirement of respect for all traditions. He stresses that respect for traditions, as such, has led people to keep certain beneficial ones for long enough to allow them to increase their wealth and then to prevail. But, if one accepts that people in general tend to follow their own particular traditions, and if one accepts Hayek's contention that certain traditions spread because they enabled the people who followed them to prevail, then one has to accept that only certain, and not all, traditions are efficient. Thus, respect for traditions is not in itself a guarantee that a particular group will prevail, since it may well happen that these traditions are not the 'right ones'.

This leads us to a crucial problem: which traditions should be followed and which should not? How can one know whether one specific tradition is or is not beneficial? According to Hayek, moral considerations must be kept apart from this evaluation. We are not actually free to choose our morals. If we choose as 'good' certain rules which in fact contradict the efficient rules that enable people to prevail, the natural selection of morals will give its indisputable verdict: our 'good' rules will simply be thrown away in the dustbin of history. Thus, Hayek's reply to the question 'which traditions should be followed' seems to be that each group should follow its own specific tradition, leaving the choice of the beneficial ones to the historical process of evolution. However, Hayek also knows that this historical evolution will choose, or select, liberal traditions as the efficient or beneficial ones.

Now it should be recalled that Hayek developed an impressive normative theory of liberal principles, which was briefly presented in the first chapter of this study. Especially in *The Road to Serfdom* and *The Constitution of Liberty* he tried to justify the moral desirability of these rules. Later, however, he told us that we are not free to choose our moral principles, and added that even the idea of 'good' must be seen as an illusion. That which is efficient is good, for it enabled certain human groups to prevail.

If we take Hayek seriously, we must then conclude that all his former intellectual effort to justify liberal principles morally has to be put aside. It was pure 'anthropomorphic illusion', only one more of the several 'justifications which are always being invented for particular traditions'. Nevertheless, one must realize that Hayek's moral preferences of the former period were somehow spared by his late theory of evolution. Although declaring 'we have never been able to choose our morals', his moral preferences constitute an exception to this rule of thumb of natural evolution: Hayek started by choosing in moral terms the rules of the extended order, and ended by verifying that these rules were, rather curiously, the only *viable* and *efficient* rules. In other words, Hayek's theory of evolution puts him in a somewhat unique position of being the only one who may have the privilege of *choosing* his morals and *being sure* that these morals will prevail.[33]

Somehow, Hayek is a moralist of sorts: his theory has a strong moral component, although he argues that people cannot choose their morals because, in crude reality, evolution selects morals. It just happened, however, that Hayek knows that the morals he chose will be selected by evolution.

Now, two major problems stem from this, one moral, the other epistemological. The moral one, which was mentioned in Chapter 2, consists of wondering what the moral value of a moral choice is which one knows in advance to be bound to prevail. The crude truth is that there is no room for any kind of moral judgement here, since we simply have to know which cause will win and then adopt it as our 'moral' one. One must be aware of the devastating relativist consequences of this kind of moral reasoning which actually drains morals of any kind of intrinsic value.

One of the best illustrations of these relativist consequences is the fact that Hayek himself changed his critique of social justice as he moved from a normative to an evolutionist view of liberalism. Whereas in *Law, Legislation and Liberty* Hayek maintained the distinction between procedural and social justice – thus endorsing the first and denying the second – in *The Fatal Conceit* he excludes the very concept of justice:

> If market coordination of individual activities, as well as other moral traditions and institutions, result from natural, spontaneous, and self-ordering processes of adaptation to a greater number of particular facts than any one mind can perceive or even conceive, it is evident that demands that these processes be just, or possess other moral attributes derive from a naive anthropomorphism. Such demands of course might be appropriately addressed to the directors of a process guided by rational control or to a god attentive to prayers, but are wholly inappropriate to the impersonal self-ordering process actually at work.[34]

Needless to say, if this argument of Hayek's were taken rigorously, not even the concept of civil and political rights could be accepted. At the core of these rights is the requirement, praised by Hayek in his early works, that individuals must be treated as equals by the law. However, as he himself has highlighted, individuals are in fact very different. To treat them as equals is therefore a convention which arises from moral considerations, namely that:

> No man or group of men possesses the capacity to determine conclusively the potentialities of other human beings and [. . .] we should certainly never trust anyone invariably to exercise such a capacity. However great the differences between men may be, we have no ground for believing that they will ever be so great as to enable one man's mind in a particular instance to comprehend fully all that another responsible man's mind is capable of.[35]

According to Hayek's later theory of general evolution, however, these moral considerations could only be seen as 'moral attributes [which] derive from a naive anthropomorphism'. There is no ground for believing that a 'natural, spontaneous and self-ordering process of adaptation' must conform to moral demands that people be treated equally. In fact, even civil and political rights would be discarded by Hayek's later theory of evolution.

ORACULAR PROPHETISM

But the second problem, the epistemological one, is no less important. Are we really able to know in advance which cause will win? How does Hayek know that the principles of a liberal order are going to prevail? Apparently, this prediction is based on the observation of past experience in which liberal principles allowed those groups who adopted them to prevail over others (by means of the comparative increase of population and wealth). Because these groups have prevailed, the others have adopted their practices.

One should probably note that there are at least three different assumptions in this reasoning: (1) liberal order allowed those groups who adopted it drastically to improve their material condition; (2) this led other groups to adopt their practices; (3) this will happen again in the future. The fact is, however, that only the first assumption deserves rational credit. The second is disputable. And the third is a mere prophecy without rational foundations.

The economic superiority of a liberal order may be analytically justified – as Hayek has done – on the basis of the impossibility for a central system to deal with the amount of information inherent in complex systems. On an empirical level, this assertion is corroborated by the prodigious achievements of capitalist societies. But this must not obliterate the fact that these achievements are not only a product of economic behaviour, or of the observance of moral traditions which make certain economic behaviour compulsory. These moral traditions – namely the Protestant ethics which is undoubtedly associated with the rise of capitalism – have their own rationale and have produced their own moral consequences. The idea of personal liberty and personal responsibility is paramount within this Protestant tradition. It has entailed the commitment to those moral values that Hayek praises so much – private property, saving, entrepreneurship, etc. – but it has also entailed the commitment to intellectual free enquiry. One cannot praise the economic consequences of a particular moral tradition which favours rational controversy, and at the same time criticize the ambition of criticizing traditions.

Even if this were possible, it is by no means certain that it would work. As de Tocqueville has observed, the people who obtained the richest material fruits of liberty were those who did not primarily try for these fruits, but for liberty itself:

Je ne crois pas non plus que le véritable amour de la liberté soit jamais né de la seule vue des biens matériels qu'elle procure; car cette vue vient souvent à s'obscurcir. Il est bien vrai qu'à la longue la liberté amène toujours, à ceux qui savent la retenir, l'aisance, le bien-être, et souvent la richesse; mais il y a des temps où elle trouble momentanément l'usage de pareils biens; il y en a d'autres où le despotisme seul peut en donner la jouissance passagère. Les hommes qui ne prisent que ces biens-là en elle ne l'ont jamais conservé longtemps.

Ce qui, dans tous les temps, lui a attaché si fortement le coeur de certains hommes, ce sont ses attraits mêmes, son charme propre, indépendant de ses bienfaits; c'est le plaisir de pouvoir parler, agir, respirer sans contrainte, sous le seul gouvernement de Dieu et des lois. Qui cherche dans la liberté autre chose qu'elle-même est fait pour servir.[36]

These words of de Tocqueville's lead us to the second assertion of Hayek, that the moral practices of the extended order have spread fairly rapidly because groups who did not previously adopt them tended to do so when they saw that these practices enabled other groups to prevail. This seems to be a typical assumption of a book written in 1988, when communism was on the verge of collapse and liberal ideas were gathering momentum. But this was not the assumption of Hayek when he wrote *The Road to Serfdom*, in 1945. He then wrote, much more reasonably, that men's foolishness, their collectivist and organicist passions, the cult of organization and hierarchy, were leading civilization to disaster. And nevertheless, Hayek argued, there was an alternative successful experience, that of liberal Anglo-American civilization, which had proved that individual freedom and tolerance, free trade and love of peace could work. Why did men not want to follow this path? This illustrates the crucial problem that the fact that a liberal civilization has already shown its achievements does not guarantee that other peoples will adopt its practices.

One might probably reply that cultural selection has worked since then. Collectivism of both right and left have had their day, and the liberal order of democratic capitalism has prevailed. This only corroborates Hayek's theory of cultural evolution, it might be said. But two lateral remarks are to be made. First of all, the fact that liberal order has prevailed cannot alone constitute the source of its legitimacy, since otherwise Hayek could not have legitimately argued for the liberal order when, in the years 1939–45, it was about to be overthrown by totalitarianism. Secondly, Hitler might have kept the power over continental Europe if only Britain had not stood in his way. In this tragic case, world history would have been quite different after 1945. Would this quite different possible outcome have proved the weakness of the liberal order in terms of cultural evolution?

* * *

To sum up: even if Hayek's view of the past as an avenue for the progress of liberal capitalism might be accepted, it could never have been accepted as a sort of historical law of cultural evolution. In fact, as Karl Popper has argued, these laws simply do not exist. The past is not composed of events that have necessarily occurred, but only of events which could have occurred in a total different manner. The task of the historian, then, is not to reveal the iron law that made these past events inevitable, but precisely the opposite: to throw light on the singularities that made these events possible, when they could just possibly have occurred differently.

Hayek's faith in the future inevitable victory of liberal capitalism reveals itself to be merely a faith. Like many theories of very wide scope, Hayek's evolutionism is not susceptible to testing. If one asks what kind of historical event will be capable of refuting his evolutionism, one has to conclude that none will do. Even if all liberal societies ceased to be so, this would not necessarily refute Hayek's thesis that the liberal order is simultaneously the product and the destiny of evolution. Hayek's theory could always explain away the disappearance of liberal societies asserting that this was only an ephemeral episode of evolution and that the necessary future collapse of illiberal societies will soon give rise to a liberal revival. In other words, as evolution is never finished, one can always say that the future will do him justice.

This illustrates the very limited empirical content of evolutionist theories with respect to the future. And rightly so, because the future is open. But the absence of test to Hayek's evolutionism reveals another point, perhaps more important in this particular. If its goal is perceived as being the provision of a natural and necessary foundation for the moral rules of liberal societies, it fails conspicuously. Even if one endorses the argument that these moral rules should be accepted because they have prevailed so far, because they have enabled the groups which have adopted them to survive and prevail, even then it will not be possible to prove that they will always prevail in the future.

This would leave us with the problem of having to decide which rules to choose if, in the future, the spontaneous evolution suggested that liberal rules did not coincide with the efficient ones. According to Hayek's evolutionist thesis that we are not free to choose our morals, the only solution should be to choose the efficient rules and to abandon the liberal ones. Nevertheless, and since the evolutionist theory does not allow room for refutation, the reverse would still be possible: one could stick to the liberal rules on the grounds that their failure in face of the efficient ones was only a frothy episode and that the superiority of liberal rules would soon become apparent again. In other words, Hayek's attempt to underpin liberal morality on 'natural' and 'scientific' grounds fails, since the same 'natural' fact of evolution could be given two different moral responses. This, of course, is merely another way of saying that there is no such thing as 'scientific morals'.[37]

It is important to emphasize this point. We just know nothing about the future. Neither can we be sure that liberal societies will prevail over others in the future, nor have they always done so in the past. Commercial democracy arose in Athens in the fifth century BC. Since her breakdown, almost two thousand years have passed before democracy has been rediscovered. That democracy is either an ephemeral episode of history or it is the fate of history we cannot know. We know nothing about the meaning or the sense of history for the simple reason that this meaning does not exist. We can only try to give history some meaning. The only thing we can know is that *it is not impossible* to build democracies where and when people want to try. As Karl Popper has said,

> True, we need hope; to act, to live without hope goes beyond our strength. But we do *not* need more, and we must not be given more. We do not need certainty . . . If we think that history progresses, or that we are bound to progress, then we commit the same mistake as those who believe that history has a meaning that can be discovered in it and need not be given to it . . . Instead of posing as prophets we must become makers of our fate.[38]

PRESUMPTION OF TRADITION AND RULES OF OPENNESS

Having argued that Hayek's evolutionist theory of cultural selection is untenable, it is now worth stressing that this is not meant to deny all his insights on the value of traditions, or on the impossibility of starting afresh and the menaces of unrestrained constructivism. In fact, if one puts aside the prophetic dimension (liberal societies will necessarily prevail) and the 'normative' dimension (liberal rules should be accepted because they have prevailed so far), Hayek's work on social evolution still has several seminal insights. The most crucial of these should certainly be his highlighting of the fact that a decentralized or spontaneous order has a capacity to deal with information that is not matched by any made order or organization. This is a decisive advantage from the point of view of evolution, because it allows liberal societies an extraordinary capacity to evolve and adapt to changing circumstances.

Under closer examination, however, this insight of Hayek's hints at a possible view of evolution which is different from the one he has embraced. The capacity to adapt to changing circumstances is an active feature which presupposes an active view of the evolutionary process; a view according to which the creative reaction of individuals is at least as important as the pressure to adapt from the external environment.[39] In this perspective, the advantage of liberal societies lies not mainly in their undesigned commitment to those traditions that have been selected so far, but in their intentional commitment to specific traditions whose rational advantage can be established. These traditions are mainly those of experimental openness, of trial and error, traditions which undoubtedly underpin the working of free markets as well as the functioning of liberal political democracies, with their mechanisms of checks and balances, limited majority power, etc. These are undoubtedly very important mechanisms to allow the widest room for piecemeal experiments, for different courses of action and the comparative observation of their corresponding results – in a word, for change without bloodshed, for conflict without revolution. Although we can by no means foresee that this will enable liberal societies to prevail in the future, we can by all means assert that this is an important advantage, both in moral and efficiency terms.

Liberal traditions, namely those inherent in a spontaneous order, should be carefully preserved, then, not because they are merely part of tradition, but because they constitute specific traditions that allow trial and error and, thereby, favour piecemeal change and adaptation. Certain traditions, then, may and ought to be preserved by design, and not only by a blind reverence to tradition as a whole. In fact, tradition as a whole is a misleading expression that obliterates the fact that there are always several traditions – even within a very single society, not to mention across different societies – that very often they clash, and that sometimes alternative choices are to be made.

Therefore, Hayek's contention that tradition as such should be followed is an empty contention that should be distinguished from his important insight (inspired by the work of Karl Popper) that we can neither start afresh nor justify all the traditions that we stick to. This would amount to asserting a critical presumption of tradition, not an overall commitment to it.[40] A critical presumption of tradition puts the burden of proof on a proposed change, rather than on the justification of an established tradition. This implies the recognition – present in Hayek's argument, but still different from his overall approach – that one should keep a tradition even when, at a certain moment, its rationale is not completely clear. Assuming that a tradition which has resisted the test of time must embody some tacit wisdom, the critical presumption of tradition puts the burden of proof on a proposed change – but does not close the door to change. Furthermore, even when the case for a change is reasonably presented, a critical presumption of tradition will add that all changes should be cautiously made so that even the worst failure of one single change could not threaten the rules of openness (or of trial and error) that have allowed that change to be endeavoured. In other words, one should rely neither on tradition nor on change, but rather on the perpetual controversy between tradition and change which is allowed only by rules of openness.[41]

According to this active view of evolution, which we could also call a critical or self-restrained constructivism, a similar correction to the one just mentioned about tradition should be introduced in Hayek's view of a spontaneous order. As opposed to a made order or an organization, a spontaneous order is still to represent a liberal ideal, mainly because it allows individuals to use the best of their knowledge to pursue their own ends under general rules of just conduct rather than under specific commands issued by the rulers. In this sense, the concept of spontaneous order is akin to the one of a decentralized order and represents mainly the old liberal ideal of the rule of law as opposed to the rule of men.

But Hayek failed to see that the rules that govern a spontaneous order are the very condition of its existence, rather than its product. As illustrated by several empirical examples (of which one of the best known is the Mafia), there is no guarantee whatever that unfettered exchange between individuals gives rise to liberal laws able to protect and foster free exchange. On the contrary, there is every reason to believe that only when free exchange is properly protected by liberal laws – i.e. laws intended to protect individual liberty – is free exchange able to survive and prevail.[42]

In this sense, a spontaneous order is not a natural product of spontaneous evolution, not a product of human action rather than human design. Although it might well have historically arisen as an unintentional or undesigned product of human interaction, its maintenance requires constant protection by design, namely protection by a liberal framework of laws. So, in the sense that it has to be protected by design, a spontaneous order is a social institution, a social and cultural artefact, which should not be seen as a product of spontaneous evolution. The order in itself, however, can still be seen as spontaneous because it is one of its chief characteristics that it evolves by the separate action and association of its components, not by the design of any central authority. The liberal rules which are intentionally produced to protect this order are mainly made with the design of preventing any such authority from concentrating power enough to command the movements of the elements of this spontaneous order. Obviously enough, in this sense, liberal societies based on market economies are spontaneous orders protected by the rule of law in which their elements are free citizens.[43]

A LIBERAL CRITIQUE OF HAYEK'S DOCTRINE

Before we come to the conclusion of this chapter dedicated to an evaluation of Hayek's argument on social rights, it is perhaps appropriate to stress the liberal character of the critique of Hayek's evolutionism which is being presented here. Several authors have criticized Hayek for his denial of the concept of 'social justice' and social rights, but not necessarily all agree upon the reasons for this denial. Socialist-oriented scholars, such as Raymond Plant,[44] have argued that the deep roots of Hayek's hostility to social rights lie in his foundationist concept of (negative) liberty as absence of coercion. Egalitarian liberals, as is probably the case with Roland Kley,[45] have attributed the flaws of Hayek's political theory to his concept of spontaneous order. And in a recent paper,[46] John Gray – the author of possibly the best scholarly study on Hayek[47] – has also asserted that the acceptance of social rights entails the endorsement of autonomy as the crucial liberal value.

Although some of these points will be discussed at a later stage, it must be emphasized now that the critique of Hayek's argument, sketched here, does not necessarily entail the endorsement of any of the assumptions mentioned above. This critique is perfectly compatible with what has been called the tradition of classical liberalism: it does not contest the view of liberty as absence of coercion, it accepts (perhaps with some qualifications) the concept of a spontaneous order of the market (although not of spontaneous evolution), and does not necessarily require the definition of autonomy as the main liberal value, although it does not preclude it either.

The crucial point of this critique may be said to lie, somehow paradoxically, in the assertion that a negative view of social rights is perfectly compatible with Hayek's normative theory of liberalism. If Hayek has failed to recognize this point, this is not due to his normative theory, but to the other component of his doctrine: the naturalist evolutionism of cultural selection or, in other words, his dogmatic and untenable comprehensive anti-constructivism. This critique, it must be said, goes along the lines of what has been presented by James Buchanan,[48] John Gray,[49] Samuel Brittan,[50] and Ralf Dahrendorf.[51] In a way, it is also akin to the work of Chandran Kukathas,[52] who has detected serious difficulties in Hayek's justification of his own liberalism. The crucial point was probably mentioned by James Buchanan when he asserted that:

In a positive, empirical sense many of our social and legal institutions have grown independently of design and intent. But man must look on *all* institutions as potentially improvable. Man must adopt the attitude that he can control his fate.

He must accept the necessity of choosing. He must look on himself as man, not another animal, and upon civilization as if it is of his own making.[53]

In a certain sense, however, this critique of Hayek's anti-constructivism is more radical than those which aim at the classical liberal principles he professed. The critique sketched here may be said to recapture the main target addressed by Karl Popper's critique of Marx's historicism, applying it now to the evolutionist system created by Hayek. Since this may sound surprising – Karl Popper and Friedrich Hayek seemed siblings, as Ralf Dahrendorf put it[54] – some further considerations must perhaps be added.

MARX, POPPER AND HAYEK

In *The Open Society and its Enemies,* Karl Popper has asserted that the most central point of his critique of the political consequences of Marx's historicism lay in the clash between two concepts of the hierarchy of power. For Marx, political power comes in third place. It is the least capable after the real and decisive power pertaining to the development of productive forces, and after the second most important, economic class relations – which themselves arise from the state of development of productive forces. Karl Popper, on the other hand, believes political power to be the most important factor – or more accurately, that political power can become the most important, the 'vanguard of power' and, according to him, it should control economic power.

Yet this clash between different evaluations of the hierarchy of power does not result from a simple technical controversy regarding what it is possible to do at a given time or in a given society. This clash frames and illustrates the most radical difference between Popper's and Marx's political theories, the difference between a technological and nominalist approach to social problems and a historicist and essentialist approach – which for Popper reflects one of the greatest contemporary superstitions. He says:

Marxism claims to be more than a science. It does more than make a historical prophecy. It claims to be the basis for

practical political action. It criticizes existing society, and it
asserts that it can lead the way to a better world. But according to Marx's own theory, we cannot at will alter the economic
reality by, for example, legal reforms. Politics can do no more
than 'shorten and lessen the birth-pangs'. This, I think, is
an extremely poor political programme, and its poverty is
a consequence of the third-rate place which it attributes to
political power in the hierarchy of powers.[55]

Against this resigned attitude to intrinsic forces, the very
essences which inevitably govern history – and which condemn
mankind simply to accelerate or retard the predetermined path
– Karl Popper proposes a constructivist attitude, which he has
called, somehow awkwardly, piecemeal social engineering.
Instead of asking what is the origin or the essence of such and
such institution, the constructivist asks 'what aim do I intend
to achieve or should I intend to achieve with such and such
institution?' As a function of this aim and of recognition of the
social constraints, the constructivist reformer tries to operate,
transform and reform institutions. Popper claims that it was
precisely because the liberal democracies put this 'social engineering' into practice that capitalism has been reformed, thus
clearly rejecting Marxist prophecies which considered political
reform to be impossible.

It may be noted that Popper attributed the salvation of capitalism precisely to the same kind of political interventions
which for Hayek constitutes the source of the disfunctions of
capitalism – and further the source of totalitarian threats against
liberal democracies. But this should not be understood as a matter of evaluation of concrete political measures. Popper wrote
The Open Society between 1938 and 1943, and from then on until
now many of the interventionist measures he supported have
been applied and sometimes overtaken. We know that the praise
he gave to the economic interventionism of what he called
'small democracies', particularly social democratic Sweden, has
now become criticism of the excessive bureaucracy in these
countries. Therefore, the issue at stake here is not evaluating
this or that concrete measure. We are not discussing whether
the state has or has not gone too far, interventionism has or
has not produced ill effects, whether the welfare state has or
has not become economically unsustainable.

What is at issue – much before this kind of specific immediate evaluation – is the very desirability of political intervention to regulate the so-called spontaneous evolution of traditions
throughout cultural selection. What is at issue is the tension
between constructivism and anti-constructivism within the same
framework of liberal values. This tension differentiates liberal
meliorism from liberal conservatism. And the fact is that
Popper's theory is clearly constructivist (though of a very special
and cautious type) whereas Hayek's evolutionist theory is solidly
anticonstructivist.

CONSTRUCTIVISM AND ANTICONSTRUCTIVISM

Contrary to Hayek's resolutely anticonstructivist theories, Karl
Popper supports a technological type of constructivism against
social problems and institutions. He is sensitive to some of
Hayek's arguments but maintains that they do not nullify the
general constructivist attitude, and that they can and should
actually be incorporated by it.

What is characteristic of this constructivism (social engineering) is the manner of seeing or perceiving social institutions;
not as a product of historical forces which determine them, not
as the result of a spontaneous process which we cannot interfere with, but as 'means to certain ends or as convertible to the
service of certain ends; as machines rather than organisms'.[56]
This is what Popper calls the 'functional or instrumental'
attitude towards social institutions.

But he immediately warns that there are several important
differences between institutions and machines. The first and
perhaps most important is that '*only a minority of social institutions are consciously designed while the vast majority have just "grown",
as the undesigned results of human actions*'.[57] A significant limitation
of social engineering arises from this difference, and it is precisely that of being impossible to foresee all the consequences
of a particular intervention. This was an argument of Hayek's
against interventionism but, although Popper also uses it, he
stresses that it does not nullify the possibility of a certain type
of interventionism.

Social engineering must be based on the knowledge of social
sciences (which Popper calls social technology) whose 'most

characteristic task is *to point out what cannot be achieved*.[58] Just as natural laws can be expressed in the form of prohibitions (you cannot carry water in a sieve), so too can sociological laws: 'you cannot have a centrally planned society with a price system that fulfils the main functions of competitive prices.'[59]

Popper explains that, in this light, anti-interventionism may be seen as a technological doctrine which asserts that some interventions will produce worse results than would non-intervention. But, Popper adds, this is different from universal anti-interventionism, the passive concept according to which 'if we are dissatisfied with existing social or economic conditions it is because we do not understand how they work and why active intervention could only make matters worse'. And he continues:

> Now I must admit that I am certainly out of sympathy with this 'passivist' view, and that I even believe that a policy of *universal* anti-interventionism is untenable – even on purely logical grounds, since its supporters are bound to recommend political intervention aimed at preventing intervention.[60]

The point is that the existence of unintentional effects which arise from all human actions and cannot be totally foreseen is not a reason for doing nothing. Rather is it a rule to be taken into consideration by those who intend to do something. It is a law similar to the law of conservation of energy, which says 'you cannot construct a perpetual motion machine'. Or the law of entropy which says 'you cannot build a machine which is a hundred per cent efficient'. Just as no engineer draws from these laws the conclusion that it is not possible to build any machine whatsoever, so the 'social engineer' does not draw from the existence of unintended effects the conclusion that it is not possible to do anything intentionally to reform social institutions.[61]

Popper's constructivism clearly has many nuances. One of the most important and best known is its gradualist or reformist character, as opposed to Utopian or revolutionary constructivism. Bearing in mind that the method of natural sciences is trial and error based on correctly controlled experiments designed to test daring hypotheses, Popper stresses that the analogy between the technology of gradual social action and true technology could and should be maintained. He claims that supporters of utopianism are those who disparage the method of natural sciences, and he therefore again disagrees with Hayek when the latter globally attributes intellectual responsibility for the disasters of utopianism to 'scientism'.

Popper's criticisms of utopianism are therefore essentially rationalist. It is not a question of knowing in advance whether certain ideals can or cannot be achieved in the future, 'for many things have been realized which have once been dogmatically declared to be unrealizable, for instance, the establishment of corresponding institutions for securing civil peace, i.e. for the prevention of international crime *within* the state'.[62] The real problem is that Utopian social engineering, by aiming at social reconstruction as a whole, is unable to control the real consequences of each proposed change or to correct these proposals when the consequences turn out to be undesirable.

In contrast, Popper recommends gradual social engineering which approaches problems on a case by case basis and experiments with well defined solutions for each. This gradual engineering is, according to Popper, nothing more than the application to society of the experimental method.

INDIRECT AND NEGATIVE CONSTRUCTIVISM

Two further restraints are added by Karl Popper to his special kind of constructivism: it must be indirect and it must aim at mainly negative goals.

They both arise from the fact that Popper's constructivism is a liberal one, and so its main goal is the protection of individual liberty. Like Hayek, he asserted that unrestrained liberty is self-defeating and thus the need for the protection of liberty by the state arises. But, in its turn, this need creates 'the most fundamental problem of all politics: the control of the controller, of the dangerous accumulation of power represented in the state'.[63] With the purpose of ensuring that 'state intervention is limited to what is really necessary for the protection of freedom', Popper then presents his two main further restraints on constructivism.

The first is the rule of indirect or institutional intervention. It is intended to create a legal, stable and universally known framework within which individuals can act in full knowledge of the rules, drawing up projects for their lives and enjoying security of expectations. This rule – which is similar to Hayek's concern with the distinction between law and legislation – is mainly conceived to prevent arbitrary government, which Popper calls 'personal or direct intervention'.

The second rule is more difficult to assess – Popper himself refers to it from time to time but not definitely. It implies 'the method of searching for, and fighting against, the greatest and most urgent evils of society, rather than searching for, and fighting for, its greatest ultimate good'.[64] There seem to be three reasons for this negative rule of Popper's. The first is moral. He states several times that there is no symmetry from the ethical point of view between suffering and happiness, or between pleasure and pain. This asymmetry must be due to the fact that human suffering produces a direct moral appeal for help, while the promotion of the happiness of someone who is not suffering does not produce such an appeal. This leads Popper to propose that the utilitarian principle of 'the greatest happiness for the greatest number' should be altered, and similarly the Kantian principle of promoting the 'happiness of others' by a negative principle:

> A further criticism of the Utilitarian formula 'maximize pleasure' is that it assumes, in principle, a continuous pleasure–pain scale which allows us to treat degrees of pain as negative degrees of pleasure. But, from the moral point of view, pain cannot be outweighed by pleasure, and especially not one man's pain by another man's pleasure. Instead of the greatest happiness for the greatest number, one should demand, more modestly, the least amount of avoidable suffering for all; and further, that unavoidable suffering – such as hunger in times of an unavoidable shortage of food – should be distributed as equally as possible.[65]

The second reason, which Popper only refers to in passing, is that it seems to him that there is a certain analogy between this view of ethics and the view of scientific methodology which he advocated in his *Logic of Scientific Discovery*. 'It adds to clarity in the field of ethics', Popper says, 'if we formulate our demands negatively, i.e. if we demand the elimination of suffering rather than the promotion of happiness.'[66]

As regards the third reason, partly a synthesis of the previous ones, it consists of claiming that the principle of 'the greatest happiness for the greatest number' would tend to produce benevolent dictatorships. This is precisely because, there being no symmetry between suffering and happiness, the proposal of promoting the happiness of others becomes a difficult target to specify, while 'a systematic fight against suffering and injustice and war is more likely to be supported by the approval and agreement of a great number of people'.[67] At the same time, and for the same reason, the target of promoting the happiness of others too often involves interference in their scale of values, and this threatens their freedom.

*   *   *

So much for Karl Popper's special kind of constructivism. It is probably sufficient to suggest how liberal values and goals may give rise to a positive agenda whose main purpose is still to secure liberty.[68]

A CIVILIZATION BASED ON PERSONAL DECISIONS

It might be said that the understanding of Hayek's political theory presented here is artificial. Wishing to separate his normative defence of liberalism from his evolutionism, this view would be falling into the awkward position of one who implies he knows Hayek's doctrine better than does the author himself. Although this critique deserves attention, it is not accurate.

In fact, the political problem which Hayek has tried to resolve has always been the same, even if his answer has somehow evolved throughout the decades. This problem was formulated by him in a very telling way in the introduction to the first volume of *Law, Legislation and Liberty*, in 1973:

> It appears to me also that the same factual error has long appeared to make insoluble the most crucial problem of political organization, namely how to limit the 'popular will' without placing another 'will' above it. As soon as we recognize that the basic order of the Great Society cannot rest entirely on design, and cannot therefore aim at particular foreseeable results, we see that the requirement, as legitimation of all

authority, of a commitment to general principles approved by general opinion, may well place effective restrictions on the particular will of all authority, including that of the majority of the moment.[69]

Hayek's political problem is the same classical one of liberals: how to protect liberty against tyranny, be it either tyranny of only one, of several, or of all gathered together. In the case of Hayek, his main problem is to prevent democracy becoming a dictatorship by the majority. In a way, Hayek's answer to this problem has always been the same, although his own view of the answer has undergone deep evolution. Obviously the answer was that democracy will remain liberal as long as the power of the majority submits to the rule of law. But Hayek's concept of the rule of law has not always been the same.

In *The Road to Serfdom* and *The Constitution of Liberty*, Hayek understands the concept of law as liberals have traditionally understood it: a set of stable and general rules, abstract and equal for all, which limit the power of majorities and cannot be altered by the arbitrary will of simple majorities.

In this regard, *Law, Legislation and Liberty* seems to be a work of transition. Hayek highlights the role of laws and tries to show how this role is decisive to a distinction between a spontaneous order and an organization. But Hayek introduces the concept of spontaneous evolution of laws, thus applying the remarkable English tradition of 'common law' as a backbone of the liberal conception of law. His effort is understandable: he wants to remove the laws from the intervention sphere of political majorities, fearing as he does that the unrestrained constructivist mirage might destroy the decisive bulwark of liberty – that is to say, the rule of law. He therefore wants the laws to remain at the guard of separate decisions of judges, thus being submitted to a slow evolution which depends upon evolving general opinion which, in its turn, judges must always try to interpret and express.

In *The Fatal Concept*, however, Hayek does not trust the judges any more. He completely removes any possibility of altering laws by design from individuals. He now says that those laws which survive are not the product of choice but of cultural selection produced by spontaneous evolution throughout the centuries. Hayek's enemy – the menace of unrestrained constructivism legitimated by democratic majorities – is now put against the wall. Even if it wants to intervene, change laws, multiply regulations, its fate is already decided: it will be defeated by spontaneous evolution. Hayek does not invite 'socialists of all parties' any longer to rediscover the moral appeal of liberals' classical meliorism. In a certain sense, he has converted himself to the language of Marxist socialists – who believed themselves interpreters of the sense of history – and he invites them to embrace liberalism without having to dismiss their insensible historicist beliefs. It suffices that they understand that history is not following the path of socialism, but of liberalism.

*   *   *

Hayek has very well understood the intellectual disease of the twentieth century and the dangers to liberty it represents. But, unfortunately, he distrusted the possibility of persuading individuals rationally to counter those dangers. Hence he persuaded himself of the existence of a natural force or trend – the spontaneous evolution – which is able to safeguard individual liberty even when individuals themselves give up that task. However, there is no rational motive for believing in the existence of such a force, and the last hope of liberty still lies in the enlightened critical judgement of individuals.

Hayek has understood that the great instability of liberal democracies is due to the fact that they are based on the personal decisions of individuals. He feared, quite reasonably, that these decisions might become hostage to collectivist passions, the democratic disease of envy – as de Tocqueville called it – or the populist discourse of tyrants who seduce the mob, flattering it with opportunistic invitations to destroy traditions, disrespect the law, and decree a paradise on earth without sin or scarcity. Hayek has tried to face these menaces with a naturalist evolutionism that would seemingly discard the need for personal decisions, moral judgements, and the responsibility of individuals for their actions.

But this is an impossible dream. The great intellectual revolution which began in Athens and resumed in the Renaissance and Enlightenment gave men the liberty to intervene and to alter social conventions. This liberty may be used either for good or for the bad, either to protect liberty or to destroy it. But this liberty cannot any longer be ignored. As Karl Popper has recalled,

> Once we begin to rely upon our reason, and to use our powers of criticism, once we feel the call of personal responsibilities, and with it the responsibility of helping to advance knowledge, we cannot return to a state of implicit submission to tribal magic. For those who have eaten of the tree of knowledge, paradise is lost.[70]

The underlying view of the present of Hayek's naturalistic evolutionism is that he failed to understand that liberalism is itself a product of this great intellectual revolution which has liberated man from the fear of superstition. Indeed this revolution itself created new superstitions, namely those of unrestrained constructivism and unrestrained interventionism. But if we are to set limits to our power of shaping our fate, these limits can only spring from our decision to shape our fate, namely the decision to protect individual liberty and to protect the rules of openness that allow us to progress by trial and error. This seems to have been what Karl Popper had in mind when he decided to close his preface to the second edition of *The Open Society* with these powerful words:

> I see now more clearly than ever before that even our greatest troubles spring from something that is as admirable and sound as it is dangerous – from our impatience to better the lot of our fellows. For these troubles are the by-products of what is perhaps the greatest of moral and spiritual revolutions of history, a movement which began three centuries ago. It is the longing of uncounted unknown men to free themselves and their minds from the tutelage of authority and prejudice. It is their attempt to build up an open society which rejects the absolute authority of the merely established and the merely traditional, while trying to preserve, to develop, and to establish traditions, old or new, that measure up their standards of freedom, of humaneness, and of rational criticism. It is their unwillingness to sit back and leave the entire responsibility for ruling the world to human or super-human authority, and their readiness to share the burden of

responsibility for avoidable suffering, and to work for its
avoidance. This revolution has created powers of appalling
destructiveness; but they may yet be conquered.[71]

HAYEK'S EVOLUTIONISM: AN OVERVIEW

This chapter started with a question: why did Hayek rule out
a concept of basic social rights, or a negative view of social
rights, if this was perfectly compatible with what was called
the Hayekian test for the legitimate use of coercion in a free
society? The proposed answer was that Hayek had gradually
detached himself from his early normative view of liberalism,
exchanging it for an evolutionist theory which rules out all
moral and normative considerations, and drains liberalism of
any active role in the political and institutional realm. The
main points of Hayek's evolutionism were then presented and
contrasted with some of Karl Popper's views, whose work Hayek
claimed to be inspired by.

The main difficulty of Hayek's evolutionism was then pointed
out: his theory has a strong moral component, although he
argues that people cannot choose their morals. It just happens, however, that Hayek is in a somewhat unique position of
knowing that the morals he chose will be selected by evolution.
This paradoxical view – whose resemblance to Marx's historicism was recalled – gives rise to at least two crucial problems:
one moral, the other epistemological.

The moral problem lies in the devastating relativist consequences of such a theory of morality. According to it, Hayek's
own normative requirement about the rule of law as opposed
to the rule of men could only be seen as 'moral attributes
which derive from a naive anthropomorphism'. Moreover, and
still according to Hayek's evolutionism, there is no ground
for believing that a 'natural, spontaneous and self-ordering
process of adaptation' must conform to moral demands that
people be treated equally by the law. In this sense, not even
civil and political rights – which, according to Hayek, aim at the
maintenance of a liberal order – could be justified, let alone
defended, if and when a 'spontaneous process of adaptation'
countered them.

The epistemological problem is no less important. Hayek's

faith in the future inevitable victory of liberal capitalism reveals itself to be merely a faith. Like many theories of very wide scope, it is not susceptible to testing: even if all liberal societies ceased to be so, this would not necessarily refute Hayek's thesis that the liberal order is simultaneously the product and the destiny of evolution, since one could always say that this was only an ephemeral episode of evolution, and that the necessary future collapse of illiberal societies would soon give rise to a liberal revival. (The resemblance to Marx's theory of the inevitable triumph of socialism is particularly striking here.) But, precisely because there is no definite test to the theory, one could also conclude that liberal principles had been discarded by evolution. This also shows that Hayek's attempt to underpin liberal morality on 'natural' and 'scientific' grounds failed, since the same 'natural' fact of evolution could be given two different moral responses.

At this stage, one main conclusion started to gain shape: evolution cannot be the test of political morality, and liberalism cannot be seen as the necessary product of evolution; it is only one of the possible several, and its advance must therefore require an active intervention of human will. This view was then reinforced by resort to a crucial insight of Hayek's: that a decentralized or spontaneous order has a capacity to deal with information, and thus of adapting to changing circumstances, that is not matched by any made order or organization. This capacity to adapt hints at a different view of evolution, in which the creative reaction of individuals is at least as important as the pressure from the external environment.

Under this light, liberal traditions, namely those of openness and of government limited by law, become crucially important, not because they are merely part of tradition, but because they favour piecemeal change and adaptation. This would also imply two main corrections to Hayek's critique of constructivism. First, instead of a blind reverence for traditions, liberalism should favour a critical presumption of tradition, that is, a view which puts the burden of proof on a proposed change, but does not close the door to change. Second, a spontaneous order, as opposed to a made order, should still be seen as a liberal ideal, but not as a 'natural' product of spontaneous evolution. Although it might well have historically arisen as an unintentional or undesigned product of human interaction, its maintenance requires constant protection by design, namely by a liberal framework of laws.

Finally, it was argued that these considerations have consequences also in the political field. Liberalism cannot be identified with 'laissez-faire', but should rather be seen as a special sort of constructivism – one which is self-restrained precisely because its main goal is the protection of a free society. Karl Popper's case for a piecemeal social engineering, in spite of this awkward label, was then recalled to illustrate what an active view of liberalism might be. But such an active view, it was emphasized, could not be fixed in a once and for all political programme. The agenda of liberalism must vary according to circumstances and only its main attitude can be defined: it aims at the preservation of a free society, ruled by laws rather than the caprices of men. But this is an unending undertaking, which requires an active intervention in the realm of politics and institutions.

* * *

This chapter closes Part I of this study, which was dedicated to Friedrich A. Hayek and neo-liberalism. The next chapter will be dedicated to Raymond Plant and socialism. It will be argued, then, that the main difference between liberalism and socialism does not lie in the opposition between non-intervention and intervention, but precisely in the goals of political intervention, which, as was mentioned above, largely determine the type of intervention.

But it should be also recalled, that the main subject of this enquiry has not yet been concluded. Although it has been shown that a negative view of social rights is compatible with civil and political ones, it has not been shown that social rights are entailed by the moral duty to help those who cannot help themselves. This still remains an open subject of this enquiry. It will be discussed in the next stage, when socialist views on social rights are also scrutinized and critically evaluated.

Part II
Raymond Plant and
Socialism

4 Presentation: Democratic Equality

To the debacle of liberal science can be traced the moral schism of the modern world which so tragically divides enlightened men. For the liberals are the inheritors of the science which truly interprets the progressive principle of the industrial revolution. But they have been unable to carry forward their science; they have not wrested from it a social philosophy which is humanly satisfactory. The collectivists, on the other hand, have the zest for progress, the sympathy for the poor, the burning sense of wrong, the impulse for great deeds, which have been lacking in latter-day liberalism. But their science is founded in a profound misunderstanding of the economy at the foundation of modern society, and their actions, therefore, are deeply destructive and reactionary.

Walter Lippmann, *The Good Society*, 1938

SOCIALISM AND CITIZENSHIP

Several authors have recently worked on the concept of social citizenship with the explicit purpose of refuting the views of Friedrich A. Hayek and some other opponents of the concept of 'social rights' – all these being designated by their critics as belonging to the so-called 'New Right'.[1] Furthermore, some recent publications give the impression that the concept of citizenship may well be at the centre of a reflection aiming at the reformulation of socialist thought. According to these views, 'there is today wide agreement that the left-wing project is in crisis', and, therefore, new realities 'require the reformulation of the socialist ideal in terms of an extension and deepening of democracy'.[2] In this process of reformulation, the concept of citizenship, and particularly the concept of social citizenship, seem to occupy a central place.

Professor Raymond Plant, now Lord Plant, is undoubtedly one of the most representative authors of this diverse current of scholars who aim at reformulating the socialist programme on the basis of the concept of citizenship. In a Fabian Society tract published in October 1988, entitled *Citizenship, Rights and Socialism*,[3] Plant argues that:

Democratic citizenship should be the key idea at the centre
of this project (of updating and modernising Labour's programme in a manner consistent with its underlying aims
and values) and that it can provide a unifying framework
within which policy can be elaborated and a link to Labour's
historical principles can be maintained.

It should be added that Raymond Plant's reflection has been
developed in a critical dialogue with the thought of Friedrich
A. Hayek, especially with his thesis on 'the mirage of social
justice' and the denial of social rights – these being the very
same theses which were dealt with in the first part of this study.
For all this, Raymond Plant seems to be the suitable author to
pursue our enquiry into the concept of social citizenship rights.
His argument will be taken as representative of a wide set of
socialist views, and, when appropriate, other authors will be
brought into the discussion. As was the case with Hayek, Plant's
argument will first be presented. A discussion will then follow
in Chapter 5, and a critical evaluation in Chapter 6 will close
this Part II. As was also the case with Hayek, Plant's work will
be presented from the angle that is relevant to the problem
being discussed, that of social citizenship. But, here again, this
will lead to a long journey through the author's work.

In Part I, the discussion of Hayek's argument attempted to
capture the approach of what was called neo-liberalism to the
problem of social and economic rights. In this Part, one may
hope, the discussion of Plant and some other socialist thinkers
will attempt to capture the socialist view, or at least a certain
type of socialist view, on the same issue. In Part III, a final
chapter, Chapter 7, will put forward an alternative proposal,
which, in broad terms, could simply be called liberal.

* * *

At the outset of his intellectual enquiry, Plant faces two crucial
questions: (1) can claims to welfare provision be perceived or
classified as rights, and, if they can, (2) ought they to be considered as such? Raymond Plant answers affirmatively to both
questions, but the process to reach these answers is long and
complex. We shall start by seeing why he considers that the

social claims *can* be perceived as rights and then why they *ought* to be considered as such. In a further and final stage, Plant's concept of 'democratic equality' and 'democratic citizenship' will then be presented.

REPLY TO FRIEDRICH A. HAYEK

In discussing how and why claims to welfare provision *can* be perceived as rights, Raymond Plant faces two main opponents: Friedrich A. Hayek and Maurice Cranston. As far as Hayek is concerned, Plant serializes two main arguments of his against the concept of social rights (which have already been presented and discussed in Part I of this study): (1) that individuals' shares of the market outcome are not a matter of social justice because market results are unintended and unforeseeable; and (2) that, even if they were a matter of social justice, there would be no criterion of distribution or social justice.

Plant's reply to the first point has already been mentioned and we have produced a critique of Hayek's denial of social justice along very similar, although slightly different, lines to those of Plant's. He accepts that market global results may well be unintended, in the sense that they are the product of the interaction of countless small decisions. But the fact that market results are unintended, as well as the fact that some natural handicaps are also no one's responsibility does not mean that our inaction before these facts is not subject to moral evaluations.

This means that justice and injustice are not only a matter of how a particular outcome came about or arose, but rather a matter of our response to that outcome. Eleven years later, Raymond Plant adds a further insight to his case for the social responsibility on market outcomes:

> If we say that as a matter of routine my intended actions produce a foreseeable but unintended outcome for another person, then it is going to be disingenuous to claim that I am not responsible for the foreseeable but unintended consequences of my action. Indeed, if this were not so, there would constantly be a strong incentive continually to narrow down the characterization of intention so that it does not include the foreseeable consequences of action.[4]

What Plant is trying to show is that, although 'we cannot predict in a free market what the economic outcome will be for an individual', we can nevertheless foresee 'the economic consequences not for an individual but for a group', since 'those who enter the market with least will end up with least'. His conclusion is as follows:

> (a) if as an empirical fact those who enter the market with least will tend to end up with least (with exceptions for random individuals);
> (b) if this is known to be the case as a foreseeable general outcome even though it is not intended;
> (c) if there is an alternative course of action available, namely some redistribution in the interest of social justice;
>
> Then we can argue that those who support the market do bear responsibility for the least well off even if they do not intend that these people should be in this position, and, in this context, the outcome of the market should not be accepted as in principle unprincipled.[5]

Having argued that, contrary to Hayek's view, the economic consequences of the market are a matter of moral responsibility, Plant now has to overcome Hayek's next point: that there is no criterion of distribution or social justice compatible with the general rules of a free society. Plant accepts this assertion of Hayek's when it applies to criteria as those of merit or desert,[6] but he maintains that 'it is possible to secure broad agreement about some ends, namely those that are necessary conditions for achieving any other ends'.[7] Plant immediately acknowledges that 'Hayek of course denies that we can reach agreement on needs (or for that matter any other end)'. But he will set up a long and elaborated argument for the concept of basic needs which, in his view, will overcome Hayek's obstacles.[8]

THE CONCEPT OF BASIC NEEDS

The concept of basic needs is central for Raymond Plant's case for social and economic rights, and the topic is present in the whole of his discussion of social rights. Plant is committed to showing that, contrary to Hayek's argument, it is possible to define 'basic needs' in a way that is firm enough to gather wide agreement in a pluralist society.

'Are there basic human needs' therefore turns into the question of whether there are any basic human ends that are wanted by all persons, with basic needs being the necessary means for the pursuit and realization of those ends ... If there are such ends generating such basic needs, then there would be a class of things needed that, following Rawls in 'A Theory of Justice' we might call primary goods which could be the basic concern of social policy.[9]

Raymond Plant's answer is of course affirmative: there are such ends generating such basic needs. And these ends do not depend upon the particular moral creed either of each individual or even of each cultural group. Every moral code has to recognize that persons need certain minimal capacities that allow them to act and pursue the moral goals enshrined in that moral code. *The capacity to act as a moral agent* then becomes *the basic human end* that is wanted by everyone. And *the conditions or means* for that action are *unqualified or human needs*:

> There are some conditions necessary for doing anything at all, for performing any action or pursuing any goal whatsoever. No matter what morality one adopts, these conditions will be necessary for carrying it out. Needs of this sort must be acknowledged in all societies whatever their moral code or standards, and may fairly be called 'unqualified' or 'human' needs.[10]

Following the work of Alan Gewirth on moral philosophy and human rights,[11] Plant concludes that *survival* and *autonomy* are *basic conditions of moral activity*. The case for survival goes without saying, since a dead person cannot act, let alone act morally. But it must be allowed that physical survival is not enough for moral activity to become a reality, since one can literally be kept alive in total dependence on a machine. Autonomy, in the sense of 'freedom to act morally', is then presented by Plant as the second 'unqualified or human need'. And, although he is ready to admit that the precise level of satisfaction involved in the concept of autonomy is open to endless disputes, he rightly recalls that the same happens with well-established individual rights in the civil and political sphere.

Ends (however different) and duties (however varied) can be pursued and performed only by human beings acting autonomously; and therefore any moral view to be coherent must recognize the maintenance of human life and the development of autonomy as basic obligations . . . The need for life and autonomy provides the logically basic human needs that have to be recognized by any logically self-consistent moral point of view.[12]

REPLY TO MAURICE CRANSTON

Having paved the way for viewing the state provision of welfare in terms of providing for people's basic needs, Raymond Plant still faced one difficult opponent: Maurice Cranston, who maintained that there is a crucial difference of nature between traditional rights and social ones. Maurice Cranston's argument was first presented in his contribution to D. D. Raphael's *Political Theory and the Rights of Man*,[13] and was later extended and revised in Cranston's *What Are Human Rights?*[14] Although his argument is rich and challenging, it is not possible to go through its details here. Let us say, then, that the main thrust of his case against social rights may be summarized in the three tests for genuine human rights that he has put forward: the test of *practicability*, of *paramount importance* and of *universality*. According to Cranston, social rights fail each and every one of these tests. Raymond Plant, in his turn, replies that social rights do pass the three tests – as much as, at least, the traditional rights do.

The test of *practicability* stems from the relationship between rights and duties. A right to X is meaningful only when it involves a duty of someone to facilitate X (to facilitate means either the negative duty of forbearance or the positive duty of action). This entails the fact that the duty to facilitate X has to be possible and practicable. According to Maurice Cranston, however, social rights entail duties which are impracticable, because they involve resources that may not be available, whereas traditional rights always involve practicable and possible duties: there are mainly negative duties of forbearance that, by definition, do not involve resources.

Plant's reply to this point is ingenious. He remarks that the forbearance required by traditional rights (life, liberty, property, etc.) 'cannot just be legislated into existence – a right not to be killed (the right to life) will require protection by police forces, defence forces, etc. all of which are going to involve capital expenditures'.[15] The same applies, Plant adds, either to the right to a fair trial (expenditure on a legal system) or, even more strikingly, to the right to some form of representative political institutions – which involve expenditure on legislatures, elections, etc. Thus, Plant concludes, social rights pass the test of practicability just as the traditional ones do, since they all involve the allocation of resources. And, if Cranston's test is meant to require total and immediate practicability, then not even the traditional rights pass the test: as D. D. Raphael put it, and Plant endorsed, 'no amount of legislation or of police forces can prevent all murders'.[16]

Maurice Cranston's second test is that of *universality*. It requires that a human right applies to all human beings as human beings, and not because they fulfil a particular social role. Cranston's favourite example is the right to holidays with pay, which, as we have seen in Part I, was also ridiculed by Hayek. The fact is, Maurice Cranston argues, that 'this is necessarily limited to those who are paid in any case, that is to say, the employee class. Since not everyone belongs to this class, the right cannot be a universal right'.[17]

Raymond Plant rightly observes that this interpretation of universality is rather narrow – in fact it would also rule out traditional rights, such as a right to a fair trial, or the right to leave one's country, etc. since they are all limited to those who belong to the particular people in question (those who are on trial, those who want to leave the country, etc.). The point with universality is, Plant remarks, that each right must apply equally, or universally, to all those who might be in the situation in question. But this, of course, applies either to traditional or to social rights:

> Not all people are employed, not all people are destitute, not all people are at any particular time in need of education; but equally, all these are possible states of life which any person could find himself in.[18]

As for the test of *paramount importance*, Cranston's third test, the fact is that it is itself rather vague. Cranston admits that there is no definite criterion of paramount importance, and he appeals to common sense. 'Common sense knows', he asserts,

'that fire engines and ambulances are essential services, whereas
fun fairs and holiday camps are not.'[19]

Of course, Raymond Plant does not deny this observation.
On the contrary, he fully accepts Cranston's appeal to common
sense and incorporates it in his case for the paramount importance of social rights. This is done by observing that one of the
underlying assumptions of the common view of 'paramount
importance' is the involvement of human life. But, Plant adds,
it would be completely mistaken to believe that human life is
only at stake in traditional rights and not in social and economic
ones. 'People die as effectively from starvation as they do from
murder,' Plant recalls, 'and in this sense social and economic
rights could pass the test of paramount importance just as much
as rights against homicide.'[20] In fact, Plant will add, this throws
some light upon the relationship between traditional and social rights. Instead of having basic different importance, as
Cranston has argued, they are rather complementary. Social
rights provide the means to the exercise of traditional ones:
'Rights to life and liberty may require certain things – among
them health and education to make their exercise a reality –
not just negative forbearance on the part of government.'[21]

OUGHT SOCIAL RIGHTS BE PERCEIVED AS RIGHTS?

Having argued that claims on welfare provision fulfil the necessary conditions to be defined as rights, Raymond Plant faces a
no less difficult problem now: why ought they be defined as
rights, that is to say, do claims on welfare provision fulfil the
sufficient conditions to become rights? Two main difficulties
arise here: (1) whether or not there is a duty to provide for
other people's basic needs, and (2) whether or not this duty
gives rise to a correspondent right of the recipient. Raymond
Plant, as expected, responds positively to both questions.

The basis for the moral duty to provide welfare was sketched
in Plant's reply to Hayek. Having shown that global market
outcomes are foreseeable, and that it is foreseeable that
'those who enter the market with least will tend to end up with
least', Plant has concluded that 'those who support the market do bear responsibility for the least well off'. He has then
argued that this responsibility should be defined in terms of

the satisfaction of people's basic needs, that is, those minimal conditions or means which are indispensable for performing any action or pursuing any goal whatsoever. These basic needs include physical survival and autonomy, i.e. freedom from arbitrary interference, ill-health and ignorance. Providing for these basic needs then becomes, Plant added, a moral responsibility of society.

Now the problem is the nature of this responsibility. Is the satisfaction of these basic needs a duty of charity or benevolence, or any other kind of imperfect duty or supererogation, or is it a strict moral obligation? The question is absolutely crucial, since, furthermore, the nature of this duty determines the existence, or non-existence, of a corresponding right: only duties of strict obligation give rise to rights, this not being the case with imperfect duties. As John Stuart Mill put it in his *Utilitarianism*:

> Now it is well known that ethical writers divide duties into two classes, denoted by the ill chosen expressions duties of perfect and imperfect obligation; the latter being those in which, though the act is obligatory, the particular occasions of our performing it are left to our choice; as in the case of charity and beneficence, which we are indeed bound to practise but not towards any definite person, nor at any prescribed time . . . duties of perfect obligation are those duties in virtue of which a positive right resides in some person or persons; duties of imperfect obligation are those moral obligations which do not give rise to any right . . . Justice implies something which it is not only right to do, and wrong not to do, but which some individual may claim from us as his moral right. No one has a moral right to our charity or beneficence because we are not morally bound to practise these virtues towards any given individual.[22]

Raymond Plant acknowledges the difficult challenge this problem poses to the social rights theorist. Whereas traditional rights entail perfect duties of forbearance – the right of X to life entails the duty of others not to kill him, the right of X to free speech entails the duty of others, under certain qualification, not to interfere with his exercise of this right, etc. – the same seems not to be the case with social and economic rights. Even if I wanted to take my duty to help those in need as a perfect duty, I would not be able to perform that duty towards each and every person in need. Here, it seems, lies one crucial difference between traditional and social rights.

Plant's response to this problem is two-fold. He starts by saying that the right to welfare provision is not to be claimed against individuals, but to society as a whole, or more specifically to the government. And secondly he concludes that, therefore, the duty to provide for other people's basic needs cannot be seen in terms of a duty to be performed directly towards this or that individual, but as a duty to support some institutions which, in their turn, provide help directly for those in need. Hence, the duty to provide welfare may be seen as a duty of perfect obligation which assumes the form of an obligation to support welfare institutions, namely the obligation to pay taxes. These welfare institutions work as a sort of intermediary between citizens who pay taxes and citizens who, because they are in need, receive welfare support:

> To see the human right to welfare as implying the duty to support government welfare measures would be equivalent to seeing due process of law as a human right. A specific individual has not the duty to provide such due process, but rather the duty to see that the procedures of due process are in fact carried out. The perfect duties corresponding to the rights of welfare are not then the personal provision of resources and services to individuals, but rather the duty to support government and institutions that are organized to meet such needs.[23]

*　*　*

Having argued that the duty to help those in need can be seen as a duty of perfect obligation, Plant has argued, by the same token, for the right to welfare provision: duties of strict obligation, unlike those of imperfect obligation, do give rise to correponding rights.

It must be noticed, however, that Plant has not shown that the duty to provide for people's basic needs *is* in fact a duty of strict obligation. His argument about taxation showed only that this *could be* a perfect duty, since it could be performed by each individual through well-defined actions – taxation – and towards well-defined recipients – the state, which acts as an intermediary between taxpayers and welfare recipients.

But why would taxpayers have the moral duty to provide for other people's basic needs? What is the moral justification for that duty? This has not been produced yet, although the basis for it has already been provided. This basis lies in the original concept of *basic need* and in Alan Gewirth's theory of there being indispensable conditions for moral action.

If it is accepted that basic needs consist of those basic goods which are indispensable for pursuing any ends (however different) and duties (however varied), then the duty to provide for those who lack these basic goods has to be accepted simply because, without them, they would not be able to fulfil any other obligation. As Plant puts it:

> The obligation to satisfy these particular needs has to be a strict obligation because it is impossible to make sense of there being other obligations that could outweigh the obligation to meet these needs just because those whose needs in this sphere are not met are not able *ex hipothesi* to pursue any other obligations, whatever they may be, or any other ends.[24]

DEMOCRATIC EQUALITY

We have described the way whereby Raymond Plant reached the concept of 'basic needs' and how he justified the duty to provide basic goods for those who need them. According to the dichotomy about the normative basis of welfare provision, which he had presented at the outset of his enquiry, the problem seems to have been solved: he has presented his argument against the view of welfare provision as a matter of charity or generosity and, therefore, against the denial of social rights. He has also presented his case for the view according to which:

> Welfare provision is a matter of strict obligation for those who hold resources and that those who are in need have strict moral claims on those better off in society. Their needs create a right to welfare and a duty on the part of the better endowed to grant welfare benefits to meet such needs.[25]

This was the purpose of his book with Harry Lesser and Peter Taylor Gooby, published in 1980, and it seems to have been achieved. The same argument is presented and developed in his latest book, *Contemporary Political Thought*, published in 1991. Meanwhile, however, Raymond Plant has published other works, books, pamphlets and contributions to other books, in which the case for 'social rights' hitherto presented is developed further and, somehow, in a different direction. In *Conservative Capitalism in Britain and the United States*, a book published in 1989 with Kenneth Hoover, Raymond Plant refers to the concept of basic goods in a slightly different manner:

> A theory of need is central to a left critique of markets because it provides *the beginning of a justification* for arguing that there are certain goods which are so necessary for individual agency that they should be provided collectively and intentionally rather than through the market, which is the forum within which wants and preferences are satisfied.[26]

One may see here that what was 'the normative basis of welfare provision' in 1980 is now perceived as only 'the beginning of a justification'. It is important to follow the author's reasoning in this respect:

> However, the basic goods of physical survival and autonomy and the specific ways in which these are cashed in terms of health care and income maintenance are fairly minimal as they stand. They would not take the defence of the welfare state in terms of the value of freedom much beyond the idea of the welfare state as a residual institution (although this is useful in defending the welfare state against libertarians such as Nozick who really see no role for welfare state at all, even at a residual level, and against neo-liberals such as Hayek and Acton who see a residual welfare state as justifiable only on pragmatic and not moral grounds).[27]

It is now important to follow closely Plant's argument for going beyond 'the welfare state as a residual institution'. The concept of basic needs, as an indispensable condition for freedom to have value, is still at the heart of Plant's argument. But the case is not for *providing basic goods for those who need them*: the case is now for *a more equal distribution of these primary goods* in order that *liberty becomes of roughly equal value to all persons.*

The goal ceases to be to provide for those 'abilities/powers/ capabilities which are indispensable to the value of liberty', and becomes to equalize those abilities in order to achieve 'a greater equality in the value of liberty'. This metamorphosis is crucial, and crucial it is that we assess it accurately.

Raymond Plant has argued that equal negative liberty is mainly guaranteed by civil and political rights which define the same limits of non-coercion in the same way for all. But then he asked why freedom is valued. The answer was: 'to live a meaningful life'. But a meaningful life requires more than negative liberty. It requires some positive resources which individuals need to be able to live their own lives in their own way. Liberty would have no *worth* had not the individual had minimal capacities to exercise this liberty. The logical conclusion was that, although civil and political rights guarantee negative liberty, they cannot guarantee a minimal worth or value of liberty for all. For this to be achieved, we need social rights, the right to the provision of basic goods which are indispensable to the value or worth of liberty.

The problem now becomes, Plant adds, how to distribute these basic goods. His answer is that, from a socialist point of view, these basic goods should be distributed equally, or as equally as possible. And the main reason for that is not that socialists are concerned with equality for equality's sake, but that they are concerned with equality for the sake of liberty. 'The liberal is interested in equal liberty', Plant recalls. But 'socialists are concerned with trying to secure the distribution of resources which will mean that liberty is of roughly equal value to all persons'. And he adds:

> The worth of liberty to individuals is related to their capacities, opportunities and resources to advance the purposes which they happen to have. Those with greater income and wealth, fortunate family background etc. will, on the whole, be able to pursue things for which we value liberty more effectively than the person who does not enjoy these benefits. It is because we value liberty for all that we are concerned to secure a greater equality in the worth of liberty.[28]

But why does the fact that socialists 'value liberty for all' entail the goal of securing 'a greater equality in the worth of liberty'? This is a crucial point and Plant provides three reasons for that.

The first may be called, oddly enough, 'the Hayekian presumption of equality', the second 'the fair value of liberty', and the third 'the implications of equal political liberty'.

THREE REASONS FOR EQUALITY

The Hayekian presumption of equality is an interesting and somehow cunning argument of Plant's, which basically consists of applying one of Hayek's arguments for equality before the law to the field of basic goods. It will be recalled that Hayek had said that:

> No men or group of men possesses the capacity to determine conclusively the potentialities of other human beings and [...] we should certainly never trust anyone invariably to exercise such a capacity. However great the differences between men may be, we have no grounds for believing that they will ever be so great as to enable one man's mind in a particular instance to comprehend fully all that another responsible man's mind is capable of.[29]

This led Hayek to say that equality before the law was an imperative of liberty, not because all men are in fact equal, which they are not, but because all other principles would be worse than this sort of 'presumption of equality'. A similar point is now presented by Raymond Plant:

> If we accept liberal assumptions about equality of respect due to each citizen, together with the kind of view to be found in Hayek, that we lack criteria for saying that one person is more deserving than another, then *there are no moral grounds for saying that some people deserve to have more effective basic liberty*. In these circumstances, therefore, those welfare goods which define the conditions of effective agency and the value of liberty *should be distributed equally* just because there are not any a priori moral reasons for any other sort of distribution.[30]

Plant was later to admit that a strictly equal distribution might well not be possible. But the important point here is that the basic presumption must be the one of equality. Moves away from equality have to be justified, and not the other way round.

* * *

Plant's second reason for equality is 'the fair value of liberty'. As was noted above, Plant asserts that the value of liberty depends not only on the absence of coercion by others, but also on the existence of *basic goods*, those 'means necessary for us to pursue our own plan of life and to advance our purposes'.[31] In this sense, 'a fair value of liberty' cannot be reached only by means of equality before the law, since this would guarantee only equal liberty, not the equal value of liberty. It becomes then necessary to promote 'a more equal distribution of the primary goods to secure a fair value of liberty'.

Strictly speaking, Plant is not giving an independent reason for the desirability of 'a fair value of liberty' here. He seems to assume that desirability to be a corollary of the principle of equal liberty, which, as was previously mentioned, is his first argument and is mainly derived from Hayek. What Plant wants to defend now is the legitimacy of certain measures which may become necessary if the pursuit of a 'fair value of liberty' is accepted:

> In so far as this (distribution of primary goods) reduces the very high worth of liberty of those who are already better off, it is a legitimate restriction and one which we, as socialists, have to face squarely. If the better off person values liberty and his education, income, wealth, etc. as a basic means whereby his freedom can be realised, then it is difficult to see how he can respect his fellow citizens and not agree that those in worse circumstances, for which they have modest responsibility, should have the worth of their liberty improved, even at the cost of some diminution of his own.[32]

In a way, this might be interpreted as a second reason for the idea of a fair value of liberty, a reason we might call 'the reciprocity one': if the better off value liberty and the resources that make their liberty worthy, and if they accept that equal respect is due to each citizen, then, reciprocally, they would have to accept that their fellow citizens who are less fortunate should have the worth of their liberty improved.

* * *

Raymond Plant's third reason for equality is more complex and full of political consequences. It consists of saying that 'it is a naive and mistaken view, although one characteristic of liberalism, that *formal political equality* can exist independently of a high degree of material inequality'.[33] The argument again consists of starting from a largely consensual value in the liberal tradition – that political rights of all citizens must be equal – to show that, without generating further equality at the social and economic level, political equality is nothing but an illusion: 'The wealthy will have more ability than the poor to influence the selection of candidates, the media, public opinion and political authorities.'[34]

And Plant applies the same reasoning to the legal system:

> The rich and the poor have the same rights, but differences of wealth at best allow better counsel to be employed not to mention the question of whether the better off members of society can in fact secure laws which favour their interests, or whether they can exercise influence upon what kinds of crimes are prosecuted (for example, in the field of tax evasion).[35]

The same idea is applied to the equal right to free expression: 'Those in better circumstances are able to utilise this liberty more effectively and it is of greater value to them.'[36]

DRAWBACKS OF EQUALITY OF OPPORTUNITY

Having seen Plant's three reasons for an equal distribution of basic goods, one should now look at what he means by 'equal distribution'. This is to be understood in a special way, which he calls 'democratic equality', a term he borrows from Anthony Crosland and John Rawls. The concept of 'democratic equality' is based on the simultaneous critique of mere equality of opportunity – which is to be seen as 'not enough for socialists' – and of equality of outcome, which is to be ruled out on the basis that some differences of outcome are necessary because they have 'a vital economic function'.

In criticizing equality of opportunity, socialists highlight two main aspects: the limits of the attempt to equalize starting positions, and the moral arbitrariness of genetic endowment. The limits to equalize opportunities are mainly related to the family institution. If the latter is accepted as a crucial institution, as Plant does not deny, 'the influence of any action taken in the field of health, education and welfare is going to be mediated through the family with all the differentiating effects this will have upon the start of particular children in life.[37] Hence, equality of opportunity seems to be a noble ideal difficult to reach in real existing societies.

Nevertheless, and this is the second aspect of the socialist critique, even if it were possible to guarantee a common starting point to every individual, it would be highly disputable that the hierarchy of merit to which they are competing is morally acceptable in itself. The 'noble ideal' is not as noble as it might appear at first sight:

> The basic objection of the left to equality of opportunity is concerned with the fact that there is no critical approach to the differential positions to which equal access is being proposed. It takes the existing structure of inequality for granted and is concerned about recruitment to it. However this is not satisfactory to the left: it will want to probe the legitimacy of the differential reward structure, otherwise greater equality of access may give a greater legitimacy to a structure of rewards which those on the left may regard as unjust.[38]

EQUALITY OF OUTCOME

If equality of opportunity is not acceptable to the left, what then should the left's proposal be? Plant admits two alternatives. The first consists of accepting the existing structure of inequality on the basis that this cannot be altered by governments in a way compatible with individual liberty; according to Plant, this is the view of market-based conservatism, especially when it is coupled with the Hayekian view that markets do not cause injustice. The other possibility, Plant adds, is to favour equality of outcome. He sees no difficulty in the principle itself, although some instrumental difficulties will be presented later:

> The other alternative is to argue for a greater compression of the reward structure and in favour of greater equality of outcome. If the family is to be maintained and personal liberty secured so that measures to secure greater equality of opportunity must be limited, then it is wrong to reward as prodigiously as we do a narrow range of talent for which the individual does not bear responsibility, and to make the costs of failure so heavy for those whose opportunities have been more modest, and who similarly do not bear full responsibility for their condition.[39]

It is worth noting that Plant is no longer limiting his advocating of equality to the field previously defined as that of basic goods. Basic goods must certainly be the main target of equality, but a socialist policy cannot help targeting income as well:

> In our society, these [basic goods] will include *health services, education and welfare goods* generally. These resources are also going to include *income* because, as Le Grand has shown, differences in income lead to marked differences in the use of other sorts of basic welfare goods.[40]

Here again we find the idea presented at the beginning of this section about democratic equality: the idea that the welfare state as a 'residual institution', that is to say, as a set of policies and institutions aiming at providing basic goods for those in need, is not enough from a socialist viewpoint. The reason for this socialist dissatisfaction lies, as David Miller put it, in the fact that, although the welfare state has been reasonably successful in fighting against poverty, it has not been equally successful in promoting equality.[41]

Why should equality be important? We have seen Plant's three main reasons for it: the Hayekian presumption of equality, the fair value of liberty, and the implications of equal political liberty. We have then started discussing what is meant by equality. We have reviewed Plant's argument about the impossibility of equality of opportunity, and also about the illegitimacy of the unequal structure of rewards to which equal opportunities are supposed to give access. Equality of outcome has then appeared as Plant's alternative to the failure of equality of opportunity. Julien le Grand's argument about the need for targeting equality of income was also mentioned to enhance the case for equality of outcome.

Now we must introduce some qualifications to this idea of equality of outcome. Not because it is wrong in principle, Plant explains, but mainly because there might have to be *a rent of ability* which, although producing some inequalities, would still, and after deeper analysis, work to the benefit of the worst off. This is what Plant calls *a theory of legitimate inequalities*.

SOME LEGITIMATE INEQUALITIES

The fundamental reason for Plant to accept some qualifications to the concept of equality of outcome lies in *the presumptive need of incentives*. Presumptive is the right word here, since Plant is not sure about this need. Along very similar lines to those of Julien le Grand, Raymond Plant asserts that it is not plain that people really need incentives in order to work more productively and efficiently.[42] But he recalls that experiences of total egalitarianism have not been quite successful – such as the Great Leap Forward in China – and finally admits that *a rent of ability* is necessary on purely pragmatic and efficient grounds.

What, then, is this rent of ability? It is, literally, that amount of legitimate inequality that citizens should accept if they want 'to mobilize skills which otherwise would no longer be mobilised and without which we should be worse off'.[43] In a very Rawlsian way, Plant is then prepared to accept *some legitimate inequalities*, if and when it is proved they work for the benefit of the worst off:

> Incentives are not ends in themselves; they are means to ends, and they are linked to justice only in the sense of the degree of economic rent which is required to be paid to generate prosperity for the welfare of citizens.[44]

This theory of equality – which allows for some legitimate inequalities, on grounds of the need for incentives, but denies any intrinsic moral value to these incentives – is called by Raymond Plant *a theory of presumptive equality*, or *a theory of democratic equality*.

The difficulty which is usually raised in reference to this

theory of democratic equality concerns the question of 'how much equality' does the theory really advocate? Plant highlights the fact that the real problem should be 'how much inequality'? The basic presumption of the theory is for equality, certain inequalities being allowed, or justified, or accepted as legitimate if and only if it can be shown that they work for the benefit of the worst off, i.e. that they correspond to an indispensable rent of ability. Hence, equality should be the basic rule, and the burden of proof should lie in departures from equality. As for the range and nature of these rents of abilities, the theory cannot specify them in advance: 'differential rewards are to be paid after empirical investigation of the economic function of a particular task and the supply price of the skills to fulfil it.'[45]

PLANT'S ARGUMENT: AN OVERVIEW

This chapter started by pointing out that Raymond Plant's work on social citizenship rights aims at a broader goal: creating the basis for updating and modernizing the socialist programme, in a manner consistent with its historical principles. At the outset of this project, Plant faced two main questions: (1) can claims to welfare provision be classified as rights and, if they can, (2) ought they to be perceived as such?

Starting with the first problem, Plant faced the main opposition of F. A. Hayek and Maurice Cranston. Hayek's argument against social rights, extensively discussed in Part I of this study, comprised the view that market results are not a matter of social justice (because they are unintended and unforeseen), and that, even if they were a matter of social justice, there would be no criterion of distribution or social justice. Plant's reply to the first assertion consisted of showing that justice and injustice are not primarily a matter of how a particular outcome was brought about, but rather of our response to that outcome. Therefore, if one can foresee that certain situations will recurrently occur in a market system – those who start with least will end up with least – one can then argue that those who support the market do bear responsibility for the least well off. As for Hayek's second assertion – that there is no criterion of distribution – Plant agrees in so far as this applies to criteria such as merit or desert, but not to need or basic need.

Plant's next step was then to show that a general agreement upon basic need is possible in a pluralistic society. His main point was to show that every moral code has to recognize that persons need certain minimal capacities that allow them to act and pursue the moral goals enshrined in that moral code. The capacity to act as a moral agent then becomes the basic human end that is wanted by all persons. And the conditions or means for that action are unqualified or human needs. Following the work of Alan Gewirth, Plant concludes that physical survival and autonomy – i.e. freedom from arbitrary interference, ill-health and ignorance – are basic conditions of moral activity. In this sense, the right to satisfaction of basic needs appears as a right whose nature and justification are comparable to those of traditional, civil and political rights of citizenship.

But Maurice Cranston is a serious opponent of this view, for he argued that these kinds of social rights are different from the traditional ones in three main respects: practicability, para-mount importance, and universality. Plant's reply consisted of arguing that, strictly speaking, those three difficulties could apply to traditional rights as well. He then concluded that, instead of having basic different natures, social and traditional rights are rather complementary: the former provide the means to the exercise of the latter.

Having shown that claims on welfare provision could be seen as rights, Plant then moved on to his next problem: ought they to be seen as rights? This problem comprised two main difficulties: (1) whether or not there is a duty to provide for other people's basic needs and (2) whether or not this duty gives rise to a corresponding right (i.e. whether or not this duty is of strict obligation). As for the latter, Plant argued that the duty to provide for other people's basic needs cannot be seen in terms of a duty to be performed directly towards this or that individual, but as a duty to support some institutions which, in turn, provide help directly to those in need: for this reason, this duty can be of strict obligation. As for the moral justification of this duty, Plant argued that it follows from the assumption that basic needs are defined by those conditions which are indispensable to acting as a moral agent: without the satisfaction of these basic needs, individuals cannot fulfil any other obligation.

Having thus justified the duty to provide basic goods for those who need them, and having argued that this duty gives rise to a corresponding right, Plant then observed that this would not take the defence of the welfare state much beyond the idea of the welfare state as a residual institution. In fact, Plant argued, the crucial importance of basic needs for the use of liberty entails the problem of knowing how to distribute those basic goods which correspond to basic needs. Plant then asserted that basic goods should be distributed equally, or as equally as possible, for three main reasons: the Hayekian presumption of equality, the fair value of liberty, and the achievement of equal political liberty. For these reasons, Plant maintained, socialists are concerned with equality for the sake of liberty: whereas liberals are interested only in equal liberty, socialists want liberty to be of roughly equal value to all persons.

But equality of the value of liberty should be distinguished both from equality of opportunity and strict equality of outcome. What Plant called democratic equality should then be seen as a strong presumption of equality, some departures from equality being allowed if and only if they correspond to a rent of ability: that amount of legitimate inequality that citizens should accept if they want to mobilize skills which otherwise would no longer be mobilized and without which all citizens would be worse off.

5 Discussion: Satisfaction of Basic Needs or Distribution According to Need?

A true thinker can only be justly estimated when his thoughts have worked their way into minds formed in a different school; have been wrought and moulded into consistency with all other true and relevant thoughts; when the noisy conflict of half-truths, angrily denying one another, has subsided, and ideas which seemed mutually incompatible, have been found only to require mutual limitations.

John Stuart Mill, 'Coleridge', 1840

THREE MAIN ASSERTIONS

The main thrust of the critique of Raymond Plant's argument on social citizenship rights to be presented in this chapter may be expressed in three main assertions.

The first consists of admitting that he has cogently replied to the most important arguments of Friedrich A. Hayek and Maurice Cranston against social rights; in other words, Plant has refuted with reasonable plausibility the allegations that a fundamental incompatibility opposes the social to the traditional rights.

Paradoxically, however, and this is the second assertion, Raymond Plant has not been clear in presenting what he understands as social rights. Sometimes he has rightly identified them with a basic and universal entitlement to a minimum of basic goods which are seen as indispensable conditions for the use of liberty. In this sense, which is called here a 'negative view' of social rights, or a view of 'basic social rights', these rights entail a duty on the part of society to provide basic goods for those who need them. But, at other times, Plant has interpreted social rights in a positive way, as generating a general principle, or a positive pattern, of distribution according to need. As it will be argued later, these two views are not only completely different but also, to a certain extent, incompatible.

It happens that, in the third place, Plant entirely adopts the positive view – which he seems not to distinguish from the negative one – when he further develops his concept of 'democratic

citizenship' and 'democratic equality'. This leads him into an
egalitarian theory which, strictly speaking, is incompatible with
his own arguments against Hayek and Cranston, that is to say,
with his own arguments for social citizenship rights.

In other words, Raymond Plant has accurately replied to the
opponents of social rights. But he derived from this illegitimate conclusions about the identification of social rights with a
positive pattern of distribution, which, in its turn, led him to
an egalitarian theory. To tell the truth, were this egalitarian
theory to be the necessary consequence of the defence of social
rights, Hayek and Cranston would have been right in their
contention that social rights jeopardize civil and political ones
– that is to say, that they threaten the principles which liberal
societies are based on.

However, there is no necessary link between the concept
of social rights and the egalitarian conclusions reached by
Plant. If he could reach these conclusions, this was due to a
crucial flaw in his argument, a flaw that started as an ambiguity
and later evolved into an entrenched view. This flaw was the
confusion – which Plant does not seem to have been aware
of – between the negative or residual principle of providing
basic goods for those who need them, and a general principle
of distribution (or a positive pattern of social justice) according
to need. The crucial point to be presented here is that the concept of social rights, which was rightly defended by Plant in
reply to Hayek and Cranston, has nothing to do with a general
or positive principle of distribution; it entails only a principle
or pattern (which is called here negative or residual) and which
consists of meeting the basic needs of those in need, that is
to say, to provide basic goods for those who need them, or
still, to help those who cannot help themselves. Nothing more,
contrary to what Raymond Plant wants, but also nothing less,
contrary to what Hayek and Cranston would like.

*   *   *

In order to justify the above assertions, this chapter will be
organized as follows:

(1)   It will start by showing the differences between a
       principle which requires that basic goods must be pro-

vided for those in need, and a general principle of
distribution according to need;

(2) Evidence will then be presented for the contention
that Raymond Plant is ambiguous in his definition
of social rights and their consequences in terms of
distribution;

(3) Plant's reply to the critics of social rights, especially
Hayek, will then be recalled in order to show that he
has actually argued for a negative or residual principle
of helping those in need, not for a general principle
of distribution according to need. Moreover, it will be
shown that Plant's reply to Hayek would not apply to
a general principle of distribution, that is to say, Hayek
would have been right, had the issue at stake been a
principle of distribution according to need;

(4) Finally, it will be argued that, if the above contentions
are accepted, then the whole egalitarian component of
Plant's argument will become unnecessary. And rightly
so, for the simple reason that this egalitarian component
arises only from the response to one question –'how
ought basic goods be distributed?' – which has no place
to be asked within the framework of social citizenship
rights, since these do not involve any general principle
of distribution whatever.

This last point needs to be clarified. At this stage in the
critique of Plant's argument, one is not discussing whether or
not basic goods should be equally distributed amongst citizens.
The only issue at stake here is that the very problem – how
basic goods should be distributed – has no relation to the case
for social rights. This, however, does not mean that the problem
itself does not exist or is meaningless. Since we are not trying
to avoid the discussion of the problem, but only to highlight
the fact that it does not follow from the endorsement of social
rights, it will be discussed in the next chapter. Then it will be
maintained that Plant's argument for social equality is flawed
in its foundationist ambition of defending equality for the sake
of liberty, and this for the simple reason that liberty is not
compatible with social equality. But this, one should insist, is
a totally different matter, and hence it must wait for the next
chapter to be treated.

SOCIAL JUSTICE VERSUS SOCIAL INJUSTICE

The time has come to clarify a crucial distinction within the discussion of social rights, a distinction which we have already come across in Part I, when criticizing Hayek's view about the 'meaninglessness of social justice', but which has not yet been properly developed. It may be worth recalling that, at that stage, what was claimed to be a misunderstanding of Hayek's, the one consisting of erroneously identifying the impossibility of a positive pattern of distribution with the impossibility of a negative pattern of social injustice, was pointed out. There was a very telling passage of Hayek's in this respect:

> It might be objected that we might not know quite well what is '*socially just*' and yet know quite well what is '*socially unjust*'; and by persistently eliminating 'social injustice' whenever we encounter it, gradually approach 'social justice'. This, however, does not provide a way out of the basic difficulty. There can be no test by which we can discover what is 'socially unjust' because (1) there is no subject by which an injustice can be committed, and (2) there are no rules of individual conduct the observance of which in the market order would secure to the individuals and groups the position which as such (as distinguished from the procedure by which it is determined) *would appear as just to us*.[1]

It was then noted that the two reasons which Hayek has presented for denying the endeavour of 'persistently eliminating injustice' were ill-conceived. The first, which is not relevant for our discussion here, was rejected along very similar lines, although slightly different, to those of Raymond Plant. The second reason – which is the one which concerns us at this stage – was misleadingly expressed by Hayek. From the standpoint of 'persistently eliminating injustice' – which is the issue discussed by Hayek in the quoted passage – we need not know 'which positions would appear as *just* to us'. It suffices to know which positions would appear as *unjust*.

It has then been pointed out that Hayek had himself recognized the possibility of defining in broad terms the notion of 'socially unjust situations'. This is patent in several passages of Hayek, but it is sufficient for our purposes to recall only one here:

There is no reason why in a free society government should not assure to all *protection against severe deprivation* in the form of an assured minimum income, or floor below which nobody need to descend. To enter into such an *insurance against extreme misfortune* may well be in the interest of all; or it may be felt to be a clear moral duty of all *to assist*, within the organized community, *those who cannot help themselves.*[2]

This means that Hayek has himself provided a basis for defining 'socially unjust situations', that is situations of 'severe deprivation', 'extreme misfortune', or those in which people 'cannot help themselves'. Why, then, did he insist on denying the endeavour of 'persistently eliminating injustice' and the negative view of social rights arising from that endeavour?

It was then suggested – and now we come to the crucial point that interests us here – that this was due to the fact that Hayek was obsessed with the idea that conceding people a right to a certain share of market outcome would necessarily demand as its counterpart a decision that somebody (a person or organization) should have the duty of *providing what the others are to have*. And this, Hayek believed, necessarily means the substitution of a commanded economy for the spontaneous order of the market.

It was then argued that this assumption of Hayek's was based on a misunderstanding about the expression 'what the others are to have'. This may be interpreted in two totally different ways from which follow totally different consequences. If one understands 'what the others are to have' as everything or most of the things that everyone is to have, we will arrive at a situation which is drastically different from the one we would get from the other possible meaning: 'the minimum of basic things that everyone is to have.' In the first case we have the typical consequence of a decision to impose a common pattern of distribution, or of social justice. If one believes that every share that the market attributes to each person must not be accepted as morally valid, then a consequence becomes inevitable: one has to substitute a central authority (either of one, or several, or of all gathered together), in charge of attributing to each individual or group particular shares of the global outcome, for the 'game of skill and chance' of the market.

As Hayek has rightly highlighted, the particular criterion of distribution is irrelevant here. It can be 'merit', or 'desert', 'needs', or 'value to society', or equality, but there will always be a common pattern of distribution. This demands that somebody, or all gathered together, decides what everyone is to have in the sense of 'everything or most of the things that everyone is to have'. This would mean, as Hayek has maintained, that individuals would no longer be allowed to use their own knowledge for their own purposes, but would have to carry out the plan which their rulers had designed to meet the needs to be satisfied.

But the second meaning of the expression 'what the others are to have' – when it is interpreted as 'the minimum of basic things that everyone is to have, or that everyone must not be deprived of' – produces rather different consequences. There is no *positive* pattern of distribution, no attempt to establish what kind of reward or share is to be allotted to each individual. On the contrary, there is only what has been called here a *negative* or *residual* pattern of distribution which refers only to *that minimum that people must not be deprived of.* All the rest above this minimum is not subject to any kind of collective or central decision. This is exactly the same negative formulation that Hayek has used to refer to the moral duty of helping those who cannot help themselves: 'a floor below which nobody need descend'.

SATISFACTION OF NEED AND DISTRIBUTION ACCORDING TO NEED

Now, the point that should be underlined is that there is a similar distinction to the two which have just been made between 'social justice' and 'social injustice', or between 'everything or most of the things that everyone is to have' and 'the minimum of basic things no one should be deprived of'. A further distinction applies between 'a principle of distribution according to need' and the imperative of 'helping those in need'.

In order to relieve situations of 'severe deprivation' or 'extreme misfortune', or 'to help those in need' with the provision of those basic goods they lack, for this to be done, there is no necessity for any general criterion of distribution or social justice. In fact, it suffices to have a criterion of *basic needs*, or social minimum, that is to say, a negative criterion about social injustice, about those situations which are not tolerable, a common floor below which it is not acceptable that someone might fall. Having this criterion (whose precise definition is, of course, subject to debate), it suffices to find a method of identifying people who are below that line and, then, to find a method whereby they can receive the necessary help in order to pass over the threshold of basic need.

It seems absolutely clear that there is no general criterion of distribution here, since we are not discussing how the goods are generally distributed, but only *how some basic goods are to be guaranteed or channelled to those who need them.* A general principle of distribution, by contrast, should not envisage basic goods only, but *all the goods.* And even a principle of distribution of basic goods only could not simply say that basic goods should be delivered to those who need them. It would have to say how, in general, basic goods should be distributed to *each and every person.* For example, it would have to say that basic goods should be distributed equally to all, or unequally, but then according to some criterion, namely according to each one's merit, or his needs, or his contribution to the general welfare, and so forth. In other words, a comparative evaluation of what is due to each person, by comparison to what is due to his fellow citizens, is always inherent in a general principle of distribution.

This is what a principle of distribution really is, and it seems indisputable that, when one says 'to provide basic goods for those who need them', there is no general principle of distribution involved, not even a general principle of distribution of basic goods only. The most one could say is that there is a residual principle here (we have called it negative) which is equivalent to asserting something like this: we do not care about how basic goods are generally distributed, unless in those particular cases in which some people do not have what we consider to be a minimum of basic goods that we believe no one should be deprived of. In these cases, and in these cases only, we will provide for those people's basic needs.

It might be replied that the imperative of 'helping those in need' is still a principle of distribution since there are resources which are being transferred, hence redistributed, from those who pay taxes to those who receive welfare benefits. But of course this is a game of words. This transfer of resources is only a consequence of the necessity of funding the help to those in need. In other words, there is of course a *distributive effect* in the imperative of helping those in need, but it is a *residual consequence* of this imperative, not its *raison d'être*. (For this reason, incidentally, we have called this imperative a residual or negative pattern of distribution or justice.) On the contrary, the *raison d'être* of a positive pattern of distribution, be it according to merit, or desert, or need, or equality, is always to give to each one what is thought to be due to him, and only as a consequence will those in need be helped. Strictly speaking, by the way, in a positive pattern of distribution or justice there would cease to be room for the concept of those in need, since each and every one is supposed to receive exactly what is due to him – whatever the criterion of 'due' might be. In the case of the imperative of helping those in need, by contrast, we know nothing, and want to know nothing, about what is due to each one in general terms. We know only that there is a minimum of basic goods which is due to everyone, or that no one should be deprived of.

It is worth discussing still another misunderstanding, which consists of perceiving progressive income tax as inseparable to the imperative of helping those in need. This is hardly so. This imperative really implies that some will pay, so that the needy can receive. But it says nothing about how the contributions should be raised among those who pay. The idea that progressive income tax is inseparable from welfare provision for the needy is to a good extent a result of the confusion we are trying to undo. It is thought that helping those in need is associated with reducing inequalities. But the fact is that, once again, if there is effective help to those in need, inequalities will in principle be reduced, *as a consequence* – since the common floor of society will move upwards and, therefore, the distance to the ceiling will in principle be reduced. But this is true even if the ceiling is not pulled down on purpose, that is to say, even if the income tax system is not progressive. (Incidentally, it is often forgotten that rich people pay more, in absolute terms, even with a proportional system.)

It is not our purpose to discuss the income tax system here, and this is not a critique of the progressive system in itself, but only of the confusion that more often than not is associated with its defence. The relevant point in this respect is that the reduction of inequalities may well be a *consequence* of the imperative of helping those in need, but it is by no means its *raison d'être*. By contrast, in a positive principle of distribution, for instance in an egalitarian one, the reduction of inequalities would be its *raison d'être* – although it might be justified by the concern for the needy.

A practical illustration of this distinction may be as follows: imagine that, in an ideal society, efficient measures are being taken to help those in need, so that one could say that basic needs are roughly fulfilled. At the same time, however, a minority at the top of the social scale is getting richer. In these circumstances, inequalities are not being reduced: although the common floor is moving upwards, the ceiling is also moving upwards, so that the distance between the two is not being reduced; maybe it is stable, or it is even being enlarged if the ceiling moves at a higher pace than the floor. What is to be done? From the standpoint of the imperative of helping those in need, nothing is to be done: if the needy are being cared for, if the common floor is at a decent level, the fact of remaining inequalities or even of increasing inequalities is of no importance. On the contrary, from the standpoint of a general principle of distribution the fact that the needy are being cared for is not decisive in itself. What matters is the comparative position of each member of the whole. And, if the principle in question is an egalitarian one, then the rich must not be allowed to get richer, even if the needy are having their basic needs fulfilled.

One might probably reply that, if the global wealth of a given society is increasing, then a likely consequence should be that the definition of the common floor would accordingly move upwards. Although this is very likely, it should be noted that it does not affect our distinction. The common floor may move upwards because there are more resources available, or because the perception of basic needs is not static, actually depending on the general welfare of a given society. In this sense, one can say that there is a comparative or relational element involved. But the relevant point is that this relational element is not the *raison d'être* of the principle of satisfaction of basic needs. It may well intervene as an auxiliary principle, in the sense that it is helpful in order to define the content of basic needs in each society at a given moment. Thus,

the relational element may intervene in order to establish
whether or not the common floor is at a decent level. But it
does not intervene on its own; as the crucial yardstick it actually
is in every general principle of distribution, regardless of what
its specific criterion of distribution may be.

THE AMBIGUITY OF PLANT'S APPROACH

Now it will be shown how Raymond Plant did not perceive this
distinction between the imperative of helping those in need
and a general principle of distribution, including one according to need. This is apparent at the beginning of Chapter 2
('Needs, Rights and Welfare') of his book with Harry Lesser
and Peter Taylor-Gooby, *Political Philosophy and Social Welfare*.
At the outset of the chapter, written by Raymond Plant, it is
said that:

> The concept of need is absolutely fundamental to the under-
> standing of contemporary social policy and the welfare state.
> In the view of some commentators, *the recognition and satisfac-
> tion of need marks the welfare function of the modern state from its
> other functions* [. . .][3]

Then, to illustrate this centrality of the concept of need in
welfare philosophy, Plant presents several quotations which, in
his view, go in the same direction. Two of them, however, are
simply opposed to each other. The first runs as follows:

> The concept of social need is inherent in the idea of social
> service. The history of the social services is the history of
> the *recognition of social needs* and the organisation of society
> *to meet them*. The Seebohm Report was deeply concerned
> with the concept of need, though it never succeeded in defin-
> ing it. It saw that the personal social services are large scale
> experiments in ways of *helping those in need*.[4]

And this is the second:

> The fundamental principle of radical social policy is that
> resources, whether in the field of health, education, hous-
> ing or income, *should be distributed according to need*. Con-
> temporary welfare capitalism in the form of the welfare state

cannot meet this basic objective, for it is guided by the social values and economic interests of the dominant class in society.[5]

Perhaps this contradiction between 'helping those in need' and 'distributed according to need' is viewed as not very important since it appears in quotations from other authors. But the proof that Plant actually shares this confusion comes on the following page. He says:

The economic market is usually to be the institution within which *wants as preferences* are satisfied, and it is *just because people have needs that are not being satisfied via the market that the social services have developed*. Needs and their satisfaction characterize the social services on the general welfare aspect of society: *the market exists to satisfy preferences and wants*.[6]

It is worth observing that the second sentence of the above paragraph does not follow from the first, unless there is a confusion between 'helping those in need' and 'distribution according to need'. In fact, when one says that 'social services have developed just because people have needs that are not being satisfied via the market' what is in principle understood is that *when* the market is not able to satisfy *certain* needs of *certain* people, *then* social services must provide for *these* needs of *these* people. This is what J. Bradshaw, quoted by R. Plant, appears to mean when he says that 'social services are large scale experiments in ways of *helping those in need*'.

Now this is completely different from saying that 'the market exists to satisfy preferences and wants', whereas 'needs and their satisfaction characterize the social services'. If this assertion were to be accepted, then food – which is undoubtedly a basic need – ought to be distributed by social services, and not via the market (which could perhaps supply exquisite food only, such as champagne and caviar, which would correspond to *wants and preferences*).

The point to retain here is that this division of functions between markets and social services follows from a principle of distribution according to need, and not from an imperative of 'helping those in need'. In fact, were that principle in place, then goods should be necessarily divided into 'needs' and 'wants', so that those corresponding to 'basic needs' – as for instance food and housing – might be centrally distributed to all, and not only to those in need. This distribution would then take place according to a general criterion, namely that of the needs which a central authority ascribed to each person, or maybe each family. Simultaneously, the market would allocate those goods which, because they were not considered as basic needs but as 'wants' and 'preferences', would be seen as secondary or irrelevant to the principle of distribution in place.

The fact is, however, that not only does this not happen in western societies, but also that Raymond Plant is perfectly satisfied with – or perhaps only resigned to, this we shall discuss later – the fact that the market supplies basic goods such as food and housing. What he is claiming, when he argues for social rights, is that those who cannot satisfy their basic needs in the market are entitled to claim their rights, instead of simply begging for help. This is the appropriate view of social rights, and it is what Plant means when he asks:

> When these transfers are made *to the needy* are they made in response to a right that *the needy* have on the resources of others, a right that requires a corresponding obligation on those with the resources to make that transfer? Or is the transfer made on the basis of a sense of humanity, or charity, or generosity towards *the least advantaged members of society*?[7]

It is absolutely evident here that Plant wants to provide for the basic needs of *the least advantaged members of society* and that, for this to be done, he proposes that the basic needs of those who could not satisfy them in the market should be guaranteed by resources transferred from those who are better off. In this view, obviously enough, social services have not the role of providing basic needs to all according to a hypothetical principle of distribution, but only of providing them to those in need.

Unfortunately, Raymond Plant presents the same misunderstanding in a crucial point of his reasoning. After having shown that in a pluralist society it is possible to pinpoint some necessarily agreed notion of need ('those needs the satisfaction of which is necessary for the pursuit of any end whatever'), Plant has put forward the intellectual basis to underpin the concept of *basic need*. And he rightly took a step forward in his response to Hayek:

> So it is arguably a precondition of Hayek's view that men should be free to pursue their ends as spontaneously as possible, that there should be an obligation to provide not merely the legal framework that is a necessary condition for this, but also those needs that are equally necessary conditions for the pursuit of any end.[8]

Having reached this point, Plant finds a quotation from Hayek which, had it not been for Plant's confusion between 'helping those in need' and 'a principle of distribution according to need', would have been tailor-made to prove that Hayek himself was constrained to recognize the moral duty of helping those in need – and, therefore, the possibility of social rights. Hayek's passage runs as follows:

> It is essential that we become clearly aware of the line that separates a state of affairs in which the community accepts the duty of preventing destitution and of providing a minimum level of welfare from that in which it assumes the power to determine the 'just' position of everybody.[9]

Rather surprisingly, Raymond Plant does not use this passage to show how Hayek is only half a step from accepting the concept of social rights. On the contrary, Plant explicitly repeats the confusion between 'helping those in need' and 'distribution according to need':

> It is clear that Hayek would seem to mean by destitution absolutely basic need, in which case *the duty to meet absolutely basic need could be seen as a principle of distributive justice – to each according to his basic need –* despite Hayek's rejection of the terminology of 'justice'.[10]

There can be no doubt here that Raymond Plant refers indistinctively to 'helping those in need' and to 'a principle of distribution according to need'.

*   *   *

What turns out to be paradoxical, however, is that in his final argument for the concept of 'democratic equality', Plant gives up definitely the reference to distribution according to need, and replaces it with the defence of 'an equal, or as equal as possible, distribution of basic goods'. It is widely acknowledged, however, that an equal distribution is not one according to need, since people's needs are strikingly different. A question then arises about what is the precise role in Plant's theory of the concept of 'distribution according to need'.

The most plausible response seems to be as follows: 'distribution according to need' plays merely the role of preventing Plant from recognizing the difference between what he has actually shown – the view of social rights based on the concept of basic need – and a general principle of distribution. Having used indistinctively 'helping those in need' and 'distribution according to need', Plant got used to the idea that, when arguing for social rights to certain basic goods, he was actually arguing for a general principle of distribution.

This was the reason why he asked the question 'how should basic goods be distributed?' However, there is no reason to ask this question within a theory of basic rights based on the concept of basic need – unless, obviously, this theory is misleadingly identified with one about a general principle of distribution. It has already been shown how different both theories and their consequences actually are. Our remaining task is now to show that Plant has actually made the case for social rights on the basis of basic need, and not for a principle of distribution. If this endeavour succeeds, it must then be allowed that Plant's question about 'how should basic goods be distributed' simply has no place in a theory of social rights.

WHAT PLANT HAS, AND WHAT HE HAS NOT, REALLY SHOWN

As has already been recalled, Raymond Plant has serialized two main arguments of Hayek's against social rights: (1) that individuals' shares of market outcomes are not a matter of social justice, because market results are unintended and unforeseeable; and (2) that, even if they were a matter of social justice, there would be no criterion of distribution or social justice. Plant has rightly replied to the first point, showing that social justice does not depend on how situations are brought about, but on our moral perception and corresponding response to those situations. For this reason, therefore, problems of poverty, deprivation, or in general avoidable human suffering should be considered matters of social justice, regardless of the specific way they were brought about. Since it is possible to foresee that the market will not be able to avoid these problems, we have the duty to take serious and permanent measures to deal with them.[11]

Having shown that there are matters of social justice in market outcomes, Plant then went on to reply to the second point of Hayek's argument: that there is no criterion of distribution or social justice in a free and pluralist society. It is interesting to note that Plant has interpreted this contention of Hayek's in the unique sense of not being possible *to reach an agreement* on a criterion of distribution in a pluralist society (a point which was of course put forward also by David Hume). We shall see later that this was by no means the only sense of Hayek's contention. Plant has, however, produced a very interesting reply to this point. He has said that it was not actually possible to reach an agreement on merit or desert, but that the same was not true for the concept of *basic need*.

Plant has then concentrated on showing that an agreement about *basic need* did not involve any uniformization whatever of the ultimate ends of individuals. On the contrary, Plant asserted, every moral code has to recognize that persons need certain minimal capacities that allow them to act and pursue the moral goals enshrined in that moral code. *The capacity to act as a moral agent* then becomes *the basic human end* that is wanted by all persons, whatever their moral codes might be. And the conditions or means for that action – which Plant, following Alan Gewirth, defines as *physical survival* and *autonomy* – turn out to be *unqualified or human needs*.

This is the way whereby Plant has shown the possibility of reaching an agreement on the concept of *basic need*. In order to make clear that he has not shown the possibility of reaching an agreement on a *criterion of distribution according to need*, we have still to recall the next step of Plant's argument. For he faced a second difficulty, possibly greater than defining the concept of basic need. He had to show that the duty to respect individuals' basic needs involves a positive obligation to provide certain goods they need, and not only a negative duty of forbearance. For it is clear enough that the right of someone to physical survival and autonomy (defined by Plant as constitutive of basic need) entails the negative duty of others not to kill or injure, and the qualified duty not to interfere in another's attempt to pursue his or her own ends. But why should the right to physical survival and autonomy entail a positive duty to supply goods which are indispensable to the pursuit of other people's ends?

It is important to recall that Plant has acknowledged the difficulty of this issue, and that he has admitted that some ambiguity in this respect could be found in Kant's work.[12] Finally, Plant has reached the conclusion that the only possible justification for a positive duty to provide for other people's basic needs has to lie in the assumption that *the lack of basic goods*, or *the unfulfillment of basic needs*, prevents people from fulfilling any other duties:

> The obligation to satisfy these particular needs has to be a strict obligation because it is impossible to make sense of there being other obligations that could outweigh the obligation to meet these needs just because *those whose needs in this sphere are not met* are not able *ex hypothesi* to pursue any other obligations, whatever they may be, or any other ends.[13]

In fact, if it is accepted that basic needs consist of those basic goods which are indispensable for pursuing any ends (however different) and duties (however varied), then the duty to provide for *those who lack these basic goods* has to be accepted simply because, without them, they would not be able to fulfil any other obligation.

In this sense, Plant has presented a powerful case for the duty to provide for other people's basic needs to be considered as a duty of strict obligation, even a precondition of other rights and duties. Doing so, however, Plant has also undoubtedly restricted the recipients of this duty to *those whose needs are not met*, that is to say, those who lack the basic goods indispensable to physical survival and autonomy. In fact, it has to be allowed that, if the basis of a moral obligation is *the lack of basic needs*, and the assumption that this prevents people from fulfilling any other obligation, then the moral obligation ceases when those needs are met.

This may well give rise to an interesting discussion about whether or not basic needs are satiable.[14] But this is not our concern here. The crucial point (only after the consideration of which one may discuss the satiable nature of basic needs) is that Plant has argued for *a moral duty to provide for the basic needs of those who need them*. Nothing more, and nothing less. Therefore, any consideration about how basic goods should be distributed in general terms is absolutely out of place. Apart from the duty to supply basic goods for the needy, social rights do not entail any other duty whatever, according to Plant's own argument. To emphasize this restricted scope of social rights, we have sometimes called them 'basic social rights' here.

* * *

But it must be added that, had Plant tried to argue for a general principle of distribution according to need, he would not have overcome Hayek's argument against positive patterns of distribution. This is where we come across Plant's misunderstanding of Hayek's point.

Two aspects of this misunderstanding must be considered. The first lies in the fact that Plant has shown that, in a pluralist society, an agreement could be reached on the concept of *basic need*, but not that a similar agreement could be equally reached on *how to use the concept of need as a general criterion of distribution*. And this was Hayek's decisive point, when he argued that any criterion such as merit, desert or need, had to be an assessable criterion applicable to all. Plant, in his turn, replied only that *basic need* is assessable, but he did not affirm that one could assess the *comparative needs* of all persons. In other words, one can assess that homelessness is a condition of basic needs not being fulfilled, but how could one possibly decide whether someone who owns a palace really needs it? Or, alternatively, how could one possibly decide whether he needs it as compared to someone else who owns a cottage?

This brings us to the second aspect of Plant's misunderstanding of Hayek's argument. Hayek's opposition to general principles of distribution did not lie only in the impossibility of agreement. It also involved, more crucially, the possibility of compatibilizing this hypothetical criterion with general rules of just conduct.[15] And, as Hayek has rightly argued, this compatibility is simply impossible. One cannot simultaneously base a society on rules of conduct and in end-states to be achieved,[16] simply because different people applying the same rules of conduct will achieve different results, which amounts to saying that abiding by rules is not compatible with the prediction of a definite state of affairs. This is a very important issue to which we have to return later, after the discussion of liberty and social equality, in the next chapter.

A CRITIQUE OF PLANT'S ARGUMENT: AN OVERVIEW

The crucial point of the critique developed in this chapter lies in the distinction between the imperative of helping those in need and a principle of distribution according to need. If this distinction is allowed, Raymond Plant's remarkable work on the concept of *basic needs* and on the manner in which it can underpin the concept of *social rights* can then be incorporated in a theory of basic social rights. However, and somehow paradoxically, this theory will be dramatically different from the one he himself has reached.

Plant's reply to the critics of social rights – namely Hayek and Cranston – is certainly an important contribution to a theory of social rights. Basically, he has refuted with reasonable plausibility the allegations that a fundamental incompatibility opposes the social to the traditional rights.

More specifically, Plant has produced a solution to the question that has remained suspended since the critique of Hayek's argument presented in Chapter 2. At that stage, it was shown that Hayek had himself accepted a duty to help those who cannot help themselves. We then postponed, for reasons of methodological convenience, the discussion of whether or not this duty could and should give rise to a right. We temporarily admitted that it could, and have gone on to discuss whether or not this hypothetical right is compatible with the maintenance of a liberal order. The conclusion reached has been that it is. But the connection between the duty accepted by Hayek and the hypothetical right has remained unfulfilled. Raymond Plant has made the connection resorting to the work of Alan Gewirth: if it is accepted that basic needs consist of those basic goods which are indispensable for pursuing any ends (however different) and duties (however varied), then the duty to provide for those who lack these basic goods has to be accepted as a duty of strict obligation simply because, without these basic goods, they would not be able to fulfil any obligation.

As a duty of strict obligation, and unlike imperfect duties of supererogation, the duty to help those who cannot help themselves can then be seen as entailing the corresponding right to the provision of basic goods. The precise definition of what these basic goods consist of should be a matter to be established by political controversy in free societies, thus being admitted that this definition may vary from society to society. But the general concept of basic goods is defined by its relationship with *basic needs*, the latter being seen as those minimal conditions which are indispensable to the exercise of liberty.

Apparently, then, Raymond Plant has overcome the difficulties raised by the opponents of social rights. This would have been so, had he not mistaken the concept of distribution according to need for the imperative of helping those in need. The latter is, in fact, at the basis of the concept of social rights, such as it has initially been defended by Plant. But distribution according to need does not follow from Plant's argument: if the basis of a moral obligation is *the unfulfilling of basic needs*, and the assumption that this prevents people from fulfilling any obligation, then the moral obligation ceases when these needs are met. No case for a general criterion of distribution can be derived from here, for the simple reason that the only duty one can justify is the duty to provide basic goods for those who need them – not the duty to share goods (either basic ones, or goods in general) according to any overall pattern or criterion of allocation of goods. For this reason, too, Plant's question about 'how basic goods should be distributed' is out of place in his own justification of social rights. To highlight this restricted or negative view of social rights, we have sometimes called them *basic social rights*.

As was announced at the outset, this chapter has intentionally avoided the discussion of Plant's egalitarian response to the question 'how should basic goods be distributed'. But we have not meant to avoid the issue, only to emphasize that the question should not have been posed within Plant's own argument for social rights. The next chapter will address this issue within a more general approach to the 'background assumptions' of Plant's argument – a similar procedure to that used in Part I with respect to Hayek's argument.

6 An Evaluation: Equal Liberty and Social Inequality

Render possessions ever so equal, men's different degrees of art, care, and industry will immediately break that equality. Or if you check these virtues, you reduce society to the most extreme indigence; and instead of preventing want and beggary in a few, render it unavoidable to the whole community. The most rigorous inquisition too is requisite to watch every inequality on its first appearance; and the most severe jurisdiction, to punish and redress it.
David Hume, *An Enquiry Concerning the Principles of Morals*, 1751

Liberty is liberty, not equality or fairness or justice or human happiness or a quiet conscience.
Sir Isaiah Berlin, *Two Concepts of Liberty*, 1958

Having presented a critique of Raymond Plant's argument, we shall now proceed to investigate why he identified the concept of 'helping those in need' with a general principle of distribution. Two main assumptions of Plant's played an important role in this identification: (1) that equal liberty entails an equal value of liberty, that is to say equality of conditions; (2) that markets do not provide for needs, but only, or mainly, for wants and preferences. This chapter is dedicated to the discussion of both.

PLANT'S ARGUMENT REVISITED

In Chapter 4 we observed[1] that Raymond Plant was not satisfied with his own argument in favour of social rights as demands to provide basic goods for those who need them. This concept, Plant asserted, 'would not take the defence of the welfare state in terms of the value of freedom much beyond the idea of the welfare state as a residual institution.'[2] Plant has then developed his reasoning and concluded that *a more equal distribution of basic goods* is indispensable if one wants *liberty to become of roughly equal value to all persons.*

This concept of 'value of liberty' is crucial since Plant is quite keen on stressing that the reason why he is arguing for a

140

more equal distribution of basic goods is not because he values equality for equality's sake, but because he values liberty and the value of liberty. In his Fabian Tract on *Equality, Markets and the State,* he is particularly committed to stressing that socialists value equality for the sake of liberty, and not for equality as an end in itself:

> Other than as a kind of aesthetic ideal it is very difficult to see what the appeal of equality, taken as an end in itself, is supposed to be. Why should people be made more equal just for the sake of it? It is much more likely that greater equality is to be seen as a means to greater liberty, or greater fraternity, or greater welfare, which are ends which it seems to make more sense to pursue for their own sake. *Equality is a method of securing other values rather than an end in itself.*[3]

And Plant then added:

> If this is so, then we have to explain *how and why we expect liberty to be extended by equality* when most of our critics seem to be convinced that the opposite is the case and how, if at all, the state organisation which greater equality might seem to require can be made compatible with the view that *we value equality for the sake of liberty.*[4]

To present the case for equality on the basis that it extends liberty was then Plant's project. This was done in two main steps. The first one consisted of showing that, although liberty is mainly a negative entity defined as absence of coercion by others, *the value or worth* of liberty is more than that. Liberty would have no worth had not the individuals had minimal capacities to exercise or use this liberty. These minimal capacities which are indispensable to the value or worth of liberty are basic goods. We have largely scrutinized this argument of Plant's and there is no reason to go through it again here.

The relevant step for our discussion is the second one, the one directly linked with equality. For the value of liberty does not lead necessarily to the goal of an equal distribution of basic goods (or an equal value of liberty), as was shown in the previous chapter. The value of liberty may simply lead to the duty of providing those basic goods which are indispensable to action and, therefore, to the duty to provide basic goods for those who need or lack them. How, then, did Raymond Plant

derive an equal distribution of basic goods from the concept
of the value of liberty?

The crucial point was his question about how basic goods
should be distributed, which we have argued to be misplaced
in a theory of social rights. But we must now face the question
in itself and discuss Plant's answer. This was that basic goods
should be distributed equally, or as equally as possible, all the
moves away from equality having to be justified in terms of
'some legitimate inequalities'. Three main reasons were provided for this view: (1) what we have called 'the Hayekian presumption of equality', (2) 'the fair value of liberty', and (3) 'the
implications of equal political liberty'.[5]

The Hayekian presumption of equality consisted of saying
that, 'if we have no way of judging people's needs, merits,
deserts and entitlements, as the subjectivist position argues,
then [...] a presumption in favour of equality can be argued
since no one can be thought of as having a more just claim than
anyone else.'[6]

The argument based on the fair value of liberty – Plant's
second reason for equality – asserted that, if the better-off
value liberty and the resources that make their liberty worthy,
and if they accept that equal respect is due to each citizen,
then, reciprocally, they would have to accept that their fellow citizens who are less fortunate should have the worth of
their liberty improved, even at the cost of some diminution of
their own.[7]

Finally, the third reason consisted of saying that equal political liberty cannot really exist against a background of material
inequality. The case of an equal right to free expression is one
of Plant's favourite illustrations of this point: 'those in better
circumstances are able to utilise this liberty more effectively
and it is of greater value to them.'[8] And Plant maintains that
this is not acceptable because, according to the Hayekian presumption of equality, 'there are no moral grounds for saying
that some people deserve to have more effective basic liberty'.[9]

* * *

Let us then discuss these three reasons of Plant's for equality. One might start by noting that the second reason is not
conclusive in terms of why equality should be the main goal.

In fact, it says only that the better-off must accept the necessity of improving the condition of those who are worse off, even though this might imply a diminution of their own standards of living. But how much should be improved and how much should be diminished? Why should equality be the only legitimate solution? The argument says nothing in this particular.

The two decisive reasons are therefore the first and the third ones, that is to say, those we have called 'the Hayekian presumption of equality' and the 'implications of equal political liberty'. It is worth observing that a common reasoning underpins both: that equality of basic goods, or an equal value of liberty, is a 'natural' and necessary extension of equal liberty.[10] According to the Hayekian presumption of equality, Plant asserts that, for the same reason whereby one accepts a presumption of equal liberty, one has to accept a presumption of equal conditions – 'since no one can be thought of as having a more just claim than anyone else'.[11] As for the implications of equal political liberty, Plant's third reason, this amounts to saying that equal conditions are a necessary extension of equal liberty: if one wants people to have an equal right to free expression, then one has to give them roughly equal material conditions, since otherwise those in better circumstances would be able to utilize this liberty more effectively.

Now, three main difficulties should be presented with respect to Plant's argument. In the first place, it is disputable that equality of conditions can be seen as an extension of equal liberty, and there are even reasons to believe that both equalities are mutually exclusive. In other words, if one accepts the Hayekian *presumption of equal liberty*, one may well have to accept a *presumption of unequal conditions*. In the second place, equality of conditions is not a necessary extension of equal political liberty, unless the latter is understood positively as equal capacity to act. But it can be argued that this understanding is hardly tenable, since an equal capacity to act is incompatible with an equal permission (or liberty in the negative sense) to act. Hence, the goal of promoting an equal value of political liberty cannot be derived from the goal of promoting equal political liberty, or, in other words, equality of conditions is *not* a necessary extension of equal political liberty.

In the third place, and if the previous contentions are acepted, it will have to be allowed that the only view of social rights which is consistent with the goal or the ideal of equal liberty is what we have been calling the negative one: basic social rights aim at guaranteeing the *universal access* to the use of liberty, not at *equalizing* the use of liberty, which must always be unequal – if liberty is to keep any meaning.

*   *   *

In order to justify the above assertions, we shall proceed as follows:

(1)   Starting with Raymond Plant's first reason for equality, the Hayekian presumption of equality, it will be argued, merely in logical terms at this stage, that equality of conditions, or an equal value of liberty, is not compatible with liberty.

(2)   This formal argument will be then illustrated with resort to passages of Plant's substantive views which show that his concern with social equality leads him to impose severe restrictions on liberty.

(3)   This stage will be dedicated to Plant's argument about the implications of equal political liberty – which we shall argue to be based on a positive interpretation of political liberty which, in its turn, is inconsistent with the ideal of equal liberty as permission to act (or absence of coercion by others).

(4)   Finally, the consequences of the previous reasoning in terms of the concept of social rights will be presented. It will then be argued that the impossible goal of an equal value of liberty should be replaced by the goal of universal access to the value of liberty.

EQUALITY FOR THE SAKE OF LIBERTY?

One must recall that the concept of basic goods was introduced by Raymond Plant in order to give liberty effective value. In other words, the purpose of guaranteeing the access of individuals to the value, or the effective use, of liberty led to the need for providing them with a certain set of basic goods. These goods, such as health care, education and minimal economic conditions, are supposed to secure the necessary conditions for free and autonomous action.

Let us now assume that these basic goods should also be equally distributed (or as equally as possible) because, as Raymond Plant has put it, 'there are no moral grounds for saying that some people deserve to have more effective basic liberty'.[12] This is what we have called 'the Hayekian presumption of equality'.

Now, what are people going to do with their equal basic goods? According to Raymond Plant's argument, they are going to act as free agents, that is to say, they are finally able autonomously to decide what they are going to do. Having equal basic goods, they are equally able to make choices. But, unless one assumes that each and everyone is going to choose to act in the same way at the same time, it has to be allowed that people with equal basic goods will choose to act in different ways.

If this is so, and if one accepts that, most likely, different actions produce different results, it has to be accepted that people with equal basic goods at the moment T1 will act differently and that, at the moment T2, will therefore obtain different results. This of course means that, at the moment T2, they have different amounts of goods, including most likely different amounts of basic goods (which include, one must recall, things like health care, education and minimal economic conditions). Thus, at the moment T2, there are unequal 'effective basic liberties', to use Raymond Plant's terminology.

However, since we have assumed that 'there are no moral grounds for saying that some people deserve to have more effective basic liberty', something has to be done so that, in T3, one may return to the 'equality of basic liberty' that there was in T1. This can, of course, be done by several methods, namely the redistribution of income that Raymond Plant, quoting Julien le Grand, considers to be the crucial tool of egalitarian policies. Thus, in T3, no one will have more effective basic liberty than the others.

In fact, one should add, nobody has any liberty at all, that is to say, all have the same lack of liberty. All are actually equal, but not equally free: they all have only an equal lack of freedom. For one has to admit that, in order to obtain equality in T3, one had to annul the results obtained in T2, which, in their turn, were the result of equally free, and therefore different, choices produced in T1. So, what are people free to do, if everything they do makes them unequal and, hence, has to be undone?

This shows that one cannot deduce a principle of social equality from a principle of equal liberty. And it should be emphasized that this has nothing to do with a particular view of human nature, or the selfish motive and the like. The basic point is that, given exactly the same basic material conditions, it has to be admitted that different people may act differently. If it is accepted that different actions produce different results, it has to be accepted that different people with equal material conditions may act differently and, therefore, may obtain unequal material conditions. The only way to reintroduce equal material conditions again is to annul the unequal results which they obtained from their different actions. But, since these different actions were made in a situation of equal material conditions – or equally effective liberty – to annul their unequal results means to annul the product of actions taken under equally effective liberty. This is, of course, paradoxical, since the only purpose whereby equality of basic goods was introduced was to allow and enable people to act effectively as free agents.

In other words, one can equalize material conditions only if one ends up by prohibiting individuals from doing the things one initially wanted them equally to be allowed and able to do. If this is so, as it seems to be, then it has also to be admitted that liberty, in the positive sense of capacity to act, or, to use Raymond Plant's terminology, the value or worth of liberty, can never be equal: one can never create an equal capacity to act for all, unless this is understood as an equal capacity not to act at all, or, at least, not to act differently, or freely. This is, of course, only a different way of saying what David Hume said a long time ago:

Render possessions ever so equal, men's different degrees of art, care, and industry will immediately break that equality. Or if you check these virtues, you reduce society to the most extreme indigence; and instead of preventing want and beggary in a few, render it unavoidable to the whole community. The most rigorous inquisition too is requisite to watch every inequality on its first appearance; and the most severe jurisdiction, to punish and redress it.[13]

HOW SOCIAL EQUALITY REALLY MENACES LIBERTY

Now we shall illustrate the above argument about the incompatibility of liberty with equal conditions, which is merely a formal argument, with Raymond Plant's substantive views in this regard. Just before that, however, it is worth recalling that socialists usually deny that equality of conditions really presents a threat to liberty. In a very telling passage, Julien le Grand maintains that:

> The argument that greater equality of economic reward would promote sameness and discourage variety is based on a confusion between inequality and diversity. Equality before the law or equality of voting rights as between one individual and another does not imply that they have the same tastes, the same sense of humour, the same political preferences, the same psychological make-up, or the same physiology. Why then should equality of economic reward? Indeed, such equality might promote the flowering of individual differences of character, for as Tawney argues 'differences of personal quality ... in England ... tend to be obscured or obliterated behind differences of property or income.[14]

This seems to miss the point. The problem does not lie in the fact that economic equality implies that individuals have the same preferences. That individuals do not have the same preferences is a simple fact of life which cannot be altered. The problem with economic equality, by contrast with equality before the law or equality of voting rights, is that its achievement and maintenance involves the repression of the expression of that variety, although the variety in itself cannot be annulled. And that this is so becomes apparent in Raymond Plant's substantive views on equality, even though he, like le Grand, is very keen on underlining that equality does not threaten liberty but, on the contrary, is necessary for the sake of liberty.

In a Fabian Tract on *Equality, Markets and the State*, Raymond

Plant acknowledges that 'to secure a *more equal value of liberty* between citizens [. . .] may well restrict the range of choices open to individuals, for example by *prohibiting private schooling or private hospital treatment*'.[15] The important point here is that Raymond Plant is by no means embarrassed by the prospect of having to prohibit so peaceful and unharmful an activity as private schooling or private hospital treatment. He is prepared to take the defence of such prohibitions precisely on the same basis that we have just criticized, that is to say, the goal of *an equal value of liberty*:

> The kind of freedom which is envisaged in this criticism is a freedom to choose an outcome which is likely to be of disadvantage to others, and *to weaken the value of freedom to others* over a not inconsiderable period of their lives. The freedom to choose a private education, with all the non-educational advantages and influences that can bring, is not at the same level as spending money on beer and cigarettes, which is often the preferred analogy . . .[16]

It may be incidental, but it is not irrelevant that the example of an unharmful liberty chosen by Raymond Plant is the liberty to spend money on beer and cigarettes. In fact, and precisely as we have argued, within a framework of an equal value of liberty, not much more liberty is left to individuals. This point becomes clear again when Raymond Plant points out the kind of liberty he would accept in the educational system:

> For example, if we are to have a state education system on egalitarian grounds, there can be no possible basis for restricting the opportunities for schools to have diverse patterns of subjects, of specialisms, and to be innovative so long as these are not secured at the expense of others.[17]

This means that all schools would have to be state-owned, although they could be different. But one must realize that this is not to say that *in principle* schools can be different, unless they fall out of certain minimal requirements put forward by the state. This is exactly the opposite: schools *cannot be different*, since they all have to be state-owned and, therefore, each and every one of the differences has to be authorized by the state department in charge which has to take decisions about each and every new school to be launched. By contrast, should private schools be allowed to compete with state schools (as they actually are in the West), they would have to comply only with certain general rules – within which each and every difference would be a risk to be freely assumed, and borne, by the share-holders, with no need for any further authorization or agreement. Instead of the principle that everything is permitted, unless expressly forbidden, Raymond Plant's view about the monopoly of state education involves the principle that everything is forbidden, unless expressly permitted.

This was exactly the point of the formal argument about the incompatibility between the goal of liberty and the goal of equality of conditions, or, to use Raymond Plant's terminology, an equal value of liberty. And this is acknowledged once again by Raymond Plant:

> The egalitarian is therefore only interested in those restrictions which will have an adverse effect on the possibilities which others have to make their freedom effective, *to restrict those choices which will lead to an unequal value for freedom.*[18]

It is quite clear in this passage that Raymond Plant is willing to restrict certain people's freedom, not because it restricts other people's freedom, but because not all people have the means to do the same things. In fact, one could hardly say that private schooling or private hospital treatment 'will have an adverse effect on the possibilities which others have to make their freedom effective'. The only thing Raymond Plant could say is that not all have the means to afford private schooling and/or private hospital treatment. But in what sense could this argument be related to a principle of liberty? If liberty means that no one has permission to do anything that all the others have not equal means to do, or, in other words, that one can only have permission to do what the others have equal means to do, the concept of liberty loses all its specificity and one can see no reason to use it as a different expression from that of the compulsion to obtain and maintain equality of means, or equality of economic conditions.

It is still worth noting that Raymond Plant is prepared to defend that, 'except in conditions of high economic growth, the greater equality in the worth of liberty cannot be attained without a certain amount of levelling down'.[19] Although we shall come back to this point later, one might note that this is exactly what we were implying when maintaining that the equalization of the worth of liberty cannot be achieved but through severe restrictions of liberty itself – restrictions which cannot be reasonably justified on other grounds than equality alone.

Now, the relevant point here is to realize how paradoxical is the attempt to derive the goal of equality of conditions from the goal of liberty. Liberty, as F. A. Hayek has acutely pointed out, involves the possibility of some people doing things which are not yet available to all. More basically, liberty means the permission to do different things, provided they do not harm a similar liberty of others. If this permission is to be restricted whenever it produces different outcomes, it then becomes obvious that this permission is going to be suppressed altogether, unless when it happens to be a permission to do equal things which one can predict in advance will produce equal outcomes. As was pointed out before, this amounts to saying that one can equalize conditions only if one prohibits people from doing the things one initially wanted them to be equally allowed and able to do.

EQUAL LIBERTY AND UNEQUAL VALUE OF LIBERTY

Raymond Plant's next reason for equality of conditions consists of saying that equal political liberty is impossible against a background of material inequality: the rich will always use political liberty more effectively.

One should note that this constitutes a problem only if 'equal political liberty' is understood as 'equal capacity to act freely in the political realm'. By contrast, were liberty understood only as equal protection against political coercion, or as equal permission to act politically, then the way in which this permission is used or made effective would cease to be a problem.[20] There are serious reasons for thinking that the interpretation of 'equal political liberty' as 'equal capacity to act politically' is inconsistent and, therefore, must be discarded. If this is accepted, Plant's point loses much of its cogency and how people make effective use of their 'equal political liberty' is no longer a difficulty.

Political liberty as capacity to act entails that the equality of political liberty cannot be achieved only by resort to equality before the law: equality of conditions is also needed because, as Raymond Plant puts it, 'inequalities of conditions will make some people's capacity to act more effective than others'. This means that any slight move away from equality of conditions has necessarily to be perceived as a move towards inequalities of liberty (understood as capacity to act).

Now, the problem is that Raymond Plant has himself admitted the existence of 'some legitimate inequalities'.[21] However, according to his view of political liberty as capacity to act, every inequality of capacity has to be classified as an inequality of political liberty. So, within Plant's perception of political liberty as capacity to act, his defence of some 'legitimate inequalities' has to be seen as an acceptance of inequalities of political liberty.

This is rather embarrassing because a commitment to 'equal liberty' is an axiom shared by the two views of liberty: that which perceives it as permission to act as well as that, here subscribed to by Plant, which sees it as capacity to act. The only possible solution for this embarrassment would be to stick to a strict equality of conditions. But rare are the egalitarians who predicate so strict an egalitarianism, and Raymond Plant is definitely not one of these. On the other hand, it has been previously shown that a strict equality of conditions is incompatible with the humblest amount of liberty: to promote equality of conditions is to create a situation in which people are equally unfree.

This shows the inconsistency of the view of liberty – be it political liberty, or any other – as capacity to act. To be consistent, it has to advocate total equality of conditions, which may easily be shown to be incompatible with permission to act differently. Then, to overcome this difficulty, the theory has to allow room for certain legitimate inequalities. But all inequalities of capacity to act have to be seen, by definition, as inequalities of liberty.

Now it might be noted that this inconsistency does not arise if liberty is perceived as a negative concept, meaning absence of coercion by others, or permission to act under the laws. This view does not need to aim at material equality as a means to achieve equal liberty. Equal liberty, as absence of coercion, is guaranteed by equality before the law, i.e. by guaranteeing that each and every citizen is restricted in his 'natural' liberty by the same restrictions enshrined in laws which are equal for all. These restrictions mainly aim at guaranteeing that the liberty of some does not interfere with a similar liberty of others. Material inequalities, therefore, do not pose a problem to equal liberty. On the contrary, except when they enable some to deny the liberty of others, they should in principle be seen as a *legitimate product* of different courses of action – which, in their turn, are the very goal of liberty.

One should also note that the conflict between liberty and equality which is described here is not perceived in the generalistic way which has been rightly criticized by Steven Lukes in his *Moral Conflict and Politics*. In fact, as the author has pointed out, the general assertion that equality and liberty must conflict 'is radically incomplete, for it leaves open whose equality, whose liberty, what is equalized and which liberties are in question.' The argument presented here follows Lukes' demand that the proposition be made more precise: 'to say that equality must conflict with liberty is to say that equalizing some aspects of the conditions of all must reduce the liberty or liberties of some.'[22] In fact, what the argument presented here asserts is not that equality undermines liberty, but that equality of the value of liberty is incompatible with equal liberty.

*   *   *

Does this amount to saying that only liberty as absence of coercion is important and that the value of liberty is irrelevant? Not necessarily. This amounts to saying that *only the equality of liberty* as absence of coercion *is important*, and *not the equality of the value of liberty*. But, once the erroneous goal of equality of the value of liberty is ruled out, we can then pay attention to the serious problem of *making liberty real for all*. This means making the use of liberty *accessible* to all – *not equal* for all.

UNIVERSAL ACCESS VERSUS EQUALITY

If the previous argument is accepted, that is, if a presumption of inequality of conditions is accepted as a necessary part of a theory of equal liberty for all, then interesting consequences must follow. A deep change in the perception of the concept of 'use of liberty' or 'value of liberty' will then take place and this must have inevitable consequences in our discussion about social rights.

It might be recalled that the discussion between Friedrich A. Hayek and Raymond Plant, and in general the debate between supporters of a negative and a positive view of liberty, tends to be concentrated in the following dichotomy: liberty includes only *the absence of coercion* by others, or does it also include *the means* for taking those actions that the absence of coercion allows to be taken? The radical position of Hayek in favour of negative liberty is to be epitomized in his contention that, under the rule of law, the beggar and the millionaire are equally free since the law is equal for both of them and, therefore, both have equal legal permission to act. Raymond Plant, in his turn, has disagreed with this view and maintained that, even though both the beggar and the millionaire may have *the same formal liberty*, they have by no means *the same effective liberty*, or, in other words, *the value of their liberty is clearly unequal.*

Now, the argument presented here has started by accepting Raymond Plant's contention that *some means* are indispensable for liberty to have any value, or, more precisely, to be used. This was the stage in which we have accepted Plant and Gewirth's concept of *basic needs* as minimal conditions to act, therefore, as minimal conditions for the use of liberty.

But it should be noted that, having accepted the concept of *basic needs for the use of liberty*, we were going to disagree, immediately after, with Raymond Plant on a no less crucial point. Plant thinks that, in order to equalize liberty, it is also necessary to equalize the value of liberty (or the capacity to use liberty). On the contrary, it has been argued that the use of liberty cannot be equalized unless liberty is itself abolished, or severely restricted. For that reason, it was added, if one wants equal liberty for all, one has to accept a presumption of unequal material conditions.

In this sense, it might be said that we have subscribed to Hayek's view to the extent that we still define liberty as a basically negative concept which means absence of coercion by others. This is true: the argument presented here assumes that this is the only concept of liberty which is consistent with the goal of an equal liberty for all. And this equal liberty is guaranteed by resort to equality before the law. However, it should now be added that Hayek has misleadingly identified the defence of negative liberty with the simple denial of the concept of worth or value of liberty. But this is hardly so. The defence of negative liberty necessarily implies the denial of the *goal of equal value of liberty,* but by no means entails the denial of the concept of value of liberty. It is perfectly possible to maintain that the beggar and the millionaire have the same liberty under the law and, simultaneously, to admit what common sense tells us: that they cannot make the same use of liberty.

Now, it is important to stress that the problem posed by common sense does not really lie in the fact that the beggar and the millionaire do not have the *same* or an *equal* capacity to use their equal liberty. In fact, who has the same capacity to act? The doctor and the nurse, the professor and the lecturer, the senior and the junior minister, none of them has the same capacity to act. The real problem posed by common sense is that we think the beggar does not have *the minimum of means to use his liberty.* The problem does not lie in inequalities in general, but only in those inequalities which we consider to be excessive because they prevent individuals from *having access to the use of liberty.*

The argument presented here agrees with this common-sense perception. That the capacity to use liberty cannot be equal for all was shown by the fact that the simple free use of equal capacities produces immediate inequalities. From this it follows that only negative liberty can be equal for all, and this is guaranteed by equality before the law. After this, and since the use of liberty cannot be equal, it has then to be unequal. But, as we have accepted that there are certain minimal conditions to use liberty, the problem then is restricted to guaranteeing a universal access to the minimal means which are indispensable for the use of liberty: the basic goods.

In other words, whereas for Plant all material inequalities are in principle illegitimate, because they are perceived as obstacles to liberty, for the argument presented here inequalities are in principle legitimate because they are necessary consequences of liberty. Plant has been compelled to accept *some legitimate inequalities,* which he does with unease because that represents a twist in his view that the value of liberty should be equal. For our argument, however, inequalities are in principle legitimate, except for *some illegitimate inequalities* which are those that deprive some individuals of the access to the use of liberty.

Here lies the crucial practical distinction: Plant's view entails the goal of *an equal use of liberty*, which he ends by admitting not to be an entirely achievable goal. The argument presented here entails the goal of *universal access to the use of liberty*, which amounts to saying that nobody should be deprived of a certain amount of basic goods which are perceived to be indispensable for the use of liberty. But this does not mean that, once guaranteed no one is deprived of these 'basic goods', nobody should be allowed to have more basic goods than others, or, in other words, that all ought to have the same amount of basic goods.[23]

It is important to stress this distinction. When it is said that nobody ought to be deprived of certain basic goods, this is a universal assertion which applies to everybody, regardless of a comparison with what is happening to others. The criterion of equality, or inequality for that matter, is absent here: to deprive someone of certain basic goods is wrong in itself, and it would not become less wrong if all the others were deprived of these goods as well.[24]

One of the best examples of this point is the case of torture. When we say that all have the same right not to be tortured, we mean that nobody should be subject to torture, certainly not that, if all are equally tortured, torture becomes acceptable. The same applies to the concept of an equal right to basic goods. It must be understood as *all having an equal right not to be deprived of basic goods*, which is of course totally different from saying that *all have an equal right to an equal amount of basic goods*.[25]

THE VIRTUES OF INEQUALITY

We have seen hitherto the drawbacks of social equality. Because of them, especially because of the threat that social equality produces against liberty, we have come to the conclusion that, if we want equal liberty for all, we have to endorse a presumption of material inequality. Now, it might be said that this argument has been a negative case for inequality. It is so, and it might be said that the main case for inequality has to be mainly based on negative arguments, that is, not in the virtues of inequality but on the serious drawbacks that would arise from its abolishment. This does not necessarily mean that the case for inequality is a weak one: the main case for liberty and democracy is also a negative one, as was immortalized by Winston Churchill, and one could hardly say that these are weak causes.[26]

But this is not to say that social inequality has no advantage of its own. In fact it has, and, not surprisingly, these are mainly related to the advantages of liberty. One of the first great advantages of inequality is precisely the variety of experiences it allows, and the comparative judgements it allows people to make about different choices and its consequences. We usually call this openness to experiment, i.e. the capacity of a certain state of affairs to allow room for different courses of action, different experiments, and their relative success or failure. Friedrich A. Hayek has rightly perceived the importance of this openness and, especially in his *The Constitution of Liberty*, he has rightly underlined several of its dimensions. Since this work of Hayek has been largely referred to previously, we need not go through it again here.

Joseph Raz has also produced an illuminating critique of equality which, by way of contrast, allows a second virtue of inequality to be perceived. It consists of saying that the principle of equality always permits waste, which the principle of inequality does not, or not necessarily:

> *Egalitarian principles often lead to waste.* If there is not enough of the benefit to go round then whatever of it we have, should be wasted rather than given to, or allowed to be retained by some. [. . .] The crucial point is that egalitarian principles always permit waste as a way of satisfying them, and in quite common circumstances require it as the only way to satisfy them.[27]

Finally, a third and decisive virtue of inequality was put forward by Ralf Dahrendorf, in a chapter of his *Life Chances* significantly entitled 'Inequality, Hope and Progress':

> The possibility of progress, however, implies the necessity of social and political change.

But how does change come about? ... It is the vision of the different, of new and improved life chances, which turns resentment, or any kind of latent desire, into action and thus into change. *Whoever has given up hope has in fact accepted the conditions around him; in this sense there is no change without hope.*
... Hope itself, in order to be realistic, must be based on the reality of the conditions hoped for. It is based on the knowledge that some individuals, groups or countries possess what others aspire to ... The very least that can be said is that *existing inequalities add an element of reality to hope and thus give substance to the demand for change*; it may well be that without this admixture hope would not be relevant for change, and thus for progress at all.[28]

This seems to be the crucial positive argument for inequality. As Ralf Dahrendorf puts it, 'a society in which all are equal in all respects is also one devoid of realistic hope and thus of incentives for progress.'[29]

PROCESS, END-RESULT AND PATTERNED PRINCIPLES

A short diversion must now be introduced in order to avoid a foreseeable misunderstanding: the misleading identification of the argument presented here, about the incompatibility between equal liberty and social equality, with Robert Nozick's argument about the conflict between liberty and end-state principles as well as distributional patterned principles of justice.[30] Although there are important similarities between the two, they are by no means equivalent.

The first and most important distinction lies in the scope of each argument. Nozick's, based on the now famous example of Wilt Chamberlain, asserts the existence of a conflict between liberty and whatever patterned or end-state principle. By contrast, the scope of the argument presented here is much more limited and modest: it asserts only that *one particular end-state principle* – that of social equality – is incompatible with a presumption of equal liberty. Nothing else is said about other end-state principles or in general about patterned principles.[31]

A second interesting distinction is yet as follows: although Nozick's argument has a *broader* scope, the nature of the conflict he detects between liberty and end-state or patterned principles is *weaker* than the one between equal liberty and social equality which is put forward by the argument presented here. Whereas Nozick considers only that 'no end-state principle or distributional patterned principle of justice can be continuously realised *without continuous interference* with people's lives,'[32] the argument presented here maintains that social equality cannot be achieved and preserved *without annulling* equal liberty. Thus, whereas Nozick refers to an interference with liberty, the argument presented here refers to a fatal interference, a total obstruction of liberty.

Under further analysis, one might say that these two features of Nozick's argument – its broad scope and its weak final contention – constitute two important drawbacks. In fact, to assert that liberty upsets patterns, or that patterns interfere with liberty, is not to say much, since it is well established that no unrestricted liberty is ever viable. In other words, liberty has to be limited and regulated – thus interfered with – for the very sake of liberty itself. This is known as the paradox of freedom.[33]

For this reason, and as Alan Gewirth has replied to Ronald Dworkin on a different issue, 'since there cannot be completely unrestricted freedom, it is no objection to there being a general right to freedom that certain freedoms must be restricted'. Or, to apply it to the present case, the fact that end-state principles and patterns interfere with liberty is not sufficient in itself to rule out end-states and patterns, since some interferences with liberty are acceptable, and even indispensable, to preserve liberty itself. Why, then, should all possible interferences with liberty produced by whatever end-state or patterned principles be ruled out, irrespective of the particular justification for that interference?[34] The idea that any restriction of liberty should be ruled out just because it is a restriction seems to presuppose the view that the right to liberty is absolute, in the sense of not being justifiably infringeable in any circumstances. But, as Alan Gewirth has pointed out, this is hardly so:

Indeed, it is difficult to see how any human right, including the right to life, can be absolute in the sense of not being justifiably infringeable in any circumstances. The important question about the right to freedom, then, is: when, and on what grounds, may freedom be restricted? It will be noted that this question already suggests (although it does not prove) that there is a general right to freedom, for it implies that there is a general presumption in favour of freedom. This is, moreover, a strong presumption: it requires compliance on the part of all persons so that, without special justification, no one's freedom is to be restricted. There is no similar presumption in favour of coercion or unfreedom, except in so far as unfreedom is required for freedom (as the above mentioned paradox suggests).[35]

Thus, the problem with Nozick's argument is that he has to explain why the interferences of end-result principles and patterns with freedom are not justified in any situation whatever and irrespective of the specific content of those principles and patterns. Two sorts of explanation could be envisaged within Nozick's argument. One would consist of strengthening his contention about the nature of those interferences, asserting that in fact they amount to fatal interferences with liberty, that is, they actually annul liberty. But this is hardly conceivable. Since the scope of his argument is so wide and therefore accounts for so many different types of interference under the action of end-state principles and patterns, it is in principle possible to find at least one of these principles which does not annul liberty. Incidentally, Rawls' difference principle is of course an example of an end-state non-patterned principle (but not a current time-slice principle, as Nozick rightly points out) which does not annul liberty, although it might be said that it seriously restricts freedom without plausible justification.[36]
Another possible explanation would be for Nozick to say – as in fact is implied in his argument – that only process principles, and never end-states or patterned principles, are compatible with liberty, because all the results that arise from a process which is free have to be accepted, whatever their specific content might be. This is of course the main contention of Nozick's entitlement theory of justice:

> Entitlement theory specifies a process for generating sets of holdings. The three principles of justice (in acquisition, transfer and rectification) that underlie this process, having this process as their subject matter, are themselves process

principles rather than end-state principles of distributive justice. They specify an ongoing process, *without* fixing how it is to turn out, *without* providing some external criterion it must meet.[37]

But this seems to be a further difficulty in Nozick's argument. It is logically conceivable that, in order to preserve liberty, certain end-results that endanger liberty have to be ruled out, even if they may be brought about as a result of free actions of individuals under process principles of fair procedure, namely those of acquisition, transfer and rectification envisaged by Nozick. In fact, this is more than a logical possibility, it is what actually happens with regulations aiming at the preservation of competition and free markets. Anti-trust laws and competition watchdogs are aimed at avoiding certain end-results – such as monopolies or other concentrations of power which are perceived as jeopardizing competition – even though these end-results can be reached and are actually reached by legal procedures of buying and selling, i.e. by voluntary exchange between individuals or groups of individuals. So, contrary to what is implied in Nozick's argument, there can be some external criteria about end-results which, although they actually interfere with results brought about by free actions, are nonetheless perceived as being necessary to preserve freedom.

This is not to say, however, that Nozick's contention about the conflict between liberty and end-states as well as patterns is pointless. It is not, and there is an important insight of Nozick's which becomes apparent when one takes into account two 'nuances' of the end-result principles embodied in laws of competition. First, it should be noted that they are 'external criteria' of a very special kind: they are not chosen because of their independent desirability *as a result*, but because they are instrumental for the maintenance of a *process* of free exchange. Secondly, because of this, they do not really establish *end-states to be achieved*, but rather some *residual end-states to be avoided*. That is to say, apart from certain results that are considered to endanger liberty – and that, for this reason, are not to be accepted, even if they may have been produced under liberty – all other results are allowed.

Perhaps this can provide a different angle to look at Nozick's argument. He is right when arguing that liberty upsets patterns, but this does not necessarily mean that liberty is only compatible with process-principles and incompatible with end-result and patterned principles. Some end-result principles, as in the case of regulation of competition, appear even to be necessary in order to preserve liberty itself. However, if there is a presumption of liberty and if it is accepted that liberty upsets patterns and end-result principles, as Nozick has recalled, then, it is most likely that, for non-process principles to be compatible with liberty, they must be mainly of a negative and residual nature: they should mainly *exclude certain* residual situations, rather than *demand* that *all* results produced by a free process conform to a certain predetermined pattern or criterion.

Unless the presumption of liberty is questioned, it seems then that liberty requires the most extensive range of possible end-results to be allowed, although the preservation of liberty may well require that certain residual end-results are excluded. A presumption of liberty would then entail, as Nozick has suggested, a presumption that end-result and patterned principles are not be to imposed on results emerging from free processes. However, and contrary to what Nozick has argued, these principles should be distinguished from residual end-states that must be avoided in order to preserve liberty. These kinds of negative and residual end-result principles seem to be quite compatible with, if not indispensable to, a presumption of liberty.

* * *

Now, it might be interesting to note that the view of basic social rights proposed in this study is perfectly compatible with this reformulation of Nozick's argument. Corresponding to the imperative of helping those in need, basic social rights do not involve any general principle of distribution, and do not aim at any specific end-result to be achieved. On the contrary, they express only the aim of end-results to be avoided, that is, those situations in which people are deprived of certain basic goods which are perceived as being indispensable for the use of liberty. Apart from these situations which are not tolerable, nothing is said about particular states of affairs which should be the result of free exchange among free individuals. For this reason we have argued that the best formulation for basic social rights is a negative one: the right not to be deprived of a certain minimum of basic goods. Above this minimum, we know nothing about which reward should be attributed to each individual, all rewards being perceived as just so long as they arise from just processes of acquisition and transfer, and, of course, so long as they do not deny basic rights – civil, political or social – of other individuals.

THE ROLE OF MARKETS AND SOCIAL SERVICES

At the outset of this chapter it was said that two main basic assumptions lay at the origin of Raymond Plant's identification of the concept of 'helping those in need' with a general principle of distribution: one, which has been just discussed, was his contention that equal liberty entails an equal value of liberty; the other, which will be discussed next, was his misapprehension of the role of markets and, thereby, of the corresponding role of social services. Basically, it will be argued that Plant has overlooked two important features of market mechanisms, one moral, the other technical, as it were; for this reason, he has underestimated the crucial role of markets in what could be called an active (but still liberal) view of social citizenship rights.

However, before developing these contentions, it should be emphasized that Raymond Plant has powerfully renovated the traditional socialist view of market mechanisms. Without going into unnecessary details here, one should note that Plant has acknowledged three important insights into markets, which, in their turn, are not usually acknowledged by socialist oriented scholars.

Firstly, Plant has clearly stated that 'in theoretical terms, the work of Menger, Mises and Hayek still stands as a formidable challenge to the economic assumptions of central planning'.[38] Highlighting Hayek's contribution to the understanding of ordinary economic knowledge – namely its dispersion and its tacit nature – Plant subscribed to the Austrian school's seminal view according to which markets cannot be replaced by planning, be it central or local.

Secondly, Raymond Plant has pointed out that there are also some preconditions for markets to function, a point not always clear in the work of F. A. Hayek:

Markets cannot exist in a moral vacuum: generally they pre-suppose certain values such as honesty, fair dealing, promise keeping and some orientation towards the common good and civic virtue. The more sophisticated early defenders of the market such as Adam Smith realised this.[39]

Thirdly, Raymond Plant has pinpointed some of the market's weaknesses, rightly highlighting the fact that these only illustrate 'the fallibility of all institutions, including markets'. Asserting this, Plant has rightly presented markets as 'an instrument of policy rather than a panacea',[40] a view that we have subscribed to when criticizing Hayek's naturalistic conception of spontaneous evolution, in Part I of this study.

Having said this, it should now be recalled that Raymond Plant has nonetheless indulged in a somewhat dogmatic view of the related roles of markets and social services. As was previously shown, he ascribed to markets the satisfaction of preferences and wants by contrast with the satisfaction of needs, which he attributed to social services. 'Needs and their satisfaction', Plant asserted, 'characterize the social services in the general welfare aspect of society: the market exists to satisfy preferences and wants.'[41]

It has then been noted that, if this division of labour between markets and social services were to be observed, then basic goods such as food and housing should be produced and allocated by social services, whereas exquisite food and perhaps sophisticated manor houses would be left to markets. This is in fact what is implied in this other passage by Plant:

> There are certain goods which are so necessary for individual agency that they should be provided collectively and intentionally rather than through the market, which is the forum within which wants and preferences are satisfied.[42]

This mistaken view was at the core of Raymond Plant's identification of the concept of 'helping those in need' with a general principle of distribution according to need. It was then argued that Plant had said nothing that could have established that basic goods have to be provided collectively and intentionally *rather than* through the market; that is to say, Plant has not produced any reason whatever for basic goods to be produced and allocated according to a general principle of distribution *rather than* through the market. In fact, what he has shown is merely that, *if* and *when* the market does not provide for basic needs, *then* the state, or society, or all the members of a certain community, have the duty to provide for them intentionally. But this does not even entail that the *intentional* provision of basic goods cannot be effected *intentionally through market mechanisms*. As was mentioned in Chapter 2, it is perfectly possible to envisage a set of policies aiming at the provision of basic goods for those who lack them, in which the state, or the social services, act as an enabling agent and not as a provider.[43]

The main point now is to investigate the reasons that have led Raymond Plant to ascribe to the markets the mere satisfaction of wants and preferences, as opposed to needs, the satisfaction of which should be the task of social services. The contention to be presented here will be that this was due to a misapprehension of two crucial features of markets: (1) the fact that they are the main engine of the rise in people's standards of living, thus the main provider for people's basic needs; and (2) the fact that they are one of the most powerful schools of peaceful cooperation between free men. Because Raymond Plant has failed to take into account these two important points, he has disregarded the important role of markets in a radical policy of social citizenship rights, in other words, the crucial role of markets in the intentional provision of basic goods for those who need them.

THE EXTRAORDINARY ACHIEVEMENTS OF MARKETS

In his work *The Moral Foundations of Market Institutions*,[44] John Gray reappraises what he calls 'the epistemic argument for the market'. Recalling the work of von Mises and Hayek on the insuperable limitations of human knowledge, John Gray adds the contributions of Michael Polanyi and G.L.S. Shackle on the tacit nature of human knowledge and the unknowability of the future and the subjectivity of expectations. He argues that 'we are always, according to Shackle, ignorant of what it is that we do not know, even as (according to Polanyi) we always know more than we can ever say'. Markets appear, then, as devices 'for the transmission and utilisation of unarticulated, and sometimes inarticulatable, tacit and local knowledge'. By contrast, central planning confronts the crucial non-existence of the knowledge it would need to be successful. 'By comparison with market participants', John Gray concludes, 'planners will make large errors – errors for which there is no elimination device such as bankruptcy in markets.'[45]

It might be interesting to note that Joseph Schumpeter, too, emphasized the role of failure in the dynamic dimension of markets, as opposed to the traditional views on price competition. In his book *Capitalism, Socialism and Democracy*,[46] Schumpeter coined the expression 'creative destruction' to designate this dynamic process which is at the core of market economies:

> But in capitalist reality as distinguished from its textbook picture, it is not that kind of competition (price competition) which counts but the competition from the new commodity, the new technology, the new source of supply, the new type of organization (the largest-scale unit of control for instance) – competition which commands a decisive cost or quality advantage and which strikes not at the margins of the profits and the outputs of the existing firms but at their foundations and their very lives.[47]

This kind of competition, Schumpeter adds, 'acts not only in being but also when it is merely an ever-present threat. It disciplines before it attacks.' This amounts to saying that, even when actual competitors are not operating in a given branch of a market economy, the fact that this economy is open to free enterprise, i.e. the fact that anyone can in principle enter the market as a new supplier, exerts a terrible and well-known pressure over the actual suppliers. They know they have to compete in order to survive, and it is this ever-present threat that 'will in the long run enforce behaviour very similar to the perfectly competitive pattern'. The threatening creative destruction is then 'the powerful lever that in the long run expands output and brings down prices'.[48]

It is difficult to exaggerate the importance of this insight of Schumpeter. He is asserting precisely the opposite view of Raymond Plant's contention that markets provide mainly for wants and preferences, and not for basic goods for the common people. Moreover, Schumpeter maintains that: 'the capitalist process, not by coincidence but by virtue of its mechanism,

progressively raises the standard of life of the masses.' He is
ready to admit that 'it does so through a sequence of vicissitudes, the severity of which is proportional to the speed of its
advance.' But, he adds, 'it does so effectively'.[49] Rejecting the
widespread view that in capitalist economies the rich have grown
richer and the poor have grown poorer, he shows that 'broadly
speaking, relative shares in national income have remained
substantially constant over the last hundred years'.[50] But he
immediately adds a crucial and very often neglected point:

> This, however, is true only if we measure them in money.
> Measured in real terms, relative shares have substantially
> changed in favour of the lower income groups . . . It is
> the cheap cloth, the cheap cotton and rayon fabric, boots,
> motorcars and so on that are the typical achievements of
> capitalist production, and not as a rule improvements that
> would mean much to the rich man. Queen Elizabeth owned
> silk stockings. The capitalist achievement does not typically
> consist in providing more silk stockings for queens but in
> bringing them within the reach of factory girls in return for
> steadily decreasing amounts of effort.[51]

* * *

The relevant point for our discussion lies precisely in this
insight. It is the mechanism of open markets that is responsible for the rise of the standards of living of the masses in the
long run. This is not to say, of course, that every individual is
improving his standard of living at every given moment. On
the contrary, Schumpeter admits that the process of creative
destruction acts with severity and produces real victims, especially in terms of unemployment and exclusion of those whose
skills cease to match the permanently renewed needs of the
capitalist production.

These severe vicissitudes of the creative destruction can be
seen as providing the main rationale for the intentional provision of basic goods for those who need them. But it is now
possible to perceive how different this is from what Raymond
Plant has presented. In the first place, not social services but
market mechanisms are the main lever that expands and makes
accessible to the common people the satisfaction of their basic

needs. In the second place, and if this is so, when basic goods have to be intentionally provided for those who could not obtain them in the market, then, it will be advisable that this intentional provision can be done through mechanisms as similar as possible to those of the markets, and with the least possible interference with the process of creative destruction of open markets. These, as we have just asserted, constitute 'the powerful lever that in the long run expands output and brings down prices'. It would be a pity, and logically paradoxical, if the intentional provision of basic goods for those who need them were going to destroy or seriously damage this 'powerful lever' that in the long run raises people's standard of living.

How to bring this view of open markets into a policy of social citizenship rights, or a policy envisaging universal access to basic goods, will be one of our next topics. Just before that, however, let us turn to the second feature of markets which Raymond Plant has overlooked, the fact that they constitute one of the most powerful schools of peaceful cooperation between free men.

MORAL DIMENSIONS OF MARKETS

In his appraisal of market mechanisms, Plant points out one of their alleged drawbacks: the fact that they operate on the basis of self-interest. It is worth considering his own words:

> Finally, markets operate on the basis of the rational calculation of self-interest. This is of course a fundamental human emotion and motive and it would be difficult to imagine life without it. However, it needs to operate in only a limited framework because the more the market mentality comes to dominate our lives, its associated motives become more and more dominant. Then other values which cannot be captured in terms of self-interest and the calculation of advantage will be undermined.[52]

It would be absurd to deny that self-interest is only one of the values which underpin a free society and that one should not allow market mentality to dominate the whole of our societies. But the relevant point here is to note that Raymond

Plant faces self-interest with the same uneasy resignation with which he faces the inevitability of 'some legitimate inequalities'. The rational calculation of self-interest is, Plant asserts, 'a fundamental human emotion and motive and it would be difficult to imagine life without it'. As was the case with inequality, this is hardly the main reason to accept self-interest. It is not only that we are bound to fail if we attempt to abolish it. There is also a moral case for self-interest, – or rather for 'self-interest rightly understood', as de Tocqueville put it, or for 'enlightened self-interest', as Bertrand Russell used to say – and this must go beyond the mere acceptance of a fact of life. Moreover, market procedures constitute an irreplaceable mechanism to foster a proper view of self-interest, one which may contribute to a peaceful cooperation between free men and the mutual advancement of their well-being, not to violence or oppression.

It goes without saying that a proper discussion of the moral dimension of self-interest goes far beyond the scope of this study. But it might suffice for our purposes to mention that even altruism could not possibly be conceived without reference to self-interest. In fact, if, according to the *Oxford English Dictionary*, one understands altruism as a 'principle of considering the welfare and happiness of others before one's own', there has to be a way of assessing both one's own and others' welfare and happiness. Needless to say, if all the others decide to abolish their individual self-interest, there will be no way of discovering what their welfare and happiness should be. Unless one assumes that the needs and wants of others are the same as one's own needs and wants, the only other way of assessing the needs and wants of others must be to allow them to express them. For this to be done, however, they have to assess and express their own self-interest.

This is one of the reasons why classical liberals have always highlighted the crucial role of self-interest in a society of free men. Altruism without self-interest is more often then not a window-dressing for the egoism of the group, the collective oppression over individuals, the holistic suppression of individual liberty and individual assessment of his or her own needs and wants.[53]

Now, the important point consists of how and why market procedures not only allow self-interest to be expressed, but also, and more crucially, how and why they channel self-interest into a positive sum game, a game in which the pursuit of each one's interest contributes to the satisfaction of others' needs and wants. This immediately brings to mind Adam Smith's view on the invisible hand and his very sensible, but often neglected, observation that: 'it is not from the benevolence of the butcher, the brewer, or the baker that we expect our dinner, but from their regard to their own interest.'[54] A similar point was made by Walter Lippmann in *The Good Society*:

> The liberal conviction that there can be no other satisfactory regulator of work, investment, and consumption rests on the realization that when men specialize their labour, they must live by exchanging the product. If they are to exchange their own product for another product that they need, they must make a product that some other specialist needs. So there must be a place where the things they can and are willing to make are matched with the things that other men need or would like to have. That place is the market place. When the collectivist abolishes the market place, all he really does it to locate it in the brains of his planning board.[55]

This amounts to saying that my interest or utility depend on the willingness of others to buy what I have to offer. Therefore, if I want to satisfy my interest, I am bound to attend to the needs and wants of others, that is, to put on offer something that might be of any utility to others. This, of course, must lead me to give up the irrelevant ambition of ruling others' needs and wants according to my own opinions or passions. And, since under further analysis, I may well discover that the more different the opinions or preferences of the others are from my own opinions and preferences the greater the probability that they want to buy what I do not want to keep any longer, I may well end up discovering that diversity of preferences is indispensable to the exchange of commodities. At the end of the day, my own interest leads me to understand that the best way to pursue it lies in my attention to others' needs and wants, regardless of their opinions. In other words, the basic nature of the market place lies in the fact that it fosters peaceful co-operation between people, teaching them how they can pursue their own purposes by providing for other people's needs, without having to impose on them their particular purposes.

It is for this reason that liberals, of whatever particular inclination, radicals or conservatives, constructivists or traditionalists, have always praised the influence of commerce on people's manners, namely its peaceful effects and its influence in tolerance and open mindedness. Montesquieu's and Adam Smith's remarks on commerce and its impact on manners are widely known. But it is sometimes forgotten that even a radical like Thomas Paine has strongly praised the practice of commerce:

> In all my publications, where the matter would admit, I have been an advocate of commerce. It is a pacific system, operating to cordialize mankind, by rendering nations, as well as individuals, *useful to each other*... If commerce were permitted to act to the universal extent it is capable of, it would extirpate the system of war, and produce a revolution in the uncivilized state of governments. The invention of commerce has arisen since those governments began, and is the greatest approach towards universal civilization, that has yet been made by any means not immediately flowing from moral principles.[56]

MARKETS AS INSTRUMENTS OF LIBERAL POLICIES

This must suffice to draw attention to the crucial role of markets and free exchange in fostering peaceful and tolerant cooperation between free men. Contrary to what Raymond Plant asserts, market mechanisms are not only responsible for the increasing of people's standards of living in the long run, but also for 'the greatest approach towards universal civilization that has yet been made by any means not immediately flowing from moral principles' – as Thomas Paine put it. The relevant point here is that these features of markets cannot and should not be disregarded in a proper view of social citizenship rights –a view to which Raymond Plant has produced remarkable contributions, but whose overall conception cannot be accepted.

Now, it should be noted that the view of markets presented here is different from the views both of Hayek and Plant. Contrary to Hayek, markets are not regarded here as a product of spontaneous evolution, but only as a feature, although a crucial one, of a liberal order. This liberal order can be seen as spontaneous, not in the sense that it is a necessary product of evolution, but in the sense that it allows the widest room for free (and not centrally designed) action and interaction between citizens. Markets are then accepted and protected because of the normative virtues we have come to discover in their procedures.

This does not mean, however, that market results are to be accepted or worshipped as the undisputed verdicts of a natural law. Market results are to be discussed and evaluated according to standards that cannot be derived from facts alone. These standards vary greatly. Liberal standards demand that those market results which prevent some people from having access to the minimal conditions for using liberty should not be accepted. Intentional policies should be drawn up to enable people to have access to a common floor of citizenship, a common status that prevents exclusion. In this sense, liberal standards involve a discussion about the subject-matter of social justice, that is, about results and not only about processes. But their specific content is that, for normative reasons, no general pattern of social justice should be imposed on market results. Liberal standards demand that social injustice, above all exclusion, be fought against. But, contrary to what Plant has argued, it requires that no uniform pattern of distribution – certainly not equality, even in its mitigated form of presumptive equality – be imposed above the common floor of citizenship. In order to stress this restricted scope of social citizenship rights, they have been called here basic social rights.

Another important difference from Plant's view is that even the intentional provision of basic goods for those who need them is to be done *with* markets and not, as Plant asserted, *rather than* through markets. In the liberal view presented here, markets are not 'panaceas', as Hayek sometimes seemed to see them, but they are not nuisances either, as Plant sometimes seemed to perceive them. Markets can be said to be crucial instruments of liberal policies, that is, of a liberal on-going undertaking to protect and enlarge liberty and opportunities for all.

In other words, if the question is how to distinguish this sort of active liberalism from the socialist interventionism endorsed by Raymond Plant, two crucial areas of distinction have been already drawn: those of *goals* and of *methods*, the latter being to a great extent a consequence of the former. Goals are different because liberals aim mainly at negative goals (avoid exclusion and social injustice), whereas socialists aim mainly at positive ones (achieving social justice). As for the methods, it has been emphasized here that liberals should draw up policies which are based on markets, whereas socialists tend to see intentional policies as opposed to market mechanisms. It seems difficult, if not impossible, to define the precise boundaries of this distinction, since most will depend on circumstances arising from new problems which cannot be discussed in advance. But the discussion undertaken so far in this study allows the suggestion of some guidelines which can be helpful. They should be seen as proposals for a further enquiry into what might be called an active liberalism, and not as definitive standpoints. Bearing this in mind, five guidelines could then be suggested.

First, one should accept a presumption of non-intervention. This means that the burden of proof should be on a proposed intervention. In case of doubt, there should be no intervention. This seems to be a normal attitude springing from a normative priority to liberty and a spontaneous order.

Second, one should avoid monopolist supply of services, either by the state or the private sector. This seems reasonable on the grounds that competition is the real engine of productivity, and thus, of the satisfaction of needs at ever decreasing costs. This of course raises too many questions – one of which could be whether or not the state should have the monopoly of money supply – but it remains an important guideline. In case of doubt, one should follow the previous one – the presumption of non-intervention – and the common-sense view that one should not change what is working well.

Third, intervention should be indirect and institutional, rather then direct and personal. This was largely discussed when Karl Popper's piecemeal social engineering was discussed, in Chapter 3. To put it in Hayekian language, one could say that, whenever an intervention is necessary, it should mainly be done through general rules, stable, predictable, and equal for all, rather than through specific commands.

Fourth, intervention should not interfere with market signals. Strictly speaking, this is comprised in the previous guideline, but it is perhaps relevant to emphasize it. For example, instead of establishing minimum wage legislation, or rent controls, governments should rather support directly those who need it. Schemes of negative income tax, minimum income guarantees, and vouchers are usually among proposals to avoid government interference with market signals.[57]

Fifth, interventions should always aim at avoiding undesirable situations, rather than promoting precise states of affairs. This is of course our well-known distinction between residual or negative and positive criterions of distribution, but it is always important to recall that, in a free society, no authority can decide the particular place of individuals nor the precise result that free processes will bring about.

PLANT'S EGALITARIANISM: AN OVERVIEW

In Chapter 5 we have mainly discussed the difference between the principle of helping those in need and a general principle of distribution according to need. We have then admitted that Raymond Plant has reasonably replied to the main opponents of social rights, such as F. A. Hayek and M. Cranston; but we have also argued that, somehow paradoxically, Plant's understanding of social rights was ambiguous from the outset, and that he has developed it into a mistaken direction. Social rights do not involve any general principle of distribution whatever, but only a negative or residual principle of helping those in need, that is to say, a duty to provide basic goods for those who need or lack them.

In this chapter, the main question has been why Raymond Plant has identified the concept of 'helping those in need' with a general principle of distribution. It has been suggested that this is due to two main 'background assumptions' of his: (1) that equal liberty entails an equal value of liberty; (2) that markets do not provide for needs, but only, or mainly, for wants and preferences. Each of these assumptions has been discussed and criticized.

As for Plant's first assumption, three main difficulties have been detected. First, it has been argued that a presumption of equal liberty entails a presumption of unequal conditions. One can equalize material conditions only if one ends up by prohibiting individuals from doing the things one initially wanted them equally to be allowed and able to do. For this reason, it has been concluded that liberty in the positive sense of capacity to act, or, to use Plant's terminology, the value of liberty, can never be equal: one can never create for all an equal capacity to act, unless this is understood as an equal capacity not to act at all, or, at least, not to act freely.

The second difficulty referred to the inconsistency of Plant's interpretation of equal political liberty as equal capacity to act in the political realm. To be consistent, this view has to advocate total equality of conditions, which has been previously shown to be incompatible with permission to act differently. Then, to overcome this difficulty, the theory has to allow room for certain social inequalities, as Plant indeed has admitted. But all inequalities of conditions have to be seen, by definition, as inequalities of liberty. It has then been noted that this inconsistency does not arise if liberty is perceived as permission to act under the law: according to this view, equal liberty is guaranteed once equality before the law is established. Material inequalities, therefore, do not pose a problem to equal liberty. On the contrary, except when they enable some to deny the liberties of others, or when they prevent some from having access to the value of liberty, material inequalities should be seen as a legitimate product of different courses of action. The latter, in their turn, are the very goal of liberty.

The third difficulty consists of saying that, if the previous contentions are accepted, it will have to be allowed that the only view of social rights which is consistent with the goal or the ideal of equal liberty is what has been called the negative one: basic social rights aim at guaranteeing the *universal access* to the use of liberty – which must always be unequal, if liberty is to keep any meaning. In this sense, an equal right to basic goods should be understood as stating that *all have an equal right not to be deprived of basic goods*, and not that *all have an equal right to an equal amount of basic goods*.

After this, two short diversions have been introduced in the discussion of Plant's argument: a brief view of the virtues of inequality, and an equally brief discussion of Nozick's argument about process, end-result and patterned principles. As for inequality, it has been argued that its main advantages are related to the drawbacks of equality, namely the fact that egalitarian principles always permit waste, as Joseph Raz has observed. The main virtue of inequality, on the other hand, is that it provides society with realistic hope and thus with incentives for progress, as Ralf Dahrendorf has argued.

Nozick's argument has been criticized on the grounds that it overlooks the fact that even the protection of liberty requires that certain end-results that endanger liberty have to be ruled out, even if they may be brought about as a result of free actions of individuals under process principles of fair procedure – namely those of acquisition, transfer and rectification envisaged by Nozick. Nozick's argument has then been reformulated so as to state that, under a presumption of liberty, the most extensive range of possible end-results is to be allowed, although the preservation of liberty may well require that certain residual end-states are excluded. The view of basic social rights proposed in this study is perfectly compatible with this reformulation of Nozick's argument: basic social rights do not aim at achieving particular states of affairs, but mainly at avoiding certain residual ones, those in which some individuals are deprived of access to basic goods. For this reason, too, the best formulation of basic social rights is negative: they involve the general right not to be deprived of a certain minimum of basic goods.

We have then moved to the issue of the related roles of markets and social services in terms of guaranteeing the universal access to basic goods. It has been argued that Raymond Plant is not right in his contention that, because basic goods are so necessary for individual agency, they should be provided by social services rather than through the market. On the contrary, the problem is that, despite the powerful ability of markets to provide for people's basic needs at ever-decreasing costs, they are not able to avoid situations of exclusion and deprivation. The logical conclusion should then be that the intentional provision of basic goods (for those who were not able to obtain them through the market) should mainly aim at helping those in need to re-enter the market place, and, thereby, enabling them to participate in the 'powerful lever that in the long run expands output and brings down prices'. The moral dimension of market mechanism has then been recalled in order to highlight the role played by markets and free-exchange in the peaceful cooperation between free men. And a brief section on the main distinctions between neo-liberalism, socialism and the view presented here – which has been called active liberalism – has then concluded this chapter.

In other words, the argument presented here could now be summarized as follows: since we have seen that the substance of social rights lies in the legitimate claim of the needy to basic goods, and not in a general principle of distribution according to need; since we have seen that this claim is in fact a claim to universal access to basic goods; and, since we have seen that open markets are the most powerful lever for the provision of basic goods, then social policies should aim basically at providing universal access to the market place for those who have been devoid of this access, that is, for those in need.

Part III
Social Citizenship Rights: A Liberal Proposal

7 Conclusions: Citizenship, Inclusion and Opportunity

The discussions of every age are filled with the issues on which its leading schools of thought differ. But the general intellectual atmosphere of the time is always determined by the views on which the opposing schools agree. They become the unspoken presuppositions of all thought, and common and unquestioningly accepted foundations on which all discussion proceeds ... This can be very important because, as Bernard Bosanquet once pointed out, 'extremes of thought may meet in error as well as in truth ...

F. A. Hayek, *The Counter-Revolution of Science*, 1952

F. A. HAYEK'S AND R. PLANT'S COMMON ASSUMPTION

According to the argument so far presented, one might now say that, in spite of their views on social rights being opposed, Friedrich A. Hayek and Raymond Plant share in fact an important common assumption about these very social rights: they both view them as giving rise to (Hayek), or being the expression of (Plant), a common and positive pattern of distribution or social justice.

This common assumption leads each of them to different conclusions. With Hayek, because there cannot and ought not be a common pattern of distribution, and because social rights necessarily involve such a pattern, the concept of social rights should be ruled out. With Plant, because the criterion of basic needs underpins a common pattern of distribution, and because social rights are derived from basic needs, the concept of social rights should be accepted as part of a general pattern of distribution or social justice, which he calls 'democratic equality'.

Now, the argument presented here can be understood as claiming that both F. A. Hayek and R. Plant are mistaken in their common assumption that there is a necessary link between the concept of social rights and a common or positive pattern of distribution or social justice. Once this common assumption is challenged, a totally different view of social rights becomes possible.

179

According to this view, social rights guarantee only that nobody will be deprived of access to that level of basic goods which is considered to be indispensable to acting as a moral agent; these rights, therefore, involve the corresponding duty of society to provide basic goods for those who need or lack them. This amounts to saying that, apart from the satisfaction of the basic needs of those who do not have them satisfied, nothing is stated about the relative positions or rewards of individuals, nor even about their relative needs above the level of the basic ones. Because this view of social rights defines only a residual or negative criterion about those situations that cannot be accepted, or that common floor below which nobody should fear to fall, it cannot and should not be perceived as a common or positive pattern of distribution or social justice.[1]

It should be noted that, once the issue of social rights is distinguished from that of common patterns of distribution, several contributions from both Hayek and Plant can and should be retained and even integrated in a theory about social rights. In a way, it is as if both Hayek and Plant had been tilting at windmills; not because their arguments are irrelevant, on the contrary, but because they are aimed at wrong questions, or wrong problems; or still, perhaps more exactly, because the problem of social rights was perceived by them as entailing a general criterion of distribution, or an overall theory of justice. Therefore, whereas they have both been fighting either against (Hayek) or for (Plant) an overall theory of justice, the truth is that social rights do not involve any overall theory of justice whatever.[2]

It is worth recalling the main points that should be retained, as distinguished from those that should be discarded, in both Hayek's and Plant's arguments.

HAYEK'S ARGUMENT RECONSIDERED

Friedrich A. Hayek's main argument against a common pattern of distribution or social justice should certainly be retained. His most popular point is the contention, inspired by David Hume, that any common criterion of distribution had to be an assessable criterion, and that, in a free society, it would not be possible to reach and maintain a peaceful consensus about such a criterion.

A less well-known, but perhaps more crucial, point in Hayek's argument is the contention that, even if a consensus on a general pattern of distribution were reached, this pattern would not be capable of accomplishment or enforcement by resort to general rules of just conduct alone. Citizens acting in accordance with general rules of just conduct would always produce results which would not fit the final pattern of distribution agreed upon. Therefore, a central authority, either a person or an organization (or, one might add, all gathered together) would have to be endowed with the power of undoing or correcting the results produced by the actions of law-abiding citizens. In fact, this would amount to giving that authority the power to determine what each member of society is to have and, hence, is to do. In this case, a crucial feature of free societies – desirable in terms of both morality and efficiency – would be irretrievably lost: individuals would no longer be allowed to use, under the laws, the best of their knowledge to pursue their own ends, since they would have to fulfil the tasks considered to be indispensable to the accomplishment of the general pattern of distribution which they had agreed upon. Moreover, these tasks could never be described by general rules of just conduct, but only by specific commands aiming at particular results.[3]

These two points constitute a powerful argument against an overall theory of justice in a free society. However, and contrary to what Hayek argued, they should be part of a proper theory of basic social rights, instead of being perceived as arguments against any attempt to construct such a theory. The crucial reason for this lies in the fact that an overall theory of justice or a common pattern of distribution is not necessary if and when a society wants only to relieve situations of avoidable human suffering; neither is it necessary if and when a society wants only to provide basic goods for those who lack them and who, for this reason, are perceived as being in need. In both cases, a common pattern of distribution or social justice is not necessary because the goal is to avoid certain situations (of deprivation and exclusion), and not to attain a global and pre-determined state of affairs.

Avoiding certain situations does not involve any determination whatever of the relative position of individuals in a given society. Such determination may even be intentionally ruled out because of its undesirable consequences, which were brilliantly put forward by Hayek. Avoiding certain situations amounts merely to saying that free individuals, obeying general rules of just conduct, agree to build up a sort of insurance system in order to assist whoever of them happens to fall into a condition which they have all agreed should be avoided. Apart from this safety net, which defines only residual situations to be avoided, nothing is said about the other positions in society – which are to be perceived as just, so long as they are attained and maintained according to the general rules of just conduct that govern that society. In this sense, it could be said that Hayek's argument against the pursuit of social justice does not apply to the avoidance of social injustice.[4]

A similar point has been made regarding Robert Nozick's global critique of end-result and patterned principles of distributive justice. To be acceptable, this critique should be reformulated. Instead of arguing against all end-result and patterned principles, it should be understood as stating that liberty requires the most extensive range of possible end-results to be allowed, although the preservation of liberty may well require that certain end-results are excluded – even if they may be brought about as a result of free actions of individuals under process principles of fair procedure. The view of basic social rights presented here is then compatible with this reformulation of Nozick's argument: basic social rights do not aim at achieving particular states of affairs, but mainly at avoiding certain residual ones, those in which some individuals are deprived of access to basic goods. For this reason, too, it has been argued that the best formulation of basic social rights is negative: they involve the general right not to be deprived of a certain minimum of basic goods.

PLANT'S ARGUMENT RECONSIDERED

As for Raymond Plant, two main contributions of his should necessarily be integrated into a theory of social rights: (1) the contention that the subject-matter of social justice is not in itself a meaningless issue in a market economy; and (2) the contention that basic needs can be assessed and can be perceived as giving rise to a right to the satisfaction of these basic needs. As was the case with Hayek, these views of Plant should be disentangled from his overall approach.

Plant's main contribution to assert the meaningfulness of social justice as a subject-matter was his assertion that the fact that market results are unintended and, in a sense, unforeseen does not entail that one has merely to accept market outcomes as natural facts. Justice does not depend on how situations are brought about, but on our moral perception of, and corresponding response to, these situations. For this reason, problems which appeal to our moral concern, such as poverty, deprivation, or, in general terms, avoidable human suffering should be considered as matters of social justice, regardless of the fact that they may well have resulted from no one's intentional action. Furthermore, if it is possible to foresee that the market will not be able to avoid these situations, then it will be possible to say that we have the duty to take serious and permanent measures to face these problems.

Contrary to what Hayek argued, then, the concept of social justice in a market economy is not as meaningless as the concept of 'a moral stone'.[5] A discussion about the subject-matter of social justice can and should have meaning in a free society based on a market economy. But the precise boundaries of this assertion should be drawn. It means that market results are susceptible of being discussed and evaluated, but it says nothing about the necessary conclusions to be produced by this evaluation. It is the argument of this study that this discussion and evaluation should lead free citizens of free societies to conclude that it is in their best interest – the best interest of liberty and justice altogether – not to submit market outcomes to any common or positive pattern of distribution or social justice, but only to a negative or residual one based on the satisfaction of basic needs. This is so, however, not because common patterns of distribution are meaningless, or because the very discussion of social justice is meaningless. Common and positive patterns of distribution or social justice should be avoided because within a meaningful discussion and evaluation of market mechanisms, there are good reasons to avoid such patterns. Some of these good reasons were produced by Hayek, as was noted above. But they can only make sense within Plant's contention that the subject-matter of social justice is not meaningless in a free society.[6]

Raymond Plant's second contribution to a theory of social rights is, of course, his long-pursued work on the concept of basic needs. Plant has cogently shown that social agreement about basic needs does not involve any uniformization whatever of the ultimate ends of individuals. Every moral code has to recognize that persons need certain minimal capacities that allow them to act and pursue the moral goals enshrined in that moral code. The capacity to act as a moral agent, he concluded, then becomes the basic human end which is wanted by all persons, whatever their moral code might be. And the conditions or means for that action – which Plant, following Alan Gewirth, defines as physical survival and autonomy – turn out to be unqualified or human needs.

Furthermore, Plant has argued that the satisfaction of unqualified or human needs, as those conditions which are indispensable for acting as a moral agent, can be perceived as a duty of society, and even as a duty of strict obligation giving rise to a right. If it is accepted that basic needs consist of those basic goods which are indispensable for pursuing any ends and duties, then the duty to provide for those who lack these basic goods has to be accepted simply because, without them, they would not be able to fulfil any obligation. As a duty of strict obligation, this duty gives rise to the corresponding right of access to basic goods. Here Plant has cogently shown that the traditional critique of social rights – built in the allegation that they are categorically different from civil and political ones – does not apply.

These two insights – into the meaningfulness of social justice, and into the satisfaction of basic needs as a duty of strict obligation – constitute a very powerful argument for the concept of social rights. However, and contrary to what Raymond Plant argued, they should be clearly distinguished from an argument for a general criterion of distribution or any positive pattern of social justice. Satisfaction of basic needs is not to be confused with distribution according to need: the former is a residual or negative criterion which commands that basic goods should be provided for those who lack them, only for those, and only whilst they lack them; distribution according to need is an overall criterion which commands that not only basic goods, but goods in general, should be allocated, not only to those in need, but to all members of society according to their respective needs. Satisfaction of basic needs amounts to the definition of a safety net for whose construction one has only to define a minimum level of basic goods to be provided, and a method of identifying and reaching people below that level. Distribution according to need, on the contrary, demands a general agreement about what are each and every one's needs, and demands a central authority in charge of distributing the goods according to the needs assessed.[7]

That distribution according to need (or according to any other general criterion) should be ruled out was shown by Hayek. But Raymond Plant himself has produced the arguments which are sufficient to show that the duty to provide for basic needs cannot underpin a general criterion of distribution according to need. In fact, if the basis of a moral obligation to provide for basic needs is the lack of basic goods, and the assumption that this prevents people from fulfilling any obligation, then it follows both that the obligation applies only when a lack of basic goods is discernible, and that the obligation ceases when basic needs are met.

For this reason, Plant has produced no argument whatever that could lead to a general criterion of distribution according to need; in fact, this would imply a comparative judgement about people's needs, even when their basic needs had been fulfilled, for which he has not produced any indication apart from equality – which is not a criterion of distribution according to need since people's needs vary greatly; and, moreover, it would imply a duty to provide for other people's needs even when their basic needs had been fulfilled – which, of course, goes far beyond the duty presented by Plant. He has presented the case, one must recall, only for the duty to provide for those minimal capacities that allow people to act as a moral agent, and only for this duty to apply when these minimal capacities are absent.

In other words, one should distinguish the subject-matter of social justice from a general criterion of distribution or social justice. The former designates the realm of normative discussions about *results*, as distinguished from procedures alone, in a market order. A defence of a pattern of distribution or social justice is then a *particular* view within this discussion, a view which maintains that market results should be ordered according to a common pattern or criterion. Therefore, the view presented here amounts to saying that, contrary to Hayek and according to Plant, the subject-matter of social justice is not meaningless. On the other hand, however, Hayek was right and Plant was not, when maintaining that market results should not be ordered according to any common pattern of distribution. The view of basic social rights defended here does not entail such a pattern, but only a residual principle of satisfaction of basic need.

THE CONCEPT OF BASIC NEEDS

A common temptation among scholars dealing with matters of social rights is to embark upon a definitive description of what is and what is not to be included under the label of basic need. This is important, we are told, in order to avoid either the endless expansion or the reduction of those goods which should be seen as constitutive of basic needs. However plausible this may seem, the argument presented here leads to a different view, according to which the recognition of the existence of certain situations of deprivation and misfortune which ought not to be allowed is sufficient for the purposes of a theory of social rights. It is of course understood that deprivation relates to basic goods only, that is to say, those conditions which are indispensable to acting as a moral agent. It is also understood that these conditions comprise physical survival and autonomy, as Raymond Plant and Alan Gewirth have argued, these being likely to include health care and education. But a precise and definitive criterion of these situations is not only unnecessary but also undesirable.

The point is to assert that there is a duty to provide basic goods for those who need them, to assert that this duty ceases when basic needs are fulfilled, and that there is no comparative criterion involved. In other words, the point is to admit the duty of society to provide for a safety net. What the precise level of this safety net should be is not a matter of a general theory of social rights but for an ongoing controversy which belongs to the realm of normal politics.[8] And rightly so, because such a precise definition can never be settled once and for all, since many contingent considerations should be taken into account. The level of wealth of a given society – and, therefore, its capacity to define the level of basic goods – is certainly one of these considerations. But others less easy to define should not be overlooked: the impact of social help on the willingness of those who are helped to regain self-reliance; the unintended consequences of social policies which can turn out to produce incentives for unsocial behaviour, and so forth.

It is likely, then, that the precise definition of basic goods will always tend to be a matter of dispute in a free society. But this is in fact an advantage, not a drawback: it will alert people to the necessity of assessing permanently the impact and costs of social policies and of being open to new ideas. These are tasks to be left to political controversy, not to a general theory of social rights or to constitutional definitions.[9]

METHODS OF PROVIDING FOR BASIC NEEDS

A similar point to the one previously made about the concept of basic needs can be produced with respect to the methods of providing for basic needs. There is no magic clue, no definitive recipe to establish these methods. The only recipe, if it can be called so, is again trial and error; this, in a free society, is of course the combined effort of rival views, including rival parties.

Besides this, the general point to be made is that the intentional provision of basic goods for those who lack them is inherent in the view of social rights presented here. If certain individuals had no access to the basic goods through the market place, and if it is accepted that the access to these goods is to be guaranteed for all, it follows that their provision is to be intentionally established.

But, contrary to what Raymond Plant has concluded, this does not mean that basic goods are to be provided by social services while wants and preferences are to be satisfied via the market. It has already been shown that basic goods are not to be centrally allocated to each and every citizen: they are to be intentionally provided for those who lack them, those who cannot obtain them in the market. But it should now be noted that intentional provision does not even mean provision outside the market. It may only mean to provide people with the means that enable them to enter the market.

In fact, since it cannot be shown that social services will produce better services than those already available in the market, this should be the best way of enforcing social rights. Instead of substituting state provision for market provision, social policies should address directly those in need, enabling them to enter the market place and act as consumers of basic goods normally produced by private enterprises competing with each other. Vouchers are usually presented as possible means of achieving this, especially in the field of education.

Even when state provision is considered to be the only available alternative, this should always be done so that competition can still operate and produce its beneficial effects. Monopoly, either public or private, should always be avoided because it prevents competition from pressing prices down, encouraging innovation and increasing productivity.

For a similar reason, every direct intervention by the state should not interfere with the system of signals that underpins market operations. It has been argued cogently that excessive labour regulation, namely establishing minimal wages, produces a net loss of jobs that could otherwise be created and accepted by those looking for a job. A minimum income guarantee, or a negative income tax, has been proposed as a more effective way of providing a common floor without interfering with the signals of the market.[10]

In more general terms, state intervention and public policies should aim at the creation of a stable framework of rules, rather than at the multiplication of commands. And it should always aim at complementing and improving the work of markets, rather than replacing it. But it is pointless to attempt a definition of the precise methods whereby this should be achieved. Apart from general guidelines, these methods will always depend on contingent considerations that cannot be established in advance.

PRACTICAL COMPROMISE, A THEORETICAL WATERSHED

If, for nearly all issues previously discussed, some contributions from Hayek and some others from Plant have been marshalled, it might be said that the views presented in this study are merely a compromise between those of Hayek and those of Plant. And yet this is not so.

Even though the views presented here may pave the way for such a compromise in practical and political terms, this is not its rationale; this does not correspond either to the reasoning that underpins the concept of social rights presented here or to the intellectual path whereby the concept should be reached. Moreover, the more general assumptions which foster the view presented here are conspicuously different both from those of F. A. Hayek and those of R. Plant.

As for Hayek, the main distinction lies in the refusal of the normative consequences (passive ones) which he infers from his naturalistic evolutionism. For Plant, the main distinction lies in the refusal of the normative consequences (egalitarian ones) which he derives from his view of basic needs. As was intentionally shown before, the concept of basic social rights argued for in this study can be justified with no further mention of the disagreement above referred to as involving 'the more general assumptions'. None the less, if the argument of this study is to be properly understood and its consequences properly explored, it should be noted that it involves in fact a deeper disagreement with the general assumptions of both Hayek and Plant.[11] It is worth recalling briefly the scope of these disagreements and some of their implications.

F. A. HAYEK'S EVOLUTIONISM

The main difficulty of Hayek's evolutionism can be illustrated by the fact that it comprises a strong moral component, although Hayek argues that people cannot choose their morals. Because Hayek's early work has been mainly normative, he is then led to a somewhat unique position of knowing that the morals he chose on normative grounds are also those which will be selected by evolution. This paradoxical view, whose resemblance to Marx's historicism has been recalled, gives rise to two main problems: one moral, the other epistemological.

The moral problem lies in the devastating relativist consequences of such a theory of morality. According to it, Hayek's own normative requirements, namely those of the rule of law as opposed to the rule of men, could only be seen as 'moral attributes which derive from a naive anthropomorphism'. Moreover, and still according to Hayek's evolutionism, there is no ground for believing that a 'natural, spontaneous and self-ordering process of adaptation' must conform to moral demands that people be treated equally by the law. In this sense, not even civil and political rights could be justified, let alone defended, if and when a 'spontaneous process of adaptation' countered them.

The epistemological problem is no less important. Like many theories of very wide scope, Hayek's theory of evolution is not capable of being tested: even if all liberal societies ceased to be so, this would not necessarily refute Hayek's thesis that the liberal order is simultaneously the product and the destiny of evolution, since one could always say that this was only an ephemeral episode of evolution, and that the necessary future collapse of illiberal societies would soon give rise to a liberal revival. But, precisely because there is no definite test to the theory, one could also conclude that liberal principles had been discarded by evolution. This also shows that Hayek's attempt to underpin liberal morality on 'natural' and 'scientific' grounds failed, since the same 'natural' fact of evolution could be given two different moral responses.

Hence, Hayek's faith in the future inevitable victory of liberal capitalism reveals itself to be merely a faith. Evolution cannot be the test of political morality, and liberalism cannot be seen as the necessary product of evolution. It is only one of the possible several, and its advance must therefore require the active intervention of human will. This view can even be reinforced by resort to one of Hayek's own insights: that a decentralized or spontaneous order has a capacity to deal with information, and thus of adapting to changing circumstances, that is not matched by any made order or organization. This capacity to adapt hints at a different view of evolution, in which the creative reaction of individuals is at least as important as the pressure from the external environment.

According to this view, liberal traditions, namely those of openness and of government limited by law, remain of crucial importance, not because they are merely part of tradition, but because they favour piecemeal change and adaptation. This would also imply two main corrections to Hayek's critique of constructivism. First, instead of a blind reverence for traditions, liberalism should favour a critical presumption of tradition, that is, a view which puts the burden of proof on a proposed change but does not close the door to change. Second, a spontaneous order, as opposed to a made order, should still be seen as a liberal ideal, but not as a 'natural' product of spontaneous evolution. Although it might well have arisen as an unintentional and undesigned product of human action, its maintenance requires constant protection by design, namely by a liberal framework of laws.

Finally, and if the above assertions are accepted, liberalism cannot be identified with *laissez-faire*, and should rather be seen as a special sort of constructivism – one which is self-restrained precisely because, as Karl Popper has suggested, its main goal is the protection of a free society. This active view cannot be translated in a once and for all political programme. The agenda of liberalism must vary according to circumstances and only its main attitude can be defined: it aims at the preservation of a free society, ruled by laws rather than by the caprices of men. But this is an unending undertaking, which requires an active intervention in the realm of politics and social institutions.

PLANT'S EGALITARIANISM

Citizenship rights, including social citizenship rights, should then be seen as part of that framework of laws which protect liberal societies. They are made by design, although in the specific way described above under the label of 'a critical presumption of tradition', but one should not overlook that it is not an arbitrary design. The purpose of citizenship rights is to protect an order of liberty, and they should be carefully designed – and corrected, when necessary – in order not to undermine but to advance this goal.

Now, the argument presented here comprises the view that Raymond Plant's attempt to associate the concept of social rights with that of 'democratic equality' would, if followed rigorously, seriously undermine a liberal order. This does not follow only from the contention, presented earlier, that such association is based on a confusion between the residual principle of 'satisfaction of basic needs' and a positive pattern of distribution. It follows also from a more general contention that the search for social equality is intrinsically incompatible with the maintenance of liberty.

This incompatibility can be illustrated by resort to a very simple 'thought experiment' which consists of imagining that, at a certain moment, all individuals are in equal social or material conditions. According to Plant's argument, this equality of conditions had been promoted with the goal of guaranteeing an equal effective liberty for all (as contrasted with equal formal liberty). For this reason, once equality of conditions is achieved, citizens will be allowed to act freely – in fact, they will finally be able to act with equal liberty.

Acting with equal liberty, thus, they will be equally able to adopt different courses of actions. If one admits that different courses of action lead to different results, one has to admit that these citizens will end up in different material conditions which were the result of different actions taken under equality of material conditions. This means that the natural consequence of liberty of action is inequality of conditions.

But it should be added that it is not impossible to recreate the equality of conditions initially achieved. This can certainly be done by annulling the different results produced by different actions. The only problem is that, from the point of view of the goal of equal liberty for all, to annul the different results of different actions is paradoxical: these actions were produced under equality of conditions, and the latter was created with the aim of guaranteeing equality of effective liberty. It is pointless to give equal effective liberty to individuals if every different result freely produced by them is to be undone. In fact, in this case, they are indeed equal, but not equally free: they are only equally unfree. In other words, one can equalize conditions only if one ends up prohibiting people from doing what one initially wanted them to be equally free and able to do.

This is why a principle of liberty necessarily implies a presumption of social inequality, and not a presumption of equality as Raymond Plant has proposed. Plant has argued that this view of liberty is merely formal and that in fact it covers deep inequalities of liberty. Liberty, he said, is not only the absence of intentional coercion by others, but also the ability to develop the actions which are open by the absence of coercion by others. Liberty, if it is to have any meaning, is inseparable from the worth of liberty, the latter being defined by those conditions which enable one to use liberty. If liberty is to be equal for all, Plant concluded, the worth of liberty, too, has to be equal, or as equal as possible.

It should be noticed that the only goal which is compatible with the goal of an equal worth of liberty is absolute equality of capacities or conditions. But since Plant himself has argued that some legitimate inequalities are to be allowed (namely those resulting from the 'rent of ability'), this means he himself is arguing for some inequalities in the worth of liberty. Moreover, since he has maintained that equal liberty is only possible with equal worth of liberty, this also means that he himself is accepting inequalities of liberty. Now, it should be recalled that the starting point of his critique of a negative view of liberty, and of his case for equality of the worth of liberty, was the allegation that a negative view of liberty covers deep inequalities of liberty. However, he arrived at the same result.

In other words, for those who perceive equality of the worth of liberty as a pre-condition of equal liberty, all the moves away from strict equality of conditions have to be perceived as moves away from equality of liberty. Since it is widely acknowledged nowadays that a strict equality of conditions is not feasible, this leads to a deadlock: for those who perceive equality of the worth of liberty as a pre-condition of equal liberty, the infeasibility of strict equality of conditions necessarily means that equal liberty is not feasible.

This inconsistency can be overcome only within a theory which views liberty as absence of intentional coercion by others. As such, equal liberty can be guaranteed by law, that is to say, by equality before the law. As it was shown before, a presumption of inequality – material inequality, or inequality of the worth of liberty – follows necessarily from this view of liberty. But this does not involve any inconsistency whatever, because, according to the negative view of liberty, an unequal worth of liberty does not entail inequalities of liberty. On the contrary, this view asserts that equal liberty will necessarily entail unequal worth of liberty.

SOCIAL CITIZENSHIP RIGHTS: A LEVEL PLAYING FIELD

This is not to say, however, that the worth of liberty is irrelevant, or that it should be dismissed as irrelevant once equal liberty is enshrined in law. The point presented here consisted merely of showing that equality of the worth of liberty is irrelevant, not necessarily the worth of liberty in itself. It should be recalled that, conversely, the critique of Hayek's views on social rights consisted precisely of arguing that the worth of liberty is relevant, and that it does not suffice to guarantee liberty in law. It is also necessary, it was argued, to guarantee that all can have access to those basic goods which are perceived as being the minimal conditions for acting as a moral agent – in other words, to act freely, or to make use of freedom. This amounts to saying that, although equality of the worth of liberty should be ruled out, the access to the means whereby liberty is worthwile is part of the goal of making liberty real for all.

Needless to say, this is the realm of social citizenship rights: the realm of the worth of liberty, of those material conditions that enable people to use their liberty. According to the argument presented here, therefore, social citizenship rights should not aim at establishing equality of the worth of liberty, but only at guaranteeing the universal access to the worth of liberty.

Now, it might be said that there is also a principle of equality involved in this view of social rights: all citizens are equally entitled to accede to the worth of liberty, or have an equal right to the satisfaction of their basic needs. This is true, but it is important to note the contrast between this liberal view of equality and the one defended by Raymond Plant. According to Plant, all citizens should have an equal right to an equal (or as equal as possible) worth of liberty, or an equal share of basic goods. According to the view presented here, this equal right concerns only the access, not the result. It is better designated, then, by universality: equality of social rights means here universality of social rights, a common set of entitlements for all that provide a level playing field. But, above this common floor, inequalities will flourish.

In this sense, T. H. Marshall's questions about the conflict between equality of citizenship and the inequalities of social class can now be seen under new light. It is true, as he observed, that equal citizenship has limited the areas in which markets work: by providing a common floor below which nobody need fear to fall, social citizenship provides a common status for all, which does not depend on the vagaries of the market. But this common status does not aim at replacing markets by a common pattern of distribution which defines the rewards that should be allotted to each and every one. It aims only at providing entry-tickets for all to enter the market place, or to put it differently, it aims at avoiding exclusion from the market place. Once inclusion is guaranteed, free exchange among individuals remains the basic 'criterion of distribution', that is, there is no single criterion at all. Thus, if it is true, as T. H. Marshall said, that the inequality of the social class system can be acceptable provided the equality of citizenship is recognized, it is no less true that, for liberty to be preserved, the equality of citizenship is desirable provided social inequality is accepted.

As Ralf Dahrendorf has argued, citizenship rights are entry-tickets, opportunities of access, demolishers of barriers, guarantees of inclusion in a world of liberty and, thus, of unequal conditions. The goal of citizenship rights is not to promote equality, but to promote opportunity, not to avoid inequality but to avoid exclusion from a world of opportunities. Because people are free and equal as citizens, they can be free and unequal as individuals.

* * *

At the outset of this enquiry into social citizenship rights it was said that it aimed at criticizing two rival views, those of Neo-liberalism, as represented by Friedrich A. Hayek, and of Socialism, as represented by Raymond Plant. It was then added that the view to be presented here, if it deserved any label, could still be called Liberal. We hope to have been able to provide a consistent alternative view of social citizenship rights throughout these pages. We would be happy, too, if it had hinted at an alternative view of liberalism – one which, unlike Hayek's neo-liberalism, is not passive in the political and institutional realms, and, unlike Plant's socialism, is not egalitarian and does not underestimate the role of markets. Anyway, this has been a thrilling exploration which, as is often the case with intellectual explorations, has created as many new problems as those it has attempted to solve. Among the former is certainly that of whether a consistent view of an active liberalism – or, as we have also called it, a self-restrained constructivism – can challenge, in global terms, those of neo-liberalism and socialism. This might well be the subject of a further exploration.

Notes

INTRODUCTION: EQUAL CITIZENSHIP & SOCIAL INEQUALITY

1. One should probably note that the terms 'Neo-liberalism' and 'Socialism' are not terribly important in themselves, other terms being possible. Neo-liberalism, for instance, is sometimes called Libertarian Liberalism, and some authors identify both with what they call the 'New Right'. The kind of socialism which is going to be discussed here, certainly not a Marxist socialism, is sometimes referred to as a specific version of 'Egalitarian Liberalism'. Since the arguments of each view will be defined and discussed in great detail, discussions about which label should be attached to which view do not seem to be of paramount importance.
2. The expression 'overall theory of justice' is borrowed from J. Gray's lecture at Nuffield College, Oxford, on 3 March 1993, entitled 'Why There Cannot Be an Overall Theory of Justice'.
3. T. H. Marshall (1950/1992).
4. A. Marshall (1873/1925).
5. A. C. Pigou (1925), pp. 101–18.
6. A. Marshall (1873/1925), p. 102.
7. T. H. Marshall (1950/1992), p. 6.
8. Ibid. It is interesting to note that T.H. Marshall acknowledges the fact that Alfred Marshall did not identify the life of a gentleman with the status of citizenship. 'To do so', he added, 'would have been to express his ideal in terms of legal rights to which all men are entitled. That, in turn, would have put the responsibility for granting those rights fair and square on the shoulders of the state, and so led, step by step, to acts of state interference which he would have deplored.'
9. T. H. Marshall (1950/1992), p. 8.
10. Ibid., p. 6.
11. Ibid., p. 7.
12. Ibid.
13. Ibid.
14. Ibid., p. 47.
15. Ibid., p. 49.
16. The classical reference for the classification of legal rights is W. Hohfeld (1919). Two excellent introductions to this work may be found in A. L. Corbin (1923) and J. Feinberg (1973), chapters 4–6, pp. 55–97. This overview will follow mainly Feinberg's work.
17. In fact, Hohfeld mentioned two further categories besides claim-rights and mere liberties: abilities or powers, and immunities. But only the first two are relevant to our discussion.
18. J. Feinberg (1973), p. 56.
19. In this sense, of course, all rights comprehend liberties, but not all liberties comprehend rights. But one should not confuse 'a liberty'

197

(or 'liberty-right') with a claim-right to liberty. As D. D. Raphael puts it, in (1970/1990), p. 106, 'the first is called a liberty because it is a freedom to do what you want to do. The second is one kind of claim-right, a claim against someone else to be left free, that is to say, a claim that he is obliged to leave you alone.'

20. As J. Feinberg rightly observes, in (1973), p. 62, when one speaks of duties entailed by rights one does *not* mean 'that a person's rights ought to be contingent upon performance of his own duties' (moral correlativity), but only that 'his rights are necessarily linked with the duties of other people' (logical correlativity). The problem of moral correlativity will not be addressed here, unless in so far as it relates to the general status of citizenship, which includes rights and duties.

21. J. Feinberg (1973), p. 60: 'The right of an accident victim to be assisted by anyone who happens to be in a position to help is positive and *in rem*'; whereas 'if you promise me to stay off the public road near my home, then I have a right... which is *in personam*... and negative'.

22. J. Feinberg (1973), p. 60.

23. This Declaration may be consulted in UNESCO (1948), where a 'Memorandum Circulated by UNESCO on the Theoretical Basis of the Rights of Man' and also a 'Report of the UNESCO Committee on the Theoretical Basis of Human Rights' may be found. Henceforth the whole document will be referred to as the UN Declaration. And yet, some earlier versions of social rights appeared in France, in a Jacobin declaration of 1793 and a socialist Manifesto of Babeuf in 1796, both republished and discussed in Marcel Gauchet (1989). In *Rights of Man* and *The Agrarian Revolution*, Thomas Paine refers also to some sort of social rights, namely the right to social security.

24. J. Feinberg (1973), p. 84.

25. R. Aron (1974), p. 75.

CHAPTER 1: PRESENTATION: THE MIRAGE OF SOCIAL JUSTICE

1. F. A. Hayek (1976), p. 103.

2. Cf. Unesco (1948).

3. We shall see later that the concept of 'rules of just conduct' is crucial to Hayek's political philosophy. But, for the time being, it is sufficient to cite the author's own basic definition of these rules: 'those end-independent rules which serve the formation of a spontaneous order, in contrast to the end-dependent rules of organization', in F. A. Hayek (1976), p. 31. Hayek identifies these rules of just conduct generally with rules of private and criminal law (but not with public law) and he assigns them the features of generality, abstractness, non-retroactivity and universality. At this stage, we may say that those rules of just individual conduct constitute for Hayek the hard core of what liberals usually refer to as *Law*, which must be equal for all and whose empire is the first condition of a liberal regime, whether it may or may not be democratic. At this point of our inquiry it is not to indulge in a major lack of rigour to identify those rules of just conduct with the

Law, general, abstract and equal for all, which is so much praised by liberals. In due course we shall introduce necessary precision and corresponding complication.

4. F. A. Hayek (1976), p. 101.
5. Ibid.
6. Ibid., p. 102.
7. Hayek cites Article 22 (everyone 'is entitled to the realization ... of the economic, social, and cultural rights indispensable for his dignity and the free development of his personality'), Art. 23(1) (a claim to 'just and favourable conditions of work'), Art. 23(3) (a claim to 'just and favourable employment'), Art. 27(1) (the right 'freely to participate in the cultural life of the community and to share in the scientific advances and its benefits'), Art. 28 (everyone is 'entitled to a social and international order in which the rights and freedoms set forth in this Declaration are fully realized'). Later on he cites Article 24 whereby every one has a 'right to just and favourable remuneration, including reasonable limitations of working hours and periodic holidays with pay'. Cf. F. A. Hayek (1976), pp. 104–5.
8. F. A. Hayek (1976), p. 104.
9. Ibid.
10. Ibid., p. 105.
11. Ibid., p. 106.
12. Ibid., p. 105.
13. Ibid., p. 102.
14. Ibid., p. 103. I must here recall that Hayek at this stage identifies the duties corresponding to social and economic rights as the government's duty to determine the particular material position of individuals or groups. I shall argue later that this identification is not necessarily true and that one of the crucial errors of Hayek lies precisely in the assumption that it is. For the time being, however, I accept the identification.
15. F. A. Hayek (1976), p. 103.
16. Ibid., p. 106.
17. See above, p. 14.
18. On the distinction between a spontaneous order and an organization, cf. below, pp. 15–16. Cosmos and Taxis.
19. F. A. Hayek (1960), especially chapter 6, 'Equality, Value and Merit', pp. 85–102.
20. F. A. Hayek (1978), ch.9, pp. 119–51.
21. F. A. Hayek (1973), (1976), (1979).
22. F. A. Hayek (1978), ch.5, pp. 57–68.
23. F. A. Hayek (1988).
24. F. A. Hayek (1960), pp. 85–102.
25. Ibid., p. 88.
26. Ibid., p. 87.
27. 'Coercion, however, cannot be altogether avoided because the only way to prevent it is by the threat of coercion', in F. A. Hayek (1960) p. 21. On the paradox of unlimited freedom see Karl R. Popper (1945 vol. I), pp. 123–4, 265–6.
28. F. A. Hayek (1960), p. 11.

29. Ibid., p. 21.
30. Ibid.
31. Ibid., p. 85.
32. Ibid., p. 87.
33. F. A. Hayek (1976), p. 82.
34. F. A. Hayek (1960), p. 95.
35. F. A. Hayek (1976), p. 72.
36. F. A. Hayek (1960), p. 98.
37. F. A. Hayek (1976), p. 74.
38. Ibid., pp. 75–6.
39. Hayek understands order as 'a state of affairs in which a multiplicity of elements of various kinds are so related to each other that we may learn from our acquaintance with some spatial or temporal part of the whole to form correct expectations concerning the rest, or at least expectations which have a good chance of proving correct', in F. A. Hayek (1973), p. 36.
40. F. A. Hayek (1973), p. 36.
41. Ibid., p. 40.
42. Ibid.
43. Ibid.
44. Ibid., p. 173.
45. Ibid., p. 49.
46. Ibid.
47. Ibid., p. 50.
48. Ibid., p. 133.
49. Ibid., p. 46.
50. F. A. Hayek (1978), p. 73, emphasis added.
51. F. A. Hayek (1973), p. 46.
52. Robert Nozick, in (1974), pp. 149–50, presents a similar view in a very telling manner: 'Hearing the term 'distribution', most people presume that some thing or mechanism uses some principle or criterion to give out a supply of things . . . However, we are not in the position of children who have been given portions of pie by someone who now makes last minute adjustments to rectify careless cutting. There is no central distribution, no person or group entitled to control all the resources, jointly deciding how they are to be doled out. What each person gets, he gets from others who give to him in exchange for something, or as a gift. In a free society, diverse persons control different resources, and new holdings arise out of voluntary exchanges and actions of persons. There is no more a distributing or distribution of shares than there is a distributing of mates in a society in which persons choose whom they shall marry. The total result is the product of many individual decisions which the different individuals involved are entitled to make'.
53. F. A. Hayek (1976), p. 71.
54. 'The order of the Great Society does rest and must rest on constant undesigned frustration of some efforts – efforts which ought not to have been made but in free men can be discouraged only by failure', in F. A. Hayek (1976), pp. 2–3.

55. F. A. Hayek (1976), p. 72.
56. 'Social justice does not belong to the category of error but to that of nonsense, like the term "a moral stone",' in F. A. Hayek (1976), p. 78.
57. F. A. Hayek (1976), p. 69.
58. Ibid., p. 64.
59. Ibid., p. 70, emphasis added.
60. Ibid.
61. Ibid., p. 62.
62. Ibid., p. 71.
63. Ibid., p. 70.
64. Ibid., p. 83. It is worth noting that Robert Nozick has produced a similar argument which will be discussed in Chapter 6.
65. F. A. Hayek (1976), p. 78.

CHAPTER 2: DISCUSSION: THE DUALISM OF FACTS & STANDARDS

1. F. A. Hayek (1976), p. 78.
2. Henceforth we shall use the expression 'social justice' or 'social justice as a subject-matter' to designate the realm of normative discussions about *results*, as distinguished from *procedures* alone, in a market order. A defence of a pattern of distribution or social justice is then a *particular view* within this discussion, a view which maintains that market results should be ordered according to a common pattern or criterion. But, as it will be shown later, there can be other views within the subject-matter of social justice – i.e. within a normative discussion about results – which do not argue for any common pattern or criterion of distribution or social justice. For the time being, however, the relevant point is to distinguish the realm or subject-matter of social justice from particular conceptions about criterions of distribution.
3. F. A. Hayek (1976), p. 69, emphasis added.
4. Ibid., p. 70, emphasis added.
5. Ibid., emphasis added.
6. 'In every system of morality, which I have hitherto met with, I have always remark'd, that the author proceeds for some time in the ordinary way of reasoning, and establishes the being of God, or makes observations concerning human affairs; when of a sudden I am surpriz'd to find, that instead of the usual copulations of propositions, *is*, and *is not*, I meet with no proposition that is not connected with an *ought*, or an *ought not*. This change is imperceptible; but is, however, of the last consequence. For as this *ought*, or *ought not*, expresses some new relation or affirmation, 'tis necessary that it shou'd be observ'd and explain'd; and at the same time that a reason should be given, for what seems altogether inconceivable, how this new relation can be a deduction from others, which are entirely different from it.' David Hume (1739/1978), p. 469.
7. This argument was actually put forward by Hayek in his last book, *The Fatal Conceit: The Errors of Socialism*, and this will be extensively discussed in Chapter 3.

8. Other difficulties might be raised. Are we really able to predict which cause will be the ultimate winner? Given two opposite predictions, is there any test that allows us to know which corresponds to what is going to happen? Moreover, is there any such test other than the one consisting of waiting for the future to become present and then verifying which of the two predictions did not actually correspond to the facts? If other tests do not exist, then we shall never be able to know in advance which is the winning cause.

9. P. H. Wicksteed (1910), p. 184, quoted by F. A. Hayek (1976), p. 63.

10. F. A. Hayek (1976), p. 63.

11. Ibid., emphasis added.

12. Ibid., pp. 64–5, emphasis added.

13. Ibid., p. 70, emphasis added.

14. Ibid., p. 71, emphasis added.

15. Ibid., p. 72, emphasis added.

16. One should note that I am not discussing whether or not this is the best moral justification for the market order. We shall return to this point later. For the time being I am only highlighting the fact that Hayek himself is constrained to justify in moral terms the moral neutrality he attributes to the market system of rewards.

17. F. A. Hayek (1976), p. 70.

18. Ibid., emphasis added.

19. Kenneth Hoover and Raymond Plant make this point in a slightly different way: 'Hayek has to accept existing inequalities in property, income and power as given because to seek to change these would be an illegitimate exercise in distributive justice. Given this initial inequality, then it does seem plausible to suggest that those who by and large enter the market with least in the way of income and property will have less capacity to act effectively in the market. If this can be foreseen as a rule of thumb, and we believe it can, then Hayek's argument about foreseeability loses much of its power'. (K. Hoover and R. Plant (1989), p. 207). I do not believe this to be the most powerful argument in order to show that market results may be globally foreseen. Nevertheless, it helps to suggest that they are.

20. F. A. Hayek (1976), p. 72.

21. Ibid., p. 87.

22. J. N. Shklar (1990), p. 81.

23. Karl Popper's expression 'minimize suffering' in *The Open Society and its Enemies* is intentionally used here: '[...] I may perhaps briefly formulate what seems to me the most important principles of humanitarian and equalitarian ethics: (1) Tolerance towards all who are not intolerant and who do not propagate intolerance [...]. (2) The recognition that all moral urgency has its basis in the urgency of suffering or pain. I suggest, for this reason, to replace the utilitarian formula "Aim at the greatest amount of happiness for the greatest number", by the formula "The least amount of avoidable suffering for all", or briefly, "Minimize suffering" [...]. (3) The fight against tyranny; or in other words, the attempt to safeguard the other principles by the institutional means of a legislation rather than by the

benevolence of persons in power.' See K. R. Popper (1945), vol.II, p. 235.

24. F. A. Hayek (1976), p. 87.
25. Ibid., p. 103.
26. Ibid.
27. Ibid., p. 87.
28. Ibid., p. 78.
29. Ibid., emphasis and numbers 1 and 2 in parentheses added.
30. Ibid., p. 87, emphasis added.
31. F. A. Hayek (1960), p. 303.
32. It is worth noting that the distinction between a negative criterion of justice (or injustice) and a positive one has somehow been acknowledged by other authors. Samuel Brittan, now Sir Samuel Brittan, has noted that Hayek's critique of the myth of 'just reward' was unnecessarily extended to the critique of *any* public policy towards the distribution of income and property. Distinguishing between *redistribution* (narrowing the gap between the rich and poor ends of the existing income scales) and *reassignment* (changing people's order on that scale), Samuel Brittan believes that Hayek's argument against a common pattern of distribution was in fact able to refute the idea of a political pattern for reassignment, but not of redistribution. The latter, he argues, acts mainly through progressive and negative income taxes, reducing absolute rewards at the top and increasing them at the bottom, *without* attempting to evaluate jobs or merit and without interfering with market rankings (Samuel Brittan (1983), pp. 48–79). In other words, one may well accept Hayek's case against a common *positive* pattern of distribution – which Brittan calls reassignment – and still allow room for a *negative* one, which he calls redistribution.

A similar kind of distinction between negative and positive views of justice is introduced by Ralf Dahrendorf, now Lord Dahrendorf, in his essay on 'Liberty and Equality', (Ralf Dahrendorf (1983), ch.7, pp. 179–214). He introduces the distinction between equality of citizenship and equality of social status and argues that, whereas the former is a condition of liberty the latter would lead to its destruction. In other words, Dahrendorf is criticizing a particular view of social rights which falls within what Hayek called a common pattern of distribution, in this case a pattern of equal distribution, or 'equal status'. That is to say, a view of social rights which wants to ascribe to each individual a particular share, in this case an equal share, of the global outcome. But, at the same time, he is maintaining that this critique – of what he calls 'equality of social status' – does not entail the denial of some basic social rights, which he calls 'equality of citizenship rights'. This resembles the distinction presented here between a negative and a positive view of social rights.

We can finally observe a similar distinction in Sir Karl Popper's approach to what might be called a liberal view of social reform. In his *The Open Society and its Enemies,* Popper stresses that he prefers 'the method of searching for, and fighting against, the greatest and most urgent evils of society, rather than searching for, and fighting for, its

greatest ultimate good'. (Karl Popper (1945/1971), vol.1, p. 158).
Popper's views on this issue will be discussed in Chapter 3.

33. R. Aron (1972/1980), pp. 194–5. Conversely, Aron draws attention to the fact that some of the other characteristics that Hayek attributes to the law may in fact prevent the functioning of a liberal society for he gives each individual the right to veto. This seems to be the case of 'progressive income tax' which, having to be accepted by all, would never be viable. Samuel Brittan (1983), pp. 63–6, puts forward similar objections: 'Hayek's proposal – that a general rule should be acceptable to a majority of both those whom it benefits and those whom it harms – is much too strong. For it gives a veto to any minority in any circumstances – for instance, to the Mafia in a proposal for a new law against banditry. His illustration of progressive taxation as contrary to the rule of law, because it is not acceptable to high rate payers, hardly helps his case. There are many arguments against high marginal tax rates; but the objections of those who pay them are hardly conclusive' (p. 64).

34. One should however note that Raymond Aron, as well as for that matter Samuel Brittan, are not denying the normative role of the ideal of government limited by law. They both contested that the formal characteristics Hayek attributes to law suffice to define *liberal laws*. But they both subscribe to the ideal of the rule of law which Hayek also shares. Aron said that 'taken one by one, each of the criteria is never decisive, but the whole suggests an ideal: the society in which the state would leave to individual initiative as great an area as possible; in which the rulers would be subject to the same obligations and authorizations as the ordinary citizens; where privileges and discrimination would be reduced to a bare minimum' (R. Aron (1972/1980), p. 197).

35. F. A. Hayek (1960), p. 149.
36. Ibid., pp. 152–3.
37. Ibid., p. 153.
38. Ibid., pp. 153–4.
39. Ibid., p. 154.
40. Ibid.
41. Ibid., p. 155.

CHAPTER 3: AN EVALUATION: CIVILIZATION BASED ON PERSONAL DECISIONS

1. F. A. Hayek (1973), p. 46.
2. Ibid., ch.5: 'Nomos: The Law of Liberty', pp. 94–123.
3. F. A. Hayek (1960), p. 11.
4. James Buchanan (1977), p. 38.
5. Karl R. Popper (1945), vol.2, p. 348. A similar point is made by Michael Oakeshott in 'The political economy of freedom': 'As every schoolboy used to know, if effective competition is to exist it can do so only by virtue of a legal system which promotes it, and that monopoly has established itself only because the legal system has not prevented it.' Cf. Michael Oakeshott (1962/1991), p. 403.

6. Karl R. Popper (1945), vol.2, p. 348.
7. James Buchanan (1977), p. 30.
8. Ibid., p. 37.
9. F. A. Hayek (1979), pp. 153–77.
10. F. A. Hayek (1982), p. xxi.
11. F. A. Hayek (1988), p. 6.
12. Karl R. Popper (1934/59).
13. F. A. Hayek (1988), p. 68.
14. 'Towards a Rational Theory of Tradition', in Karl R. Popper (1963/1984), pp. 120–35.
15. F. A. Hayek (1988), p. 68.
16. Ibid., p. 16.
17. Ibid., p. 14.
18. Ibid., p. 136.
19. Ibid., pp. 136–7.
20. Karl R. Popper (1945/1971), vol.II, pp. 228–9.
21. Ibid., p. 230.
22. Ibid.
23. Karl R. Popper (1963/1984), p. 120.
24. Ibid., pp. 120–1.
25. Karl R. Popper (1963/1949), p. 129.
26. Karl R. Popper (1963/1984), pp. 126–7.
27. Ibid., p. 120.
28. F. A. Hayek (1988), p. 136, emphasis added.
29. Ibid., p. 137.
30. Karl R. Popper (1945/1971), vol.I, pp. 172–3.
31. F. A. Hayek (1988), p. 136.
32. Ibid., p. 133.
33. One must recall that Marx's theory was in a similar position: although history had been only the history of class struggle, the proletarian class – whose cause happened to coincide with Marx's own cause – was in the unique position of fighting for its own interests *and* the liberation of all classes. In other words, although class interests have no moral basis, it happens that the interests of the proletarian class coincide with the purest moral goals. For a devastating critique of Marxist views on morals, see Steven Lukes (1985).
34. F. A. Hayek (1988), p. 73.
35. F. A. Hayek (1960), p. 88.
36. Alexis de Tocqueville (1856/1986), p. 1053.
37. In his last book, *The Fatal Conceit: The Errors of Socialism*, Hayek seemed to have believed in something similar to a 'scientific morality', namely when claiming that the disagreement between liberalism and socialism concerns mainly matters of fact rather than of value. Contrary to this view, however, it is possible to argue that this disagreement involves both matters of fact and of value, which amounts to saying that it is not capable of solution on the basis of facts alone – even though facts should play a not irrelevant role. This may be illustrated by the fact that, although Marxist historicism has long ago been refuted by facts, namely by the fact that Marxist revolutions have always taken place in

pre-industrial societies, Marxist beliefs have resisted factual refutation becoming a sort of what Raymond Aron has called a 'secular religion'.

38. Karl R. Popper (1945/1971), vol.2, pp. 279–80.

39. See Karl Popper, *In Search of a Better World* (1989). In the first essay of this collection, under the same title, Popper presents an outline of what he calls an 'active and optimistic theory of evolution', whose chief characteristic is that it emphasizes the active role of individuals in the process of adaptation to the environment. In fact, Popper argues, individuals are not only influenced by the environment but they themselves change the environment, namely through their permanent search for a better world.

40. I use the expression 'presumption of tradition' in the first sense scrutinized by Joseph Raz to the expression 'presumption of liberty': 'A presumption of . . .' is sometimes used to indicate that the burden of adducing evidence and marshalling arguments is in those who favour the restriction of liberty'. Cf. Joseph Raz (1986/1988), p. 8.

41. This formulation can be rooted in Karl Popper's distinction between piecemeal and Utopian social engineering which, in spite of the somewhat awkward labels, is still of crucial importance. According to the terminology used here, piecemeal social engineering, unlike the Utopian one, respects the critical presumption of tradition.

42. In this regard, it should be noticed that, as James Buchanan has observed, Hayek's proposal for a second Chamber (to be elected by a very special process) with the exclusive task of revising and improving general rules of just conduct is inconsistent with his view of laws as part of spontaneous evolution. It is, however, perfectly compatible with the view presented here and, irrespective of the specific content of Hayek's proposal, the importance of the problem he addresses should be acknowledged: the need for a more clear separation of powers. In this sense, and as was suggested by Walter Lippmann in *The Good Society* (1938), the English tradition of the common law should be seen as a specific way of achieving the intentional goal of separating the Judiciary from both the Executive and the Legislative, and not as an indication that the laws cannot be changed by human design.

43. According to the terminological conventions used here, on might say that the American founding fathers acted by design under, or according to, a critical presumption of tradition. Like their French counterparts, they, too, broke away from some traditions. But, unlike the French doctrinaires, they did not want either to start afresh or to build a made order. Acting by design, they decided to build on the English tradition of liberty and piecemeal change, and, accordingly, they attempted to construct a framework of laws, the American constitution, that allowed and protected the evolution of a spontaneous order. The combination of the English and the American experiences is rightly called the Anglo-American tradition of liberty. As Walter Lippmann also remarked, the crucial feature of this tradition may be said to lie in the obedience to a higher law, or to the spirit of the law: 'The denial that men may be arbitrary in human transactions *is* the higher

law [...] This law which is the spirit of the law is the opposite of an accumulation of old precedent and new fiats. By this higher law, that men should not be arbitrary, the old law is continually tested and the new law reviewed' (W. Lippmann, 1938, pp. 346–7).

44. Cf. Raymond Plant (1980), (1988), (1989), (1991), (1991a).
45. Cf. Roland Kley (1990).
46. Cf. John Gray (1992).
47. John Gray (1984).
48. James Buchanan (1977).
49. John Gray (1984), (1989), (1989a).
50. Samuel Brittan (1983).
51. Ralf Dahrendorf (1990).
52. Chandran Kukathas (1990).
53. James Buchanan (1977), p. 38.
54. 'Though they seem siblings, however, they are in fact very different. Hayek has a fatal tendency to hold another system against that of socialism. It is a passive system to be sure, but one complete in itself and intolerant of untidy realities; ... Popper on the contrary is a radical defender of liberty, of change without bloodshed, of trial and error, and also of an active march into the unknown, and thus of people who try to design their destiny. This epistle is a homily to Popper rather than to Hayek.' Ralf Dahrendorf (1990), pp. 25–6.
55. Karl R. Popper (1945/1971), vol.2, pp. 125–6.
56. Karl R. Popper (1957/1976), p. 65.
57. Ibid., Popper's emphasis.
58. Ibid., p. 61.
59. Karl R. Popper (1957/1970), p. 62.
60. Karl R. Popper (1957/1976), pp. 60–1.
61. Ibid., pp. 60–2.
62. Karl R. Popper (1945/1971), vol.1, p. 161.
63. Ibid., vol.2, p. 129.
64. Ibid., vol.1, p. 158.
65. Ibid., pp. 284–5.
66. Ibid., p. 285.
67. Ibid., p. 158.
68. On more detailed views of a liberal positive agenda, see Walter Lippman (1938), pp. 203–41, and John Gray (1989a) and (1993), pp. 1–45.
69. F. A. Hayek (1973), p. 6.
70. Karl R. Popper (1945/1971), vol.1, p. 200.
71. Ibid., p. ix.

CHAPTER 4: PRESENTATION: DEMOCRATIC EQUALITY

1. Cf., among others, Desmond S. King (1987), Geoff Andrews, ed., (1991) and Chantal Mouffe, ed., (1992).
2. Presentation of 'Phronesis', a New Series from Verso edited by Ernesto Laclau and Chantal Mouffe, in Chantal Mouffe (1992), unnumbered page.

3.   Raymond Plant (1988), p. 1.
4.   R. Plant (1991), p. 92.
5.   Plant (1991), pp. 92–3. In K. Hoover and R. Plant (1989), p. 207, the
     same argument is presented on the basis that it is foreseeable 'that
     those who by and large enter the market with least in the way of
     income and property will have less capacity to act effectively in the
     market'. Incidentally, it might be recalled that, in our critique of
     Hayek's views on this same issue, we have avoided this question of
     the comparative capacity to act. We have stressed the fact that it is
     foreseeable that markets will produce, or rather will not be able to
     avoid, the appearance of outsiders, deprivation and exclusion.
          This, it has been maintained, is an inescapable moral problem.
     The relevance of the difference between these two approaches will be
     discussed in Chapters 5 and 6.
6.   'Oddly enough, there would be some agreement between the need
     theorist and a market theorist such as Hayek that distribution accord-
     ing to desert, although a well entrenched principle, trades off a vague
     and indeterminate notion of desert or merit', in R. Plant et al. (1980),
     p. 66.
7.   R. Plant et al. (1980), p. 61.
8.   In fact, we shall argue later that there is a misunderstanding between,
     or common to, Hayek and Plant, here. Hayek has not provided one
     sole argument against the concept of basic need, as we believe to have
     shown in Part I, although he seemed to think he did. What Hayek has
     criticized – and, to our mind, refuted – is the concept of *distribution
     according to need.* Because Raymond Plant, in his turn, misleadingly
     identifies 'helping those in need' with 'distribution according to need',
     he is in fact providing remarkable arguments for 'basic needs' which
     do not entail his further conclusions (on distribution according to
     need). This is a crucial point of our critique both of Hayek and Plant,
     and it will be developed in Chapter 5.
9.   R. Plant et al. (1980), p. 33.
10. Ibid., p. 38.
11. Cf. A. Gewirth (1978) and (1982).
12. R. Plant et al. (1980), p. 93.
13. D. D. Raphael (1967), pp. 43–53 and 95–100.
14. Maurice Cranston (1973), especially ch.VIII 'Economic and Social
     Rights, pp. 65–72.
15. R. Plant et al. (1980), p. 76.
16. D. D. Raphael (1967), p. 64, quoted in R. Plant et al. (1980), p. 76.
17. M. Cranston (1973), p. 67, quoted in R. Plant et al. (1980), p. 77.
18. R. Plant et al. (1980), p. 78.
19. M. Cranston (1973), p. 67, quoted in R. Plant et al. (1980), p. 78.
20. R. Plant et al. (1980), p. 79.
21. Ibid.
22. J. S. Mill (1871/1987), p. 323.
23. R. Plant et al. (1980), p. 82.
24. Ibid., p. 93.
25. Ibid., p. 52.

26. K. Hoover and R. Plant (1989), p. 210, my emphasis. It is worth noting *en passant* that the authors have said nothing whatsoever that could have established that basic goods have to be provided collectively and intentionally *rather than* through the market. In fact, what they have shown is merely that, *if* and *when* the market does not provide for these basic goods, the state, or society, or all the members of a certain community, have the duty to provide for them collectively. These, as we shall see later, are far from being merely differences of semantics.

27. K. Hoover and R. Plant (1989), p. 210.

28. R. Plant (1984), pp. 6–7.

29. F. A. Hayek (1960), p. 88, quoted and discussed in Part I of this work.

30. K. Hoover and R. Plant (1989), p. 211, my emphasis.

31. R. Plant (1984), p. 7.

32. Ibid. It is worth noting that Plant adds that 'except in conditions of high economic growth the greater equality in the worth of liberty cannot be attained without a certain amount of levelling down'.

33. R. Plant (1984), p. 7.

34. Ibid., p. 8.

35. Ibid.

36. Ibid.

37. Ibid., p. 140.

38. K. Hoover and R. Plant (1989), p. 220.

39. Ibid., p. 221.

40. Ibid., p. 222, my emphasis.

41. D. Miller (1989), p. 9.

42. Here are Plant's words: '. . . Arguments about incentives can be stood on their head, so that, if incomes above a certain level are taxed at a differentially high level, individuals will work harder to maintain their standard of living,' in K. Hoover and R. Plant (1989), p. 224. Julien le Grand says, in a more technical way, that 'it is true that a high marginal tax rate lowers the opportunity cost or "price" of leisure, and, as with any commodity whose price is reduced, thereby encourages people to consume more of it (and thus do less work). But, on the other hand, it also lowers people's incomes, and thereby may induce them to work harder so as to maintain their standard of living', in J. le Grand (1982), p. 148.

43. K. Hoover and R. Plant (1989), p. 224.

44. Ibid.

45. R. Plant (1981), p. 144.

CHAPTER 5: DISCUSSION: SATISFACTION OF BASIC NEEDS

1. F. A. Hayek (1976), p. 78, emphasis and numbers 1 and 2 between brackets added.

2. Ibid., p. 87, emphasis added.

3. R. Plant et al. (1980), p. 20, emphasis added.

4. J. Bradshaw (1972), p. 640, emphasis added, quoted in R. Plant et al. (1980), p. 20.

5. V. George and P. Wildin (1972), emphasis added, quoted in R. Plant et al. (1980), p. 21.
6. R. Plant et al. (1980), p. 22, emphasis added.
7. Ibid., emphasis added.
8. R. Plant et al. (1980), p. 61.
9. F. A. Hayek (1960), p. 303, quoted in R. Plant et al. (1980), p. 62.
10. R. Plant et al. (1980), p. 62, emphasis added.
11. This is, in fact, my own formulation of Plant's argument against Hayek, which is slightly different, as has been previously mentioned, from his own. But the differences are not very important in this particular, and one should not be distracted by them now.
12. The crucial passage of Kant's runs as follows: 'Now humanity could no doubt subsist if everybody contributed nothing to the happiness of others but, at the same time, refrained from deliberately impairing their happiness. This is, however, merely to agree negatively and not positively with *humanity as an end in itself* unless everyone endeavours also, so far as in him lies, to further the ends of others. For the ends of a subject who is an end in himself must, if this conception is to have its *full* effect in me, be also, as far as possible, *my* ends'. (I. Kant (1875/1948), p. 92).
13. R. Plant et al. (1980), p. 93.
14. On the satiable nature of basic needs see J. Raz (1986), pp. 233–44 and J. Gray (1992), pp. 57–72.
15. Cf. Part I of this work, especially Chapter 1.
16. Although, as I shall argue later, one can base a society simultaneously on rules of conduct and on end-states to be *avoided*, as opposed to end-states to be *achieved*.

CHAPTER 6: AN EVALUATION: EQUAL LIBERTY & SOCIAL INEQUALITY

1. See mainly the section on Democratic Equality pp. 109–12.
2. K. Hoover and R. Plant (1989), p. 210.
3. R. Plant (1984), p. 6, emphasis added.
4. Ibid., emphasis added.
5. See Chapter 4, especially pp. 112–14.
6. R. Plant (1988), p. 9.
7. R. Plant (1984), p. 7.
8. Ibid.
9. K. Hoover and R. Plant (1989), p. 211.
10. It might be recalled that Raymond Plant used the expressions 'equality of basic goods' and 'equal value of liberty' as synonyms, since the value of liberty is defined by those minimal material conditions which are indispensable for the use of liberty. Later on, in his defence of democratic equality, Plant maintained, quoting Julien le Grand, that a rough equality of conditions (and not only of basic goods) would be necessary to achieve an equal value of liberty. For this reason, it is not to indulge in a major imprecision if we refer to the three expressions as synonymous for the purposes of our discussion in this particular.

11. R. Plant (1988), p. 9.
12. K. Hoover and R. Plant (1989), p. 211. See also R. Plant (1988), p. 9.
13. D. Hume (1751/1975), p. 194.
14. J. le Grand (1982), p. 148.
15. R. Plant (1984), p. 8, emphasis added.
16. Ibid., emphasis added.
17. Ibid.
18. Ibid., emphasis added.
19. Ibid., p. 7.
20. In fact, it will be argued later that it ceases to be a problem provided universal access to the use of liberty is guaranteed.
21. See the presentation of Plant's concepts of 'the presumptive need of incentives' and 'a rent of ability' in Chapter 4, pp. 117–18: Some Legitimate Inequalities.
22. S. Lukes (1991), pp. 62–3.
23. In certain circumstances, however, and as was observed by Joseph Raz, relational matters play an important role as auxiliary principles. At least one of these situations has been already mentioned here: the definition of the precise content of the common floor of basic need in a given society, which of course must depend, to a certain extent, on the general welfare of this society. Another situation might possibly be the one envisaged by Karl Popper when he argues that 'unavoidable suffering – such as hunger in times of unavoidable shortage of food – should be distributed as equally as possible' (in K. Popper (1945/1971), vol.I, p. 285.
24. As Joseph Raz puts it, in (1986), p. 229, 'poverty may be no worse in a society where it afflicts only some than in a society where all are poor. It is bad or regrettable in both to the same degree and for the same reasons. The charge of inequality which can be levelled against only one of these societies is used here rhetorically. The wrong is poverty and its attendant suffering and degradation, not the inequality. But the inequality is an indication that there may be resources which can be used to remedy the situation. It is relevant to an argument about what can be done, as well as to arguments about responsibility for not doing enough to reduce the poverty.'
25. Joseph Raz has masterly presented this distinction in (1986), ch.9, pp. 217–44. See also J. R. Lucas (1966), Section 56: Equality, and 57: Humanity, pp. 243–52, as well as H. L. Hart (1979), p. 845.
26. Karl Popper has also presented a powerful negative case for democracy: this should be seen, neither as a method to choose the best government nor as the rule of the people, but as the only method to avoid tyranny, i.e., the only method to change governments without bloodshed. Cf. Karl Popper (1945/71), especially vol.I, chapter 7: 'Leadership'. Raymond Aron, too, used to say that the advantages of economic growth, such as those of liberty, are better perceived when they are not present.
27. J. Raz (1989), p. 227, emphasis added. A similar point is made by J. R. Lucas (1966), p. 252.
28. R. Dahrendorf (1979), pp. 135–7, emphasis added.

29. R. Dahrendorf (1979), p. 123.

30. See R. Nozick (1974), chapter 7: 'Distributive Justice', pp. 149–231.

31. In fact, a discussion about patterned principles was undertaken when Hayek's views were appraised, and his general contention on this issue was accepted: that we lack the knowledge necessary to assess patterns of distribution. This contention was considered insufficient in Nozick (1974), p. 158–9.

32. R. Nozick (1974), p. 163.

33. On the paradox of freedom, see for instance Karl Popper (1945/1971), vol.I, pp. 123–4 and 265–6, and Alan Gewirth (1982), pp. 16–17.

34. Incidentally, it should be noted that this kind of difficulty does not arise within the argument presented here. This argument does not refer to general interferences with liberty but to the very specific contention that social equality – which is a very specific end-state principle – annuls liberty. If it annuls liberty, and if the goal of social equality has been introduced by Raymond Plant for the sake of enhancing equal liberty (and not for the sake of equality itself), then, the goal of social equality must be consistently ruled out. On the other hand, however, other end-state or patterned principles are not necessarily ruled out by this argument. As such, they simply have not been addressed.

35. A. Gewirth (1982), pp. 16–17.

36. In fact, and since Rawls's first principle asserts a priority of equal liberty, it seems that the most plausible formulation of the second principle should be the reverse of what it actually is. Something like 'all inequalities are to be seen as justified unless they deprive the worst off of the access to certain basic goods which are indispensable for the use of liberty' appears to be more consistent with the presumption of liberty embodied in the first principle.

37. R. Nozick (1974), pp. 207–8. This theory can be encapsulated in Nozick's slogan 'From each as they choose, to each as they are chosen' (p. 160).

38. R. Plant (1988), p. 16.

39. Ibid., p. 19.

40. Ibid., p. 18.

41. R. Plant et al. (1980), p. 22.

42. K. Hoover and R. Plant (1989), p. 210.

43. For an stimulating view of an enabling welfare state, see John Gray (1992), pp. 57–72.

44. J. Gray (1992) and (1993), pp. 63–123.

45. J. Gray (1993), p. 72.

46. J. Schumpeter (1943/1987), p. 64.

47. Ibid., p. 84.

48. Ibid., p. 85. It is interesting that Andrei Sakharov has mentioned in his *Mémoires* a similar observation about capitalism which an uncle of his used to utter at family gatherings, when Sakharov was a child: 'Pour lui (oncle Vania), le système socialiste était dans son essence inefficace pour la satisfaction des besoins humains, mais en revanche, il convenait parfaitement au renforcement du pouvoir. J'ai retenu une de ses formulations: dans le monde capitaliste, le vendeur court

après l'acheteur, ce qui les forces tous deux à mieux travailler, tandis que, sous le socialisme, l'acheteur court après le vendeur (et il va de soi qu'ils n'ont plus le temps de penser au travail). Ce n'est bien sur qu'un aphorisme, mais il me semble qu'il contient une vérité profonde.' A. Sakharov (1990), p. 37.

49. J. Schumpeter (1943/1987), p. 68.
50. Ibid., p. 67.
51. Ibid.
52. R. Plant (1988), p. 18.
53. An interesting and somehow unorthodox discussion of liberal views on self-interest, altruism and egoism can be found in Karl Popper's *The Open Society and its Enemies*, especially vol.I, chapters 6 and 10. Here Popper opposes the common view that identifies collectivism with altruism and individualism with egoism, and, standing for what he calls an 'individualistic altruism', he asks (quoting Charles Sherrington's *Man on his Nature*): 'Are the shoal and the herd altruism?' K. Popper (1945/1971), vol.I, p. 258, n.28.
54. A. Smith (1776/1991), p. 13.
55. W. Lippmann (1938), p. 175.
56. T. Paine (1791/1984), pp. 212–13.
57. An interesting recent proposal in this field has been presented by James E. Meade under the title of 'Citizen's Income', J. E. Meade (1993). A similar view had been presented by Milton Friedman (1962), pp. 190–5.

CHAPTER 7: CONCLUSION: CITIZENSHIP, INCLUSION & OPPORTUNITY

1. This view of social rights is closely connected with the one maintained by Ralf Dahrendorf in several of his works, especially in 'Liberty and Equality', in R. Dahrendorf (1968), pp. 179–214. It is also close to the views presented by John Gray in 'Moral Foundations of Market Institutions', in J. Gray (1993), pp. 66–123, and by Joseph Raz in *The Morality of Freedom* (1986), especially chapter 9 'Equality'. The underlying inspiration of the argument presented here is mainly borrowed from the works of Karl Popper and Ralf Dahrendorf.
2. I have borrowed the expression 'an overall theory of justice' from John Gray's lecture at Nuffield College, Oxford, on 3 March 1993, entitled 'Why There Cannot Be an Overall Theory of Justice'.
3. A slightly modified version of this argument was produced by Robert Nozick in his well-known example of Wilt Chamberlain (see R. Nozick 1974), especially chapter 7 'Distributive Justice', pp. 149–231). For a discussion of side-constraints and end-states, see mainly Chapter 6 of the present work pp. 157–62.
4. For a discussion of the distinction between promoting social justice and avoiding social injustice, see Chapter 2, especially pp. 45–50.
5. 'Social justice does not belong to the category of error but to that of nonsense, like the term "a moral stone"', in F. A. Hayek (1976), p. 69.
6. That even Hayek has accepted the meaningfulness of a discussion

about market outcomes can be shown by the fact that he himself has discussed the general structure of these outcomes and has rightly argued that they tend to maximize the well-being of any individual taken at random (see Chapter 2, pp. 138–41).

7. An illustration of this distinction could be as follows: whereas a principle of satisfaction of basic needs would entail homelessness being a condition of basic need, a principle of distribution according to need would entail a discussion as to whether someone who owns a palace really needs it as compared to someone else who owns a flat. The same applies to education or health care. A principle of satisfaction of basic needs does not care that some go to public schools and private hospitals whilst some others do not – provided that all have access to a proper level of education and health care. On the contrary, a principle of distribution according to need would necessarily contest that some really need public schools or private hospitals, whilst others cannot afford it although it could be said that they need it as much as the others.

8. The concept of normal politics, as contrasted to constitutional politics, is used here in the sense presented by Ralf Dahrendorf in his *Reflections on the Revolution in Europe* (1990), especially pp. 30–7.

9. For this reason, this study has avoided the discussion of empirical arguments about social policies such as those produced by Charles Murray in his now famous *Losing Ground* (1984). These arguments could perfectly be perceived as part of the ongoing discussion about the best level and method of welfare provision, and, as such, they are entirely within the theory of social rights presented here. What would, however, go beyond this framework, and therefore would become unacceptable, would be a claim to the extinction of welfare provision for the needy on the grounds that this provision was producing undesirable effects. This would be unacceptable for the same reason that the empirical discovery that the right to a fair trial is allowing some criminals to escape could not lead to the dismissal of the right to a fair trial. This right is based on the assumption that it is preferable to allow a criminal to escape because of lack of evidence than to condemn an innocent person on lack of evidence. A similar argument applies to the provision of basic goods for those who lack them. Having said this, one should not dismiss on dogmatic grounds many important empirical data which have been produced about the unintended consequences of welfare: they should be seen as challenges to our capacity to improve the application of welfare principles, not as invitations to rule out the very principles.

10. An interesting proposal in this field has been presented by James E. Meade under the title of 'Citizens' Income', in J. E. Meade (1993). A similar view had been presented by Milton Friedman in (1962), pp. 190–5.

11. This two-fold discussion of Hayek's and Plant's views corresponds to the structure of this study. These views have been discussed separately in Part I and Part II. Each Part comprises three chapters, the first ones being dedicated to a presentation of each author's view, the second to their direct discussion, and the third ones to the general evaluation of their respective background, or 'more general assumptions'.

Bibliography

Andrews, Geoff, ed. (1991) *Citizenship* (London: Lawrence & Wishart).

Aron, Raymond (1972/1980) *Études Politiques* (Paris: Gallimard, 1972), quotations translated into English from the Brazilian edition, *Estudos Políticos* (Brasília: Editora Universidade de Brasília, 1980).

——(1974) 'Is Multinational Citizenship Possible?' (*Social Research*, vol. 41, no. 4).

Barbalet, J. M. (1988) *Citizenship* (Milton Keynes: Open University Press).

Barry, Norman (1979) *Hayek's Social and Economical Philosophy* (London: Macmillan).

——(1990) *Welfare* (Milton Keynes: Open University Press).

Berlin, Isaiah (1958/1969) Two Concepts of Liberty in *Four Essays on Liberty* (Oxford: Oxford University Press).

Bradshaw, John (1972) 'The Concept of Social Need', in *New Society*.

Brandt, R. B., ed. (1962) *Social Justice* (Englewood Cliffs, NJ: Prentice Hall).

Brittan, Samuel (1973/1988) *A Restatement of Economic Liberalism* (London: Macmillan).

——(1983) *The Role and Limits of Government. Essays in Political Economy* (London: Temple Smith).

Buchanan, James M. (1977) *Freedom in Constitutional Contract. Perspectives of a Political Economist* (Texas: Texas A&M University Press).

——(1986) *Liberty, Market and the State. Political Economy in the 1980s* (Brighton: Wheatsheaf).

Corbin, A. L. (1923) 'Legal Analysis and Terminology' (*Yale Law Journal*, XXIX, pp. 163–73).

Cranston, Maurice (1973) *What are Human Rights?* (London: Bodley Head).

Dahrendorf, Ralf (1968) *Essays in the Theory of Society* (Stanford: Stanford University Press).

——(1979) *Life Chances: Approaches to Social and Political Theory* (London: Weidenfeld and Nicolson).

——(1988) *The Modern Social Conflict* (London: Weidenfeld & Nicolson).

——(1990) *Reflections on the Revolution in Europe* (London: Chatto & Windus).

Drover, G. and Kerans, P., eds (1993) *New Approaches to Welfare Theory* (Aldershot and Brookfield: Edward Elgar).

Feinberg, Joel (1973) *Social Philosophy* (Englewood Cliffs, NJ: Prentice Hall).

Freeden, Michael (1991) *Rights* (Milton Keynes: Open University Press).

Fried, C. (1978) *Right and Wrong* (Cambridge, Mass.: Harvard University Press).

Friedman, Milton (1962) *Capitalism and Freedom* (Chicago and London: University of Chicago Press).

Galligan, D. and Sampford, C., eds (1985) *Rights and the Welfare State* (London: Croom Helm).

Gauchet, Marcel (1989) *La Revolution des droits de l'homme* (Paris: Editions Gallimard).

George, V. and Wildin, P. (1972) *Ideology and Social Welfare* (London: Routledge & Kegan Paul).

Gewirth, Alan (1978) *Reason and Morality* (Chicago and London: University of Chicago Press).

—— (1982) *Human Rights. Essays in Justification and Applications* (Chicago and London: University of Chicago Press).

—— (1984) 'Reply to my Critics' in Regis Jr., Edward, ed. (1984).

Goodman, Lenn E. (1991) *On Justice. An Essay in Jewish Philosophy* (New Haven and London: Yale University Press).

le Grand, Julien (1982) *The Strategy of Equality* (London: Allen & Unwin).

Gray, John (1984) *Hayek on Liberty* (Oxford: Basil Blackwell).

—— (1989) *Liberalisms. Essays in Political Philosophy* (London: Routledge).

—— (1989a) *Limited Government: A Positive Agenda* (London: Institute of Economic Affairs, Hobart Paper 113).

—— (1992) *The Moral Foundations of Market Institutions* (London: IEA Health and Welfare Unit, Choice in Welfare Series no. 10).

—— (1993) *Beyond the New Right. Markets, Government and the Common Environment* (London and New York: Routledge).

—— (1994) *Post-Communist Societies in Transition: A Social Market Perspective* (London: Social Market Foundation).

Green, David (1990) *Equalizing People. Why Social Justice Threatens Liberty* (London: Institute of Economic Affairs, Health and Welfare Unit).

—— (1993) *Reinventing Civil Society: The Rediscovery of Welfare Without Politics* (London: Institute of Economic Affairs, Health and Welfare Unit).

Hart, H. L. A. (1979) 'Between Utility and Rights' (*Columbia Law Review*, 79, pp. 828–46).

Hayek, Friedrich A. (1944) *The Road to Serfdom* (London: Routledge, reprinted in paperback 1991).

—— (1949) *Individualism and the Economic Order* (London: Routledge & Kegan Paul).

—— (1952/1979) *The Counter-Revolution of Science* (Indianapolis: Liberty Press).

—— (1960) *The Constitution of Liberty* (London: Routledge & Kegan Paul).

—— (1967) *Studies in Philosophy, Politics and Economics* (London: Routledge & Kegan Paul).

—— (1973) *Law, Legislation and Liberty, Vol. I, Rules and Order* (London: Routledge & Kegan Paul).

—— (1976) *Law, Legislation and Liberty, Vol. II, The Mirage of Social Justice* (London: Routledge & Kegan Paul).

—— (1978) *New Studies in Philosophy, Politics, Economics and the History of Ideas* (London: Routledge & Kegan Paul).

—— (1979) *Law, Legislation and Liberty, Vol. III, The Political Order of a Free People* (London: Routledge & Kegan Paul).

—— (1982) *Law, Legislation and Liberty*, first one-volume paperback edition with corrections and revised Preface, (London: Routledge & Kegan Paul).

—— (1988) *The Fatal Conceit: The Errors of Socialism*, first volume of 'The Collected Works of Friedrich August Hayek', edited by W. W. Bartley III (London: Routledge).

Hohfeld, Wesley N. (1919/1964) *Fundamental Legal Conceptions as Applied in Judicial Reasoning* (Westport, Conn.: Greenwood Press).

Hoover, Kenneth and Plant, Raymond (1989) *Conservative Capitalism in Britain and the United States. A Critical Appraisal* (London: Routledge).

Hume, David (1739/1978) *A Treatise of Human Nature* (Oxford: Clarendon Press).

——(1777/1975) *Enquiries* (Oxford: Clarendon Press).

Kamenka, E. and Tay, A. E.-S., eds (1978) *Human Rights* (London: Edward Arnold).

Kant, Immanuel (1785/1948) *Groundwork of the Metaphysic of Morals*, in Paton H. J. (1948).

King, Desmond S. (1987) *The New Right. Politics, Markets and Citizenship* (London: Macmillan).

Kley, Roland (1990) *Political Philosophy and Social Theory. A Critique of F. A. Hayek's Justification of Liberalism* (DPhil. thesis, University of Oxford).

Kukathas, Chandran (1990) *Hayek and Modern Liberalism* (Oxford: Clarendon Press).

Lippmann, Walter (1938) *The Good Society* (London: George Allen & Unwin).

Lipsey, D. and Leonard, D. (1981) *The Socialist Agenda. Crosland Legacy* (London: Jonathan Cape).

Lucas, J. R. (1966) *The Principles of Politics* (Oxford: Clarendon Press).

Lukes, Steven (1973) *Individualism* (Oxford: Basil Blackwell).

——(1985) *Marxism and Morality* (Oxford: Oxford University Press).

——(1991) *Moral Conflict and Politics* (Oxford: Clarendon Press).

Manent, Pierre (1986) *Les Liberaux*, Vols. I and II (Paris: Hachette).

Marshall, Alfred (1873/1925) *The Future of the Working Classes*, privately printed by Thomas Tofts, reprinted in Pigou, A. C., ed. (1925), pp. 101–18.

Marshall, Thomas H. (1950/1992) 'Citizenship and Social Class', in *Citizenship and Social Class, and Other Essays* (Cambridge: Cambridge University Press), reprinted in Marshall, T. H. and Bottomore, T. (1992), pp. 1–51.

——and Bottomore, Tom (1992), *Citizenship and Social Class* (London and Concord: Pluto Press).

Meade, James E. (1993) *Fifteen Propositions concerning the Building of an Equitable, Full-Employment Non-Inflationary, Free-Enterprise Economy* (London: Employment Policy Institute).

Mill, John S. (1859/1975), *On Liberty*, in *Three Essays* (Oxford: Oxford University Press).

Miller, David (1976) *Social Justice* (Oxford: Clarendon Press).

Minogue, Kenneth (1963) *The Liberal Mind* (London: Methuen).

Murray, Charles (1984) *Losing Ground: American Social Policy 1950–1980* (New York: Basic Books).

Mouffe, Chantal, ed. (1992) *Dimensions of Radical Democracy* (London and New York: Verso).

Nozick, Robert (1974) *Anarchy, State and Utopia* (Oxford: Basil Blackwell).

Oakeshott, Michael (1962/1991) *Rationalism in Politics and other Essays*, New and expanded edition with a foreword by Timothy Fuller (Indianapolis: Liberty Press).

Paine, Thomas (1791/1984) *Rights of Man*, with an Introduction by Eric Foner (Harmondsworth and New York: Penguin).

Paton, H. J. (1948) *The Moral Law* (London: Unwin Hyman).

Pigou, A. C., ed. (1925) *Memorials of Alfred Marshall* (London: Macmillan).

Plant, Raymond (1973) *Hegel* (London: George Allen & Unwin).

——, Lesser, Harry and Taylor, P. (1980) *Political Philosophy and Social Welfare* (London: Routledge & Kegan Paul).

——(1981) 'Democratic Socialism and Equality', in Lipsey, D. and Leonard D. (1981).

——(1984) *Equality, Markets and the State* (London: Fabian Society, Tract no. 494).

——(1985) 'Needs, Agency and Rights in Law', in Galligan D. and Samford, C., eds (1985).

——(1988) *Citizenship, Rights and Socialism* (London: Fabian Society, Tract no. 531).

——and Barry, Norman (1990) *Citizenship and Rights in Thatcher's Britain: Two Views* (London: IEA Health and Welfare Unit, Choice in Welfare Series no. 3).

——(1991) 'Social Rights and the Reconstruction of Welfare' in Andrews, Geoff (1991).

——(1991a) *Modern Political Thought* (Oxford: Basil Blackell).

——(1993) 'Free Lunches Don't Nourish: Reflections on Entitlements and Citizenship' in Drover, G. and Kerans, P., eds (1993).

Popper, Karl R. (1934/1959) *The Logic of Scientific Discovery* (London: Hutchinson).

——(1945/1971) *The Open Society and its Enemies* (Princeton: Princeton University Press, according to the fifth edition, revised, London: Routledge & Kegan Paul, 1966).

——(1957) *The Poverty of Historicism* (London: Routledge & Kegan Paul).

——(1963) *Conjectures and Refutations* (London: Routledge & Kegan Paul).

——(1992) *In Search of a Better World* (London: Routledge).

Raphael, D. D., ed. (1967) *Political Theory and the Rights of Man* (London: Macmillan).

——(1970/1990) *Problems of Political Philosophy* (London: Macmillan).

Rawls, John (1971) *A Theory of Justice* (Cambridge, Mass: Harvard University Press).

Raz, Joseph (1986) *The Morality of Freedom* (Oxford: Clarendon Press).

Sakharov, Andrei (1990) *Mémoires* (Paris: Éditions du Seuil).

Schumpeter, Joseph (1943/1987) *Capitalism, Socialism and Democracy*, with a new introduction by Tom Bottomore (London: Unwin Paperbacks).

Shapiro, Ian (1986) *The Evolution of Rights in Liberal Theory* (Cambridge: Cambridge University Press).

Shklar, Judith N. (1990) *The Faces of Injustice* (New Haven and London: Yale University Press).

——(1991) *American Citizenship. The Quest for Inclusion* (Cambridge, Mass. and London: Harvard University Press).

Tocqueville Alexis de (1856/1986) *L'Ancien Regime et la Revolution* in *Tocqueville* (Paris: Collection Bouquins, Editions Robert Laffont).

Turner, Bryan S., ed. (1993) *Citizenship and Social Theory* (London, Newbury Park and New Delhi: Sage).

Unesco (1945), *Human Rights. Comments and Interpretations* (London and New York).

Vincent, Andrew and Plant, Raymond (1984) *Philosophy, Politics and Citizenship. The Life and Thought of the British Idealists* (Oxford: Basil Blackwell).

Voltaire (1734/1964) *Lettres Philosophiques* (Paris: Flammarion).

Waldron, Jeremy, ed. (1984) *Theories of Rights* (Oxford: Oxford University Press).

Wicksteed, P. H. (1910) *The Common Sense of Political Economy* (London).

Index